TWENTY-FIVE YEARS
1892–1916

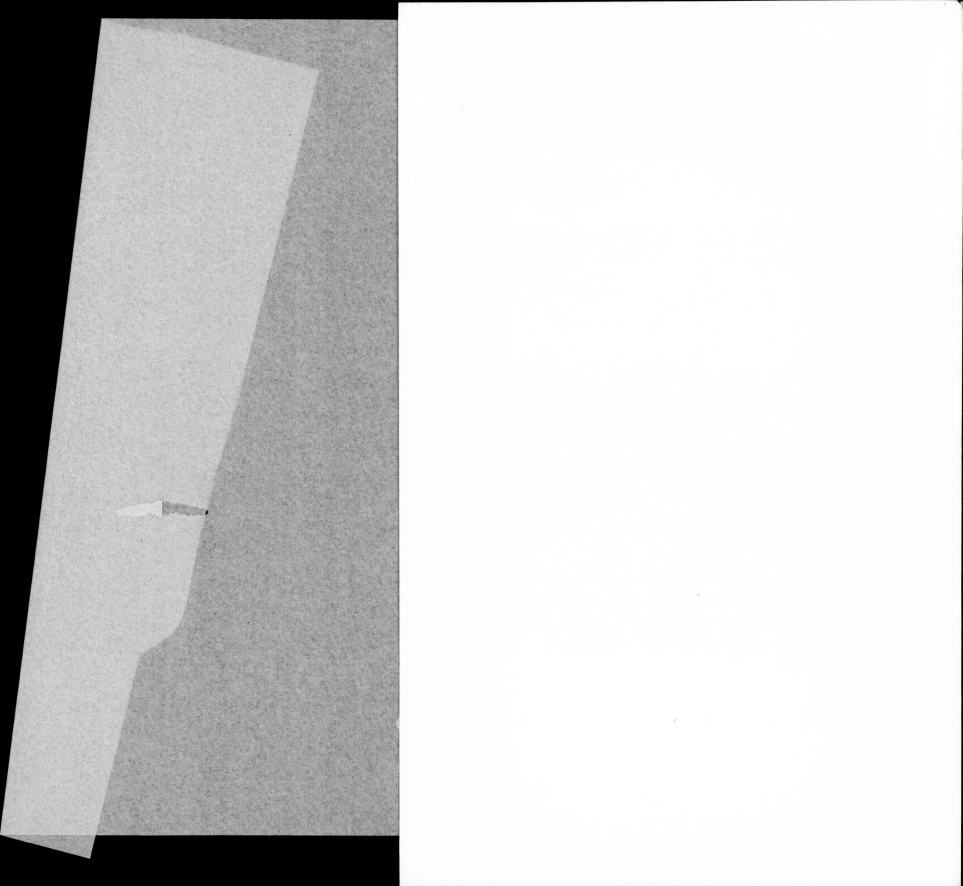

Photograph by Lafayette, Ltd.

VISCOUNT GREY

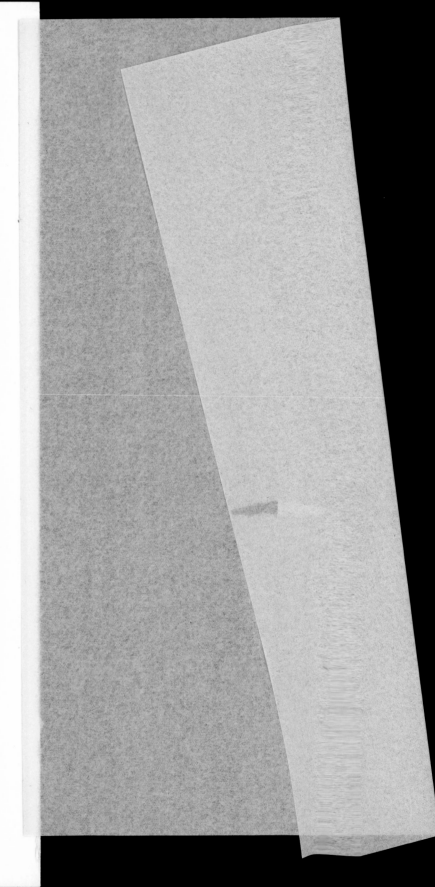

TWENTY-FIVE YEARS

YEARS

1892-1916

BY

VISCOUNT GREY OF FALLODON, K.G.

*WITH THIRTY-TWO ILLUSTRATIONS
FROM PHOTOGRAPHS*

VOLUME II

NEW YORK
FREDERICK A. STOKES COMPANY
MCMXXV

Printed in the United States of America

CONTENTS

VOLUME II

ILLUSTRATIONS

TWENTY-FIVE YEARS
1892–1916

CHAPTER XVII

(1914)

THE COMING OF WAR

A Change in the Point of View—A Question of Naval Obligations—
Examination of the Belgian Issue—Lord Clarendon's Definition of
British Obligations—The Distinction between Belgium and
Luxembourg—Mr. Gladstone's View—The Movement towards
Cabinet Unity—The Speech of August 3—Lichnowsky's Last
Questions—At War.

BY August 1 a change in the point of view of the
anti-war group was beginning to give shape to
the attitude of the Cabinet as a whole. It is not
possible to say with certainty how and why this change
was being wrought. It is not always easy for a man to
trace the inward path and steps by which he reaches his
own conclusions; so much of the working of the mind is
subconscious rather than conscious. If it is difficult to
be sure of one's own mind, one can only guess at the
processes in the minds of others. My impression is that,
as war became more imminent, men began to picture to
themselves the probable scenes and events of it; and the
more vividly they saw these, the more uneasy they became at the prospect of Britain sitting still and immovable, while great events fraught with incalculable
consequences were happening at her very doors.

The first sign of this trend of thought was the expression of an opinion that we could not stand the German

Fleet coming down the Channel, and, within sight and sound of our shores, bombarding the French coast.

It might be supposed that this suggestion came as a tactical move from a pro-French quarter made and designed to shake or sap the position of the anti-war section. It was no such thing. It came spontaneously from the anti-war quarter and was based, first, simply on the ground of feeling and sentiment. But on consideration it was reinforced by a very powerful argument of a different kind. It will appear, if the reader looks back to the record of the conversations with Cambon in 1906, that not only British and French military, but also naval, authorities were in consultation. But the naval consultations had been placed on a footing satisfactory to France in 1905 before the Liberal Government had come into office. The new step taken by us in January 1906 had been to authorize military conversations on the same footing as the naval ones. For this reason, and perhaps also because the despatch abroad of our army would denude our land defence at home, it was the military more than the naval aspect of these consultations that had preoccupied us; but both had been authorized and were covered by the letter exchanged with Cambon in November 1912. These consultations had not affected the disposition of the armies. French armies were practically placed where they would have been if no Franco-British military or naval conversations had existed. The main French Army was in France. So with the British Expeditionary Force; it was disposed as best suited British military arrangements and the probable requirements of the Empire. With the fleets it was different:

the French Fleet was in the Mediterranean; the main British Fleet in the waters of Great Britain. The French north and west coasts were therefore left entirely without naval defence. Had not the naval conversations then placed France (if we stood aside) at a positive disadvantage? Had they not, in fact, created an obligation, in spite of express stipulations that they were not to do so? This consideration did not originate the suggestion of guaranteeing the French north and west coasts, but it clinched it.

The promise to defend these coasts was given to France. The German Government were informed. They promised not to attack these coasts (of course on the understanding that we remained neutral), and this naval point ceased to have any direct influence on the decision of the British Government. But the Belgian point had then become paramount, and the naval point was therefore no longer a decisive one.

Meanwhile Germany had declared war on Russia. France was bound as Russia's Ally, and could not remain neutral; the main German army was advancing, not on Russia, but on France, and its aggression brought the Cabinet face to face with the violation of the neutrality, first of Luxembourg, then of Belgium. The Luxembourg obligation was as slight as the Belgian was formidable. Our obligation to Luxembourg was examined. The Hansard Report of the debate on the Luxembourg Treaty in the House of Lords in 1867 was brought to me. In that debate the obligation imposed by the treaty guaranteeing the neutrality of Luxembourg was defined by

Lord Clarendon, the Liberal Ex-Foreign Secretary, who agreed to it:

> With regard to the guarantee, I will go somewhat further than the noble Earl at the head of the Government, and say that, if we had undertaken the same guarantee in the case of Luxembourg as we did in the case of Belgium, we should, in my opinion, have incurred an additional and very serious responsibility. I look upon our guarantee in the case of Belgium as an individual guarantee, and have always so regarded it; but this is a collective guarantee. No one of the Powers, therefore, can be called upon to take single action, even in the improbable case of any difficulty arising. (Lord Clarendon, House of Lords, June 20, 1867.)

We were all working under great pressure, and I do not remember that more than this was brought to my notice at the time. There was, however, a subsequent debate on the Luxembourg Treaty in which Lord Derby, though not less definite in distinguishing between separate and collective guarantees, gave a longer explanation of what he considered to be involved in a collective guarantee. For the sake of completeness, Lord Derby's statement is added:

> In my reference to the treaty brought under our notice by the noble lord, I hope he will not understand me as speaking of moral obligations, but of the technical obligations imposed by the treaty. To the latter only the noble lord's question has reference, and to them alone shall I apply myself in my answer. Let me give your lordships one or two instances of separate guarantees and of collective guarantees. The first I will take is a very remarkable case—that with regard to the neutrality of Belgium. In the year 1831 a Conference of the five Great Powers laid down twenty-five articles, which were to determine the relations between Belgium and Holland, and which were to form the basis of a treaty between those two countries. The Powers who were parties to that Conference of 1831 bound themselves to uphold,

not collectively but severally and individually, the integrity of the treaty. That was a separate and individual guarantee. But, notwithstanding, in 1832, when Belgium, who had been put in possession of the territory assigned to her by that treaty, called on the Powers parties to the Conference to enforce her rights, Prussia, Russia, and Austria declined to interfere by force of arms for that purpose: while on the other hand France and England, taking a stricter view of the obligations imposed on them by the treaty, proceeded to enforce it by combined naval and military operations. In the same treaty there was comprised a guarantee for the possession of Luxembourg by the King of Holland, not in his capacity as King of Holland, but as Grand Duke of Luxembourg.

In 1839, after a treaty had been made between Belgium and Holland embodying the main provisions of the Treaty of 1831, a separate one was entered into between the five Powers and Belgium, in which the obligations of the former treaty of 1831 were repeated and renewed, and the five Powers bound themselves separately to maintain the integrity of Belgium, its neutrality and independence. The Prussian Minister must have been perfectly well aware of the terms of that treaty by which the five Powers, acting individually, guaranteed the independence of Belgium; yet, if he thought the one kind of guarantee equal to the other, I want to know why he should have studiously altered the words and asked, not for a separate and several guarantee, but for a collective guarantee by the Great Powers for the integrity and independence of Luxembourg.

If the noble Lord [Lord Houghton] is not satisfied with my view of this treaty—namely that the integrity and neutrality of Luxembourg rests upon the collective voice and upon the honour of all the Powers who are signatories to it—I should wish that he gives us his interpretation of its effect and to what extent it is binding upon us. I will put a case to him. Suppose that Prussia, with a view of making war upon France, or France with a view of making war upon Russia, were to enter the territory of Luxembourg—thereby, of course, violating its neutrality by the mere passage of an army, for I am not dealing with the question of occupation or possession, but of violating the neutrality of Luxembourg by passing an army through it—does the noble Lord mean to say that all the guaranteeing Powers in this Treaty of 1867, or each singly, would be bound by the objections thrown on them by this treaty to go to war against the Power—whichever it might be—

which entered Luxembourg with an army? Would Prussia desire this interpretation of the treaty? Suppose, in anticipation of any invasion by France, Prussia thought it necessary to make defensive advances into Luxembourg, would Prussia contend that all the other Powers would be thereby bound to take part with France in a war against her for the purpose of vindicating the neutrality of Luxembourg? And supposing, in a case, that Russia and Austria held aloof from the fulfilment of their portion of the guarantee in the event of any case for interference arising, does the noble Lord for a moment contend that England—situated as she is, and absolutely unable to put a sufficient military force on the Continent for preserving this neutrality—has contracted the obligation of enforcing the guarantee which she gave in common with all the other great Powers of Europe? Such a construction is contrary to all the rules of interpretation, and far beyond what this country should undertake or carry through. Suppose, again, that France and Prussia for the purpose of coming to a contest, should simultaneously violate the neutrality, in what position would the other Powers be? Should the remaining guarantors, or England alone, immediately begin a sort of triangular duel, to prevent the violation of the treaty by Powers who had already violated it? It is evident the conditions of the treaty must be construed with a regard to what is reasonable and practicable; and I say, again, that by a collective guarantee it is well understood that, while in honour all the Powers who are parties to it severally engage to maintain, for their own part, a strict respect for the territory for which neutrality is guaranteed, and although undoubtedly any one Power has a perfect right to declare a *casus belli* if she thinks fit, because of the violation of the guarantee, yet a single Power is not bound to take up the cudgels for all the other Powers with whom she gave a collective guarantee.—*Lord Derby in the House of Lords, July 4, 1867, in reply to Lord Houghton's question, "What is the construction which Her Majesty's Government place on the words 'collective guarantee' (garantie collective) in the Treaty of May 11 relative to the Grand Duchy of Luxembourg?"*

It was thus made clear that what Luxembourg had was a collective guarantee; that no one of the signatory Powers had an obligation to defend Luxembourg, unless all the signatory Powers did so; that no other Power had an obligation to act separately and without the others. This made our position quite clear; the violation of Luxembourg entailed no obligation upon us to take action. We could, if we wished, make the German invasion of Luxembourg a *reason* for going to war, but it was not an *obligation;* it was a question whether the interest of Britain, not its honour, required us to act. The question was further simplified by the fact that Luxembourg itself made no resistance to the German invasion, though it lodged a notification of it with the signatory Powers. The question of Luxembourg was therefore laid aside, and attention concentrated upon that of Belgian neutrality; but it must not be supposed that the violation of Luxembourg was altogether without effect.

In the first place, it was the breaking of a treaty and a breach of Germany's pledged word. That was clear; and the wrongdoing of it was not affected by the obligation, or absence of obligation, on our part to resist it. Nor did Luxembourg's submission affect this aspect of the matter. Luxembourg was helpless and had not the means to resist. There was a perceptible hardening of British feeling against Germany.

In the second place, the violation of Luxembourg had caused the study of that debate of 1867. The debate established that there was no separate guarantee of Luxembourg, but, by the contrast drawn between the Luxembourg and the Belgian guarantee, it brought into strong relief the binding character of the guarantee of Belgium. I do not remember that any of us ever questioned that, but I have a very distinct recollection of thinking with what force quotations from the debate on the Luxembourg

Treaty would be thrown in the face of any British Government that tried to maintain that the Belgian Treaty was not binding on us. It was brought to my notice afterwards that one or more British Ministers of previous years had spoken ambiguously about the binding force of our obligations with regard to Belgium. According to my recollection, no such statements were brought before us at the time. The Belgian Treaty was of old date, but it had never dropped out of view. Ever since it was made its existence had been familiar to public opinion, and to each succeeding generation of public men. We had lived in the knowledge of it and in the belief that Britain was bound to defend the neutrality of Belgium. What we had before us was the action of Mr. Gladstone's Government in 1870 and the doctrine laid down by himself and Lord Granville about our obligation to Belgium.[1] Lord Granville said plainly that British interests and honour were involved. Mr. Gladstone characteristically guarded himself against any unqualified admission that treaty guarantees should always in all conditions bind us to go to war in defence of them, but threw into the scale of British obligation to defend Belgium a tremendous assertion that this was required by a policy and a morality that were independent of time or circumstances.

And had circumstances changed since 1870? Only in this, that Germany was now more mighty than at the outbreak of the war in 1870, and the evil of a violation

[1] To meet the special circumstances of the publication of the alleged draft treaty of 1866 (in which the proposal was made that Prussia should support France if she should be led by circumstances to enter Belgium or to conquer it) Lord Granville invited both belligerents, while maintaining all the guarantees of the Treaty of 1839, to join in a new treaty giving Belgium a new and special guarantee during the war and for twelve months afterwards. This they did.

of Belgium graver than ever. For, if her neutrality were violated, and the violation submitted to by Belgium and acquiesced in by her guarantors, her independence was gone for ever. She must become the satellite and serf of the great neighbour who had used her as he pleased. It would have been proved that she had a master, and had no friends able or willing to help her.

There was no getting past the Luxembourg debate and the British declarations of 1870. How could any man, however opposed to war, stand up in the House of Commons and explain these away? In the fierce glow of this crisis such attempts at explanation would be consumed in a moment. As it became more and more certain that the German Army was going to invade Belgium, the Cabinet began all to face the same way, for we had our backs to the same straight wall.

By the end of the week, on August 1, we had before us the announcement of the Belgian Government that Belgium would, if invaded, defend her own neutrality to the utmost of her power; that made the question straight and simple. Belgium at this stage made no appeal to the guaranteeing Powers. In this she acted properly and wisely. Such information as has come to my notice goes to show that, up to the last moment, the Belgian Government did not believe that any Power intended to violate the Treaty of Guarantee. To appeal to the Powers would then have implied a suspicion that she did not entertain: to ask help from some of them, and not from all, would have laid her open to a charge of siding with some against another, and thus departing from neutrality before this was threatened. But the announcement that, if her neutrality was assailed, she intended to defend herslf, was important. If she were to acquiesce voluntarily, or even under duress, in the passage of German troops, we should be entitled to send troops to vindicate the neutrality and resist the violation of it; but it was clear that an appeal from her for help, when she was herself fighting for what we were pledged to defend, would be peculiarly strong and moving. How could we possibly resist it?

My recollection of those three days, August 1, 2, and 3, is of almost continuous Cabinets and of immense strain; but of what passed in discussion very little remains in my mind, not even what part I took in the discussions. There was little for me to do: circumstances and events were compelling decision. I remember saying more than once, to colleagues inside or outside the Cabinet, that it did not matter whether the decision was to go to war or to demand conditions from Germany. Conditions meant war just as surely as a declaration of war. Respect for the neutrality of Belgium must be one of the conditions, and this Germany would not respect. The state of mind at which the Cabinet had arrived at the end of our meeting on the morning of Monday, August 3, is, I believe, faithfully represented in the speech made by me that afternoon in the House of Commons; at any rate, that speech was intended to represent the mind of the Cabinet, though some of the arguments used may have been my own. Where I thought I might be expressing something that was outside the strict limits of Cabinet agreement, it was carefully expressed as a personal view.

It was at one of these last Cabinets that a message was read to us saying definitely that the Conservative front

Opposition benches were ready to support a decision to stand by France. There was no mention of Belgium, and all credit must be given to the Conservative leaders for their resolution and courage in making this contribution to decision at a moment when they had not before them, as we had before us, the compulsion of the imminent menace to Belgium. But the message was first read and laid aside; it could have no influence then on our discussion. It was to the good to know it, but what mattered it now, when the issue of the Belgian Treaty was bringing everyone to the conclusion that we must fight by the side of France, and to the determination to do so?

The narrative has been brought to the close of the last Cabinet before the speech in the House of Commons on August 3. It may be well now to say something first about the circumstances in which this speech had to be prepared, and then about the speech itself.

The week ending with August 1 had been most exhausting. The strain for every member of the Cabinet must have been intense. In addition to Cabinets, I had the strain of holding conversations of great moment with Ambassadors, of dictating after each the summary of it that appeared eventually as a telegram or despatch to the British Ambassador at Berlin or Paris or elsewhere. Some telegrams were not dictated, but were written with my own hand. Communications vitally important at this moment were daily being received through Foreign Ambassadors in London, verbally, or through British Ambassadors abroad by telegram. These, however critical, had to be considered and dealt with promptly, for every hour mattered. All this made what was a trying week for everyone, an exceptionally heavy one for me; but perhaps it made the week in one sense easier for me. Work, incessant, peremptory work, relieves nervous strain; it allows no vacant hours in which anxiety can prey upon an unoccupied mind; it wearies, but by that very weariness helps to ensure sleep sufficient to restore; unless or until it causes exhaustion, it stimulates. The sense of responsibility in that week was great, but responsibility elevates when it does not crush. But when the week was over, and the hope of peace was gone, the strain was felt more severely. Sunday brought no rest; there was a Cabinet in the morning and another in the afternoon. When these were over, the discussions had become definite and taken shape enough for me to forecast the lines which a speech on behalf of the Government must take in the House of Commons on Monday afternoon. Sunday evening was spent arranging into notes the material of which my head was full. There was no time for verbal preparation; all that could be done was to select and arrange what should be said, without much thought as to how it could be well or best said; and to see that such documents or quotations as I wanted to read were ready. These, of course, the private secretaries got for me.

On Monday morning there was no time for further preparation: it was necessary to see the telegrams in case there was something urgent or new to be considered. Then there was another Cabinet. It was fully two o'clock before I got back from it to my room at the Foreign Office. There was barely an hour to go to Queen Anne's Gate, where I was staying, to get some food, which was then essential, and to be in the House of Commons by three o'clock, and in that interval to give what final thought was possible to the speech.

When I entered the room at the Foreign Office, a private secretary came in to tell me that the German Ambassador was waiting and most anxious to see me. It was hardly possible that he had come with anything from the German Government, for surely they had nothing more to say to us; but if he had, it was my business to hear it, and essential for me to know what it was, before I spoke. Time must be made to see him. He came in, and his first words told me that he brought nothing from Berlin. He asked what had the Cabinet decided? What was I going to say in the House of Commons? Was it a declaration of war? I answered that it was not a declaration of war, but a statement of conditions. He asked very earnestly what were the conditions. I would have told him personally anything, for no man had worked harder to avert war than Lichnowsky, or more genuinely hated this coming war; but he was bound to telegraph whatever was said to Berlin, and the German Government, of all people, must not know an hour in advance of others abroad what was to be said. I replied that in an hour's time the whole world would know, and I could say nothing in advance. He asked, was the neutrality of Belgium one of the conditions? I could only repeat that I could say nothing before I spoke. He then implored that we should not make Belgian neutrality one of the conditions; he knew nothing, he said, of the plans of the German General Staff: he could not suppose that a serious violation was one of them; but it might be that it was part of the plan for German troops to go through one small corner perhaps of Belgium; if so, they could not alter that now. I was sure what he said of his own want of knowledge of German military plans was true; he, at least, was no party to the violation of Belgium; but I could say nothing. There was no time to make any record of the conversation, and there is none but what is set down here. It was the last time that I saw him in the Foreign Office, and the vision of it is clear now—he standing in front of the door that he had entered, and I standing with him, hard-pressed for time, and ready to go out.

When I stood up to speak in the House of Commons I do not recall feeling nervous. At such a moment there could be neither hope of personal success nor fear of personal failure. In a great crisis, a man who has to act or speak stands bare and stripped of choice. He has to do what it is in him to do: just this is what he will and must do, and he can do no other.

As for the speech itself,[1] it was never revised, and is on record as reported at the time, and must stand as it is; but one or two things may be said here about it.

At first it was in my mind to read to the House Bethmann-Hollweg's bid for our neutrality, and the reply made to it; but this was deliberately discarded. To read that would tend to stir indignation, and the House ought to come to its decisions on grounds of weight, not of passion. We were not to go into the war because Bethmann-Hollweg had made a dishonouring proposal to us. We should not be influenced by that in our decision. When the decision was made, then the communication with Bethmann-Hollweg should be published, and it

[1] See Appendix D., p. 308.

would no doubt strengthen feeling; but this ought to be later—after the decision, not before it. I was myself stirred with resentment and indignation at what seemed to me Germany's crime in precipitating the war, and all I knew of Prussian militarism was hateful; but these must not be the motives of our going into the war. It was not on the case against Germany that our treasure was to be spent and British lives sacrificed in the war. These considerations worked in my mind by flashes of instinct in the pressure of those hours, rather than by calm proofs of reasoning; but it was these considerations that decided the line of this speech. There is in it a short and passing reference to the bid for our neutrality, but not made in a way to attract special attention or arouse feeling against Germany, and used only to enforce the argument about the importance of Belgium. Let anyone, who is interested in pursuing this train of thought, read first the White Paper, which, be it noted, contains all the material things that we knew then about events immediately preceding the outbreak of the war; then let him read the speech, and he will see how little use was made of documents that could have been used to prejudice opinion against Germany. The White Paper came, later, to justify the line we had taken, to show what we had done and what Germany and others had done; but it came to confirm a decision already taken, and to give information that Parliament and the country should have.

The real reason for going into the war was that, if we did not stand by France and stand up for Belgium against this aggression, we should be isolated, discredited, and hated; and there would be before us nothing but a miserable and ignoble future. The speech was directed to presenting this consideration in the way that would convince and make the strongest appeal to the House, and which was, in fact, the way this issue presented itself from the first to some of us, and in the end to all the Cabinet, except the two, John Morley and John Burns, who resigned. I never fully understood the reason of these resignations, and will therefore say only this about them—that we felt sure they were based on deep and sincere conviction, not on any pusillanimity or opportunism; and we respected them accordingly.

One other point about the speech. It was felt to be essential to make clear to the House that its liberty of decision was not hampered by any engagements entered into previously without its knowledge. Whatever obligation there was to France arose from what those must feel who had welcomed, approved, sustained the Anglo-French friendship, that was open and known to all. In this connexion there was nothing to disclose except the engagement about the north and west coasts of France taken a few hours before, and the letters exchanged with Cambon in 1912, the letter that expressly stipulated that there was no engagement. It was not till 1923, nine years later, that a charge of having omitted the last sentence of that letter was brought to my notice. My first impulse was to deny the thing as impossible; but it is so: the last sentence of the letter does not appear in the report of the speech.

A question, according to the report, was interjected about the date of the letter and it may be that the interruption in the reading of the letter, so near the end,

Photograph by the James Press Agency

PRINCE LICHNOWSKY
German Ambassador in London, 1912-1914

caused an accidental omission, or perhaps I thought the last sentence unimportant, as it did not affect the sense and main purport of what had already been read out. I cannot say. The letter was published in full in the White Paper two or three days later; the proof of that Paper was submitted to me before publication; I certainly did not raise any question of how the letter should appear in the White Paper, and so I must either have attached no importance to the omission of a sentence in the speech, or have been unconscious of there having been any omission.

Here, too, it must be said, in answer to another allegation, that this letter to Cambon, published in the White Paper, is the actual letter written in November 1912, and is given without omission or alteration of a word.

After the speech was over, but before the House rose, the following communication was brought to me; it had just been received from the Belgian Legation in London:

Germany sent yesterday evening at seven o'clock a note proposing to Belgium friendly neutrality, covering free passage on Belgian territory, and promising maintenance of independence of the kingdom and possession at the conclusion of peace, and threatening, in case of refusal, to treat Belgium as an enemy. A time limit of twelve hours was fixed for the reply. The Belgians have answered that an attack on their neutrality would be a flagrant violation of the rights of nations, and that to accept the German proposal would be to sacrifice the honour of a nation. Conscious of its duty, Belgium is firmly resolved to repel aggression by all possible means.

If this communication had been received before I went to the House it would, of course, have been read out as part of the speech; it would certainly have strengthened the statement very much, and would probably have shortened it by making unnecessary and eliminating some hypothetical circumlocution. As it was, it had to be read out afterwards and separately. When this was done, there can have been no doubt left in any mind that war was certain and inevitable.

An ultimatum was sent to Berlin requiring a satisfactory answer about Belgium on August 4, by midnight.

That evening some of us sat with the Prime Minister in the Cabinet Room in 10 Downing Street. I was there in touch with the Foreign Office to certify that no satisfactory reply had come from Berlin, though this was, after all that had happened, a foregone conclusion and a matter of form. Churchill also was among those present, ready at the appointed hour to send out the war order, that the fleet were expecting. Midnight came. We were at war.

CHAPTER XVIII

(1914)

SOME REFLECTIONS

The Immensity of the War—The "Lamps Going Out"—The Economic Disaster—Opinion in France, Russia, and Germany—What the German Emperor wanted—The Helplessness of German Civilians —The Deciding Power in Germany—Calculations that miscarried —The German Motive—Offensive or Defensive?—The Attitude of Austria—Qualifications of the Original Judgment—Could Great Britain have stood aside?—The Probable Result, if she had—The Conditional Obligation to France—Impossibility of an Absolute Pledge—A Summary of Causes and Events.

THE endeavour of the two preceding chapters has been to give an account of what passed in the week preceding the war, so far as we knew it at the time; to give the sequence of events to the reader, as these presented themselves to me from July 25 to August 4, 1914; to tell the impressions made as they developed day by day and the thoughts to which they gave rise.

This chapter will be devoted to reviewing those impressions and those thoughts in the light of all that has happened and of what we know now; in other words, my object will be to write a chapter of history rather than narrative.

Let us examine the first of the four considerations given in Chapter XVI,[1] as dominant in my mind in the last week of July 1914. This was, that a great European war would be a catastrophe on an unprecedented scale, and

[1] Vol. I, p. 302.

that this would be so obvious to all the Great Powers that, when on the edge of the abyss, they would call a halt and recoil from it. The first half of this impression unfortunately admits of no qualification now. We know the full tale of the loss of life, of the maiming and wounding; we know this, but the amount of grief and suffering caused by it is more than human thought or sympathy can measure.

A friend came to see me on one of the evenings of the last week—he thinks it was on Monday, August 3. We were standing at a window of my room in the Foreign Office. It was getting dusk, and the lamps were being lit in the space below on which we were looking. My friend recalls that I remarked on this with the words: "The lamps are going out all over Europe; we shall not see them lit again in our life-time."

The full extent of the economic disaster of the war is not yet known. Europe is still engaged in grappling with it; we have certainly not yet seen the end of it; it is possible that we have not seen the worst of it. Some of us thought that economic disaster would make itself felt more quickly after the outbreak of war; that it would rapidly become so acute as to bring war to an end. In that we were wrong, but we were wrong only in our estimate of the time and the manner in which economic disaster would make itself felt. It might have been more merciful to Europe as a whole, if this disaster had made itself felt more quickly and imperatively, and so had shortened the war. The longer the war went on the greater the magnitude of the economic disaster was sure to be, and the more prolonged and enduring would be the effects of it. Those who had the worst forebodings of what war would mean, did not over-estimate the human suffering or the economic distress that it has actually caused.

The war has also had a great effect on the old social and political order. In some countries it has destroyed it; in all European countries it has shaken it. The crust of the old order was wearing thin already. I felt that if war came the new forces pent within must break through. If war came, and proved to be the catastrophe that was anticipated, people would not stop to apportion war guilt, to blame one country or to acquit another; they would take a wholesale view and say that, no matter who was to blame for this war, the system under which such a catastrophe was possible must be changed. This feeling found expression in an interview I had with the Austrian Ambassador which is recorded in a later chapter,[1] and it was with me constantly at this time.

How much of this forecast has actually been verified? Six Great European Powers took part in the war. France is the only one of them of which it can be said that the social and political order has not been changed to an extent and degree that seemed almost impossible or incredible to us in 1914. Russia has had a revolution and is in a condition that seems to baffle description; Germany is a Republic; Italy has had a revolution sufficient to change her whole political system; and Austria-Hungary, as a Great Power, has disappeared. Britain has had a Labour Government, though, according to our precedents, we are making our revolution slowly and by constitutional methods.

[1] See infra, p. 239.

Let us now examine the other half of this first consideration—the opinion that other European Governments
would see the abyss and recoil from it. This unfortunately was wrong.

France, indeed, dreaded war, and did all she could to
avoid it.   French minds were probably more preoccupied
with the awful peril of war to France than with the dread
of war as a general catastrophe.   The immense growth
and strength of Germany had smothered all French intention to attempt a *revanche*.   The idea of recovering the
lost provinces of Alsace and Lorraine had tacitly been
dropped, though the French Government might not have
dared to say in public that it had been for ever abandoned.
The Franco-Russian Alliance did not contemplate or
cover a French *revanche*.   I once said to Metternich,
when he was still German Ambassador in London, that
though I had not seen or been told the terms of the
Franco-Russian Alliance, I assumed that it did not cover
a *revanche*.   Metternich smiled grimly and said, "Yes;
we know very well that it does not."   France had no Ally
but Russia on whom to count even for a war of defence,
and the Russian Army was an uncertain factor.   It was
certainly big, but it was sure to be slow, and France,
therefore, in the event of war would feel the first terrific
onset of an armed nation, nearly double that of France
in numbers, with an army so highly trained and equipped
that Germany had persuaded others, besides herself, that
it was invincible.   France, therefore, in these last critical
days, went to extreme limits to avoid giving provocation.
She had the memory of 1870 and the apprehension of

something much more formidable than 1870. When the shock of war came she met it with all the desperate gallantry of a nation fighting for its life; but she never sought war, and till the last moment strove to avoid it.

Of Russia one cannot speak as of one compact, sentient unit. The Tsar certainly desired peace. No one can doubt that his suggestions to the German Emperor for a settlement by use of the machinery of the Hague Tribunal was genuine, nor can the Russian mobilization be fairly construed as evidence of a desire for war. After the veto of a Conference, with Austria mobilized and Germany ready to strike, what counsellor could have honestly advised the Tsar that mobilization in Russia was a premature, unnecessary precaution? That Russia felt that she would not submit a second time to a humiliation such as that of 1908, is probable. That the Tsar, or Sazonof, or anyone who had a decisive word in Russia was planning to provoke or to make war I do not believe. Perhaps it may be true to say, of Russia, that she was like a huge, unwieldy ship, which in time of agitation kept an uncertain course; not because she was directed by malevolent intentions, but because the steering-gear was weak.

What about Germany? Were the German people thirsting for war, or even consciously desiring it? I do not suppose so. But the outbreak of war was received in Germany with frantic demonstrations and enthusiasm. In Bismarck's time Germany had had three wars: the war against Denmark in 1864; against Austria in 1866; against France in 1870. All these wars had been short, had lasted only a few months, and had been completely successful, and out of them had come the German Empire.

That Empire was now, after forty years of consolidation and growth, the most mighty Power actually, if not potentially, in the world. Was it to dread war? On the contrary, was it not possible that war might be another stage in its growth? We need not give too positive answers to these questions; but surely it is within the mark to say that there was not in Germany a dread of war or a repugnance to war strong enough to create a determined will to peace. If German opinion did not desire war, it was at least content to leave the conduct of affairs in the hands of the Emperor and the powers behind the throne, whoever they might be.

In fact, German and French people both thought of war, consciously or unconsciously, in 1914 in terms of the experience of people in the latter half of the nineteenth century. The French thought of it as the possible end of the history of France as a great Power; to Germans it must have seemed a possible step forward in the history of their Empire. We must therefore look for the real German policy and views elsewhere than in public opinion. What was the real policy that wielded German influence in the critical days before the war? We shall never know all, for, if there were persons in power who were bent on war, the record of their views and work will not be found in official documents. No revolution will unearth them; perhaps there are none. No account need be taken of the German Emperor; we know, from the Kautsky documents, the line that the Emperor took. He had told Tschirschky (the German Ambassador at Vienna) to stop talking what the Emperor called "nonsense": the "nonsense" being that Tschirschky had urged

moderation on the Austrian Government after the murder
of the Archduke; Tschirschky was reprimanded for this
moderation, and the Austrian Ambassador at Berlin was
told that he had been reprimanded. The authorities at
Berlin did not always treat their Ambassadors with much
consideration for their dignity or feelings, though for-
eigners were expected to show this deference, as Metternich once impressed upon me, when the London police
had found some difficulty in getting way made for his
carriage.

Then the German Emperor proceeded to encourage
Austria against Serbia, not without some contemptuous
surprise that there should be so much spirit shown at
Vienna. The language of his marginal notes, "Stamp
upon this rabble," suggests a huntsman encouraging
hounds to break up a fox. He was satisfied with the
Austrian ultimatum to Serbia, he was also satisfied with
the Serbian reply. "There is now no cause for war" was
his marginal note on the reply. Austria had stamped;
Serbia had grovelled; all the materials were now ready
for staging another diplomatic triumph, with Germany
as the brilliant second in shining armour. This was all
that the German Emperor wanted; and, if matters had
rested with him, there would have been no European war
arising out of the Austro-Serbian dispute. But, when
Austria condemned the Serbian reply as unsatisfactory,
the German Emperor did nothing; and after that he let
the German and Austrian Governments veto a Conference
to settle the one or two points that the Serbian reply had
left outstanding; he made no response to the appeal of
the Tsar to get the dispute referred to the Hague Tri-

bunal; he let his own Government reply to the Russian mobilization, not with a counter mobilization of a similar character, but with an ultimatum that made war certain.

If we are to look for the real direction of German policy in the days preceding the war, we must look elsewhere than to the man who wrote the marginal comments on the Kautsky documents. It is of no use to look to the action of Bethmann-Hollweg and Jagow—the men who, having nominal direction of German policy, folded their hands after the murder of the Archduke, and, according to their own account of the matter, never asked to see the terms of their Austrian Ally's ultimatum to Serbia before it was sent; the men who, after that ultimatum was sent and the Serbian reply received, expressed some criticism of the former and thought that the latter went further in the direction of conciliation than could have been expected; and who yet let things drift or spoke only in whispers at Vienna, when a decisive word was wanted. I believe that neither the Emperor nor Bethmann-Hollweg nor Jagow planned or desired war. But the Emperor, in the critical moment after the Serbian reply, apparently withheld his influence, when it might have been decisive for peace—a moral abdication that four years later led to the material abdication of his throne; and Bethmann-Hollweg and Jagow had no influence. It has been told me that in later years Jagow said of Bethmann-Hollweg and himself that, in the days before the war, they were "Machtlos." Whether Jagow said this or not, it is a true saying, and probably Bethmann-Hollweg and Jagow knew it all along to be true. They were powerless, and they were the only Germans with whom other Governments, including our own, could deal.

What deciding power was then in Germany? The one steady, constant, organized authority was the military one; and there can be little doubt that high military opinion held that war must come and that in 1914 the time for war had come. All preparations had been made for 1914; even in finance Germans had as far as possible got in what was owed to them, and arranged matters so that, when war came, they should owe and should not be owed money abroad. The capital levy had been made, the final and supreme effort to equip the Army. Some German naval opinion was adverse to war in 1914; but that was not on the ground that war was not to come: it was solely on the ground that in two or three years more the German Fleet would be more powerful.[1] The only difference between military and naval authorities was as to the year when war should be made; there was no difference in the opinion that war would have to be made. The military authorities settled it. The operation against France would work according to plan, as in 1870; all the more certainly, perhaps, because this time the plan included an attack through Belgium, and therefore in the more over-whelming strength for which the wider front provided by the inclusion of Belgium gave fuller opportunity. If the British Expeditionary Force were sent, it would be

---

[1] See evidence of Admiral Koch before the Second Sub-committee of the Committee appointed by the National Constituent Assembly to enquire into the responsibility for the war: "We hoped to be able to delay the war for a few years in order to have the battle-fleet of quite different dimensions—that is, different in the way of numbers, so that we should then have been in a position ourselves to seek a decision ourselves off the enemy's coasts. Unfortunately the war overtook us." (*Official German Documents,* Carnegie Endowment Translation, vol. i, p. 532.)

too small to make a difference to the result.   (It is known, now, that on the outbreak of war the German military authorities told the Navy not to make an effort to prevent the British Army from landing in France, because, if it did land, the German Army could deal with it).[2]   In a few weeks not only would Paris fall, but the French armies would be defeated and out of action.   France would then be held with comparative ease, and the whole German Army might be turned against Russia.   In a few months Russia would tire of defeat and loss with no prospect of success.   All this would be accomplished before British naval pressure could have time to tell upon Germany, who would then be supreme over all the Continent of Europe and Asia Minor, for the Turk would be with a victorious Germany.

There is nothing fantastic in attributing such plans to German military authority—they very nearly succeeded; according to German calculations they must have been bound to succeed.   The examination of the error in these calculations, which German eyes could not see, must be reserved for a chapter on the war.   There seems to be no doubt that there was a military party in Germany that had decided for war in 1914 (though German diplomacy was expected to do what it could to make it appear that the war guilt was with someone else) and that no such settlement as in the year of Agadir would have been permitted.   This crisis was to be forced to the point of war. If France abandoned Russia and offered to remain neutral, that was not to suffice; France was to be required to cede, as pledges of neutrality, the two fortresses of Toul and

[2] See Von Tirpitz, *My Memories*, vol. ii, p. 290, English translation.

Verdun. There was to be no escape from humiliation, not even by neutrality.

The judgment to be passed upon all this is not a very simple matter. The German military view, assuming it to be as stated, may have one or the other of two aspects; and the historian's judgment of it will depend upon which of these aspects it is that he selects as the true one. They shall both be stated here.

The first is that Germany was deliberately aiming at world predominance. For this purpose, not content with the greatest Army the world had ever seen, she was building a big Navy as well. Her object was first the hegemony of the Continent and then predominance over Britain. Passages from the German Emperor's speeches could easily be used to show that he believed the Germans to be a chosen people, and that belief lends to the assumption that other nations have no virtues, no rights; that the interest of the chosen people is the only test of right and wrong; and it causes a general hypertrophy of patriotism. The danger of this is expressed in Latin in three words, *corruptio, optimi pessima;* the saying applies to all the best things in human life—to religion, to art, to music—and patriotism is no exception to the application of it. But it is not fair to take the Emperor as typical of anything; he was *sui generis.* It will be enough to sum up this aspect by saying that many persons in Britain thought, and still think, that Germans felt German *Kultur* to be a superior thing that ought to dominate the world; that they did not believe in "live and let live" or in equality; and that, to come to the concrete and particular, they considered that there was not room in the world for both the

British and German Empires. It is not surprising if this was a dominant notion in Germany. Most nations think better of themselves than of others, but when this opinion takes the form of an attempt at world power, other nations are justified in regarding it as an aggression, and in saying that, if the aggressor fails, he richly deserves his fate.

The other aspect in which German action may be viewed requires a different judgment. In this aspect German militarism would still seem to have made the war in 1914, but its case for doing so would be stated thus. Europe had become an armed camp. The burden of armaments was becoming an intolerable strain, which must end in war. And did not the piling up of armaments imply that force was the only thing that counted among nations? War was therefore inevitable. It was not reasonable that Germany, who was at the height of her military power, with her maximum of men and equipment and perfection of strategic railways to the frontiers of other countries, should wait till her neighbours, more particularly Russia, had increased the size and efficiency of their armies and perfected their strategic railways. If war really was inevitable surely a patriotic German was entitled to choose for war the year and the moment that best suited Germany. This case, in short, for making war is, as Germans themselves put it, that it was an offensive-defensive war.

The first comment on this aspect of German militarism is that it was Germany, more than any other nation, who had forced the pace in armaments, first in armies and then in navies. If war were really inevitable, it was Germany who had the largest share of responsibility for producing the state of affairs that made war inevitable. It was Germany who had been most quick to oppose suggestions for agreements to arrest the growth of armaments; who had resented as unfriendly, if not aggressive towards herself, the very harmless tentative of Campbell-Bannerman in *The Nation* article of 1907, and had blocked every movement in that direction, down to the Churchill proposal for a naval holiday in 1913. If military preparation and strategic railways in France or Russia were to be regarded as justification for Germany to make war, then the corresponding preparations in Germany were at least an equal justification to any other nation, for in every way German preparations and armament had been ahead of that of other nations.

There is another comment to be made. To make war, until it is impossible to avoid it, is a crime. Is it justifiable or wise to precipitate a crime, because one thinks that someone else will sooner or later commit it? The answer to this question would need a discussion on belief or disbelief in Divine superintendence and the reign of Moral Law in human affairs; this would be too great a digression here. The conclusion of this argument shall be brought within very comprehensible limits by stating its minimum. Those who argue that German militarism was justified by militarism in her neighbours must in fairness at least admit that militarism in Russia or elsewhere was justified by militarism in Germany.

The estimate formed at the time, 1914, of the attitude of Austria must be qualified. This estimate was that Austria simply and foolishly hoped for a triumph over Serbia without the danger of war with Russia; that, when

she found this to be a miscalculation, she tried to get out
of it by diplomatic settlement with Russia direct; but
found it was too late. Her Ally, Germany, had gone to
war with Russia and dragged Austria in. If this view
is put to a German I am told the answer is that Austria's
delay in going to war with Russia was a pose, intended
to clear Austria, even at the expense of Germany, of
responsibility for war. The truth probably is, that there
were sinister and reckless influences in Austria. The
persons and forces that moved in the Friedjung and the
Agram trials and made use there of forged documents
were still in existence; and they were capable of any crime
and any blunder. In Austria, as in Russia, there was no
head with direction and grip of affairs.

The upshot of all this is, that on the Continent all the
Great Powers most concerned in this crisis were thinking
of war in terms of previous experience, and of the latter
half of the nineteenth century. We were alone in fore-
boding that war in the twentieth century would be unlike
anything that had preceded it. The abyss was not generally seen even when Governments came to the edge of it.
Could more have been done to make them see it? I think
not. When once we were in the diplomatic crisis we were
so occupied in searching for practical expedients for solution that there was no time for abstract argument about
the catastrophe of modern war. In a crisis people cannot
change their settled points of view on general matters;
they are too busy with particulars of the moment. Pre-
dictions that war would bring a general social upheaval
fell flat. Even now, with all the experience of the war
behind us, it is doubtful whether Europe is penetrated

with a sense that war must be prevented in future, and that this must be the common purpose of all nations. Europe was not ready before the war for such an appeal against war; it is not certain that Europe is ready yet to respond whole-heartedly and effectively to such an appeal.

Little more need be said of the assumption (No. 2 in Chapter XVI [1]) that Germany counted for everything in the crisis, and that it was only with her we had to deal. It is clear that it was not the case that Bethmann-Hollweg could control the Austrian Government, and apparently he did more than we knew at the time to recommend a Conference or some form of mediation; but if his was not the decisive word at Berlin, it could not be so at Vienna. But it would have made no difference if we had dealt at Vienna as strenuously as at Berlin. We could have dealt only with Berchthold, the Minister for Foreign Affairs at Vienna, and he seems not to have counted at all. The military elements in Austria-Hungary had been set in their course by encouragement to take a stiff line with Serbia. Nothing but a decisive word from military elements in Berlin would have pulled them up; they would have paid no attention to anything said from London.

The statement (No. 3 in Chapter XVI [1]) that if war came we ought to stand by France must next be reviewed. Any reader of Chapter XVI may reasonably find the following question suggested to him by what is written. Ought not anyone, who thought that European war must be such a huge catastrophe, have determined to keep Britain out of it? One answer is, that a large part of the Cabinet did so resolve, and the narrative has shown how

[1] See supra, Vol. I, p. 302.

impossible it was for them to keep that resolution. But this does not explain the position of those who, seeing modern war as a great catastrophe, yet held, even before the invasion of Belgium, that British interests would require us to go into war, if war there must be, on the side of France.

The rightness of this opinion will best be made apparent by examining an opinion expressed the other day in a political speech at home. I forget who the speaker was, but his opinion was to the effect that if, in 1914, we could have known all that the war would mean, no member of the Government would have agreed to go into it. This statement, final as it sounds, is not the end of thought: it makes one begin to think. It is a commonplace of conversation that, if we had kept out at the beginning, we should have been drawn in later on. I remember once saying to a friend that, if we had not gone into the war, France must have been beaten, for the Germans would have declared steel contraband of war and with their powerful fleet have cut off from France the supply of foreign, including British steel, which soon became essential to enable France to carry on the war. "That," said my friend, "would of course have brought us in." That particular instance may seem too narrow a ground on which to base so great a conclusion. Then let us take a broader consideration. The United States was removed from the scene of war by 3,000 miles of ocean—an ocean from which the Middle West and West, the majority of their population, were remote, some by hundreds, and some even by thousands of miles. The political interests of the United States were not menaced: at the outset the

sympathies of the people were divided, where these were
not indifferent to European war altogether. As neutrals
they throve in some branches of commerce; materially
they had something to lose and nothing to gain by departing from neutrality and entering the war. Yet they came
in. It is out of all reason to believe that the forces which
moved so great a nation, from such a distance, to enter the
war would not have compelled Britain to take part in it
too. No ocean separated us from it; our shore was within
sound of the guns; our world position was bound to be
affected by the result of the war. To anyone who thinks
that we might have stood aside at the first, but must have
come in later, there is one simple reply. If we were to
come in at all, let us be thankful that we did it at
once—it was better so, better for our good name, better for a favourable result, than if we had first tried
to keep out and then found ourselves impelled or compelled to go in.

The only position to be examined at more length is that
of those who, pacifist in 1914, or who have become pacifist
since by contemplation of the ruin of war, hold that we
could have kept out of the war for good and all, and that
we ought to have done so. This opinion must be based
on the premise that a great country, though part of a
militarist continent, can escape the effects of militarism
by refusing to fight; that it can, as far as its own welfare
is concerned, limit the consequences of a great war by
refusing to take part in it. This premise, as applied to
the war of 1914, is not sound. The result of taking part
in the war is known; it entailed immense loss and suffering, but it does not therefore follow that we should have

avoided it or could have done so. Have those who think we should have kept out of the war drawn any clear picture in their thought of what would have happened if we had stood aside in 1914? They give no sign that they have thought of this at all. Let us think it out as well as we can. What would have happened?

Paris would have been taken according to the German calculation. Paris very nearly was taken; there was nothing to spare. If there had been lacking anything, French or British, that was used to stop the retreat and accomplish the battle of the Marne, the Germans would have reached Paris; the absence of the British Expeditionary Force would have made a difference that would have been fatal. How long France would have been able to hold out after Paris fell is matter for military conjecture. Her Fleet having to contain the Austrian Fleet in the Mediterranean could not have kept the Atlantic and Channel sea communications open. France would have been cut off from foreign supplies of iron and coal, of which some of her own most valuable supplies would have been in German hands, as indeed they actually were even after the battle of the Marne. The end was certain. Huge defeats of Russian armies would have followed; and, with no prospect of recovery in France, those elements in Russia that were always susceptible to German influence would have asserted themselves. Russia would have made peace probably in no very long time; especially if Germany, having gained the day, had been wise enough to make the terms appear easy. Then Germany would have been supreme on the Continent. Belgium would have been under her heel. The fear of the fate

of Belgium would have been before the eyes of every
neutral State; the position of Italy, who had refused to
join the other two members of the Triple Alliance in the
war, would not have been pleasant.

Consider what the position of Britain would have been.
We should have been isolated; we should have had no
friend in the world; no one would have hoped or feared
anything from us, or thought our friendship worth having.

We should have been discredited, should have been
held to have played an inglorious and ignoble part.
Even in the United States we should have suffered in
good opinion.   Those Americans who were outspokenly
pro-Ally and who wanted the United States to join the
Allies at once or much earlier than their own country
eventually did, would have despised us.   We would have
lost what pro-British sympathy there was in the United
States, and we should have gained nothing there: the
feeling that was indifferent about us would have remained
indifferent; the feeling that was anti-British would have
been anti-British still.   Every neutral country would have
held that we had turned our back on a clear obligation
to Belgium and done this in spite of the Belgian appeal
and of the fight she herself was making against overwhelming odds.

We should have been hated.   Even after the Franco-
Prussian War of 1870 we incurred much odium for
having stood aside.   I think the odium was then quite
unreasonable, but the *tertius gaudens* is always hated.
Our intense unpopularity on the Continent at some previous times has been due largely to the opinion that we
were always taking a hand and never taking a side.   In

those days we had boasted of a "splendid isolation"—in other words, of having no friend. Of late years we had found the position of having no friend to be unsafe; we had made friends. If we had stood aside now, we should again have had no friends. France and Russia would not have loved Germany after the war, but in one thing they would have been ready to join with her, and this would have been in a policy directed against Britain, who had stood aside while they suffered. In Germany militarism and navalism would have been supreme. The Socialism in Germany of which we heard so much, counted for nothing on the outbreak of war. For a time, after a triumphant war, it must have been still more subordinate; if it had become troublesome, its energies would have been turned into patriotic channels once more, this time in war against Britain. And that war we should certainly have had to face. Germany would have wielded the whole diplomatic strength of the Continent. For a time we might have struggled on ingloriously, squeezed and thwarted everywhere. There would have been weakness, moreover, inside the Empire. What the Dominions would have thought I do not venture to say, but quite a substantial section of British opinion would have regarded with shame the conduct of this country in standing aside; some of our self-respect would have gone. Finally, when the German Fleet was ready, war would have been forced on us, and we should have been found dispirited, half beaten before the war began. By that time the full range of the big gun, the extended use of the submarine, would have been known; the French shores would have been in unfriendly hands, and the Channel

would have been closed to us. Can anyone say that this
picture is remote from probability? If anyone thinks so,
let him read the second edition of von Bülow's book[1] and
the *Memoirs and Letters of von Kiderlen Waechter,* and
consider German feeling and the part played by German
militarism in policy before the war. Then let him
picture to himself faithfully what German militarism
and its policy would have meant for us after a war from
which Germany had emerged supreme.

It is not the intention to suggest that all that is set down
in this chapter was in our minds in the week before the
war—some of it was, some of it was not. The two
preceding chapters tell what I thought in 1914, and how
we came to act as we did. We did not then believe war
to be inevitable. We had no thought ourselves of going
into war in 1914 because we supposed that sooner or later
we should have to fight. We just strove to prevent war
happening at all. But when, in spite of our efforts, war
came, it is well that we took our place in it and at the
outset. The latent forces at work became apparent as
the war proceeded, and the incidents in which the war
originated were forgotten as these forces were revealed.
It was a great struggle between the *Kultur* that stood for
militarism and the free unmilitarist democratic ideal. It
was the perception of this, whether consciously or unconsciously, that brought the United States into the war—the
United States, which as a whole had cared little about
the incidents that caused the war at the outset, and which
did not as a whole then perceive it. But it was the

[1] *Imperial Germany,* by Prince Bernard von Bülow. (English translation,
with a Foreword by J. W. Headlam. New and revised edition, November,
1916. Cassell & Co.)

perception of it, revealed to us as the war developed, that made us know that we were fighting for the very life of what Britain and the self-governing Dominions cared for. We could not have escaped that struggle between militarism and democracy by turning our backs upon the war in August 1914. The thing would have pursued us until we had to turn and face it, and that would have been when it was even stronger and when we had become weak and isolated. We suffered grievously, most grievously after going into the war in 1914, but we came out of it honourably and with our country safe; if we had not gone into the war in 1914 we should have had later, and perhaps not so very much later, to undergo suffering at least as great, and we should have perished ignobly.

One other picture may be suggested. After a German triumph on the Continent, accomplished rapidly, while Great Britain and America stood aside, the people of the United States might have perceived what the inevitable issue was, and, when the struggle was renewed, might have made common cause with us; and so militarism might have been defeated. I will not attempt to trace to their probable conclusions all the hypotheses that this picture suggests. Such a course would certainly have been less honourable for us. If anyone is inclined to prefer it, he can ask Americans whether they think that this would have been the actual sequel; and whether they would have preferred it to what they and we actually did.

The consideration (No. 4 in Chapter XVI[1]) that no pledge must be given to France and Russia which Parliament and the country might not fulfil has been fully

[1] See supra, Vol. I, p. 303.

explained. There is no qualification to be made of what has been said about it. The pledge simply could not have been given sooner than it was. To give it on my own initiative, without consulting the Cabinet, was, of course, out of the question. To do so would have been criminal, for such a pledge would have been worthless. The Cabinet, in the earlier days, was not prepared to give such a pledge, and, with the existing state of feeling in Parliament and the country, it was not in a position to give it. The French appeal for help was brought before the Cabinet; if any of us had pressed for a pledge to be given in the earlier days of that week, we should have divided the Cabinet. The Cabinet, in such a grave matter, stood in a similar position to the House of Commons as that in which the Secretary of State stood to the Cabinet. If this Cabinet, in the earlier days, had asked Parliament to ratify such a pledge, it would have divided the House of Commons and the country. The violation of Belgium, when it came, would have found us with a divided Cabinet, possibly with one Government resigned and another not formed; with a House of Commons and a country paralysed by division of opinion, with one section vehemently committed to helping France and another section, with equal vehemence, opposed to taking any part in war. Looking back on it all, it seems to me that the course actually followed in those critical days was the only one that could have led to the entry of Britain into the war, immediately, whole-heartedly and with practical unanimity. This was the actual result. It was a result that had seemed exceedingly doubtful when the crisis first began.

As the giving of a pledge in the earlier days was impossible, it is hardly worth while to consider whether, if it had been possible, the giving of a pledge to France and Russia, and the intimation to Germany that it had been given, would have prevented war. I feel sure that it would not, though I am aware that there is much British and French opinion to the contrary.

The military authorities in Germany had made up their minds that the entry of Britain into the war would not make their plans miscarry. Their military plans, they thought, would succeed before the pressure of the British Army would have had time to tell. For this reason naval authorities who, like Admiral Tirpitz, wished political crises to be avoided until the German Fleet was stronger, were either overruled or not consulted. So little did the German military authorities consider that the landing of the British Expeditionary Force in France would upset their advance on Paris, that the Navy was apparently told that it need not attempt to prevent the landing.

Germany would naturally have preferred that we should not come in; to keep us out, she was ready to promise anything that would not interfere with her military operations (such as not to attack the north and west coasts of France), but her military authorities considered that our entry into the war would not make any difference to the success of their advance on Paris. After the capture of Paris the Channel ports must fall into German hands, and what further use would the British Expeditionary Force have been to France after that? They underrated the value of our Expeditionary Force.

Before the war the German Military Attaché in

London told Haldane that he kept reporting to Berlin that the British Expeditionary Force, though, from a continental point of view, absurdly small in numbers, was in quality the finest thing in the world, "and," he added, "they won't believe me."

Everything we know goes to prove that the German military authorities calculated on a war, not of years but of months, during which they would not be seriously hurt by anything the British Army could do; that they thought they would deal easily with the British Expeditionary Force if it came: in other words, that their plans covered the risk of Britain coming in, and that they were prepared and had made up their minds to take that risk.

If this were so, an early intimation that we should join France and Russia would not have prevented war; it would have led to an outburst of German propaganda, and to the cry that British hostility had at this last moment made war inevitable by stiffening the backs of France and Russia.   It would have been said that our entry had incited France and Russia to attack Germany.

Here it may be well to summarize the course that policy took so far as I was concerned.   I entered the Foreign Office in 1892 without experience and without preconceived ideas of policy.   I was content to follow first Rosebery and then Kimberley in what was done in the Foreign Office.   I left it in 1895 full of discontent and apprehension, feeling that we were dependent on Germany and yet had not Germany's good-will, and that we were drifting towards war with France or Russia or with both.   What happened after I left office deepened that feeling.   Friction with France or with Russia continued over incidents that would never have occurred or would never have been dangerous but for the jealousy and mistrust on their side and on ours. The impression of German ill-will towards us was confirmed by manifestations of it, as in the telegram to Krüger and in the South African War. We could understand the ill-will of France and Russia; we had more than once thwarted Russian access to an open port; France was sensitive about our occupation of Egypt, and we were often in conflict with her. But why did Germany dislike us in those days? Then came the Agreement with France in 1904, and I welcomed it as the end of quarrelling and the removal of one real danger of war. There was nothing but this in my mind when both the front opposition bench and I welcomed the Agreement in the House of Commons, and a reading of the speech I then made will bear this out.[1]

I entered the Foreign Office again in December 1905 with a fixed resolve not to lose the one friendship that we had made, not to slip back again into the frictions of 1892-5; the sense of discomfort and danger that I had felt then was so clearly remembered. But I found this friendship in peril: France had been menaced in 1905, forced to dismiss Delcassé, and to agree to the Algeciras Conference. This Conference was approaching, and the new friendship had to be tested there. It would be either broken or confirmed. I was resolved that if possible it should not be broken, and it emerged from the Conference stronger than before. That had been no part of my

[1] See Appendix B., p. 293.

design when I took office; German pressure forced it in
1906 and forced it again in 1911.

In making the Agreement with Russia there was no
thought but to do what had been done with France—
remove friction and mistrust. There was never any
thought of giving our relations with France and Russia
an aggressive turn against Germany. Support was indeed
given to France at Algeciras and over Agadir, as the 1904
Agreement openly bound us to do, and diplomatic relations with France and Russia were always close and
friendly; but on no question was our influence ever used
to make mischief for the Triple Alliance, and where we
could, as in the friction between Austria and Russia after
the Balkan Wars of 1912-13, we worked hard to make
things better.

With Germany I wanted to be as friendly as I could be
without sacrificing friendships already made; as I said
in the House of Commons at least once, if not oftener,
I was willing to make a new friend, wherever it could
be done, without losing an old one. The agreements,
which were initialled, about the Portuguese Colonies and
Bagdad Railway, and which I was ready to sign, are an
instance of this; but on the thing that mattered most, on
the navies, we could come to no agreement; and it was
not our fault. I accepted the Triple Alliance and made
no attempt, however covert, to weaken it. My object
was indeed to preserve the Entente, for British interests,
I thought, required this; but the intention and hope were
that the Entente and the Triple Alliance might go on
side by side and preserve peace by settling diplomatically
each difficulty as it arose. The London Conference over

Balkan troubles confirmed this hope, but in 1914 this intention was defeated and the hope destroyed.

Anyone who has taken an important part in public affairs, looking backward after it is over, may be amazed to see how far the results of what he did differ from what he intended them to be. He may well feel, as he reflects upon this, that he has been but an instrument for purposes of which he did not think at the time, and which are beyond his power to comprehend or fathom.

What was directly due in some measure, at any rate, to my presence at the Foreign Office was:

1. That the Government and the country were not divided, as they would have been divided, if an aggressive or pronounced anti-German policy had been adopted and pursued; and

2. That close touch with France and Russia, especially with France, was preserved for nine years, as it would not have been, unless there had been someone at the Foreign Office with a constant resolve and care to keep it; and so war was at least deferred till we were better placed to bear it.

Our coming into the war at once, and united, was due to the invasion of Belgium. That was done by the Germans.

The fact that when we intervened we could do so with any timely effect was due to our having an Expeditionary Force ready and equipped to go abroad at a moment's notice. This was due to Haldane.

The part played by Asquith, as Prime Minister, was of supreme importance; on this all the efforts of individual Ministers depended for their effect. That is dealt with in a subsequent chapter.[1] Subject to this, it may fairly be said that the Germans, Haldane, and myself were the agencies most directly used to bring about the united, immediate, and effective entry of Britain into war; but this was not what any of us had desired. Haldane and I had not wanted war, and the Germans had not wanted us to be in it.

The tragedy was great, but it was for Britain the least of the immense perils with which the time was fraught.

[1] See *infra.*

CHAPTER XIX

(1914)

COULD WAR HAVE BEEN PREVENTED?

Difficulty of dealing with Germany—Absence of Good-will—Persistence of Naval Competition—Imputation of Hidden Motives—The Atmosphere of Militarism—The Vicious Circle of Armaments—Creating Fear—If Great Britain had adopted Conscription—A Certain Result—A Personal Matter—Failing Eyesight.

AFTER the outbreak of war I sometimes lay awake asking myself again and again whether the war could have been prevented by anything that I could have done in the preceding years. Sleep came every night sufficient in amount to restore strength for the next day, but there was often a wakeful time round about four o'clock in the morning—that time when vitality is low and spirits are depressed and the mind is often a prey to doubts and anxieties. I would try one hypothesis after another, considering what hope there would have been in any of them. The one that I dwelt upon most was this. Suppose that, after the London Conference of 1912-13, I had gone to Berlin; had there pointed to the success of the Conference in tiding over a European crisis; had urged upon the Germans the value, even the necessity, of a general agreement between the Triple Alliance and the Entente to put the same Conference machinery in motion and use it directly a new crisis came! Suppose I had done this, would the appeal have been successful? Would the Germans have understood it? Could they have been trusted to use it fairly, or would some twist have been given to the overture representing it as a change of policy towards detachment from France and Russia? The answer I gave myself was never hopeful. What we know now shows how insuperable were the difficulties of satisfactory dealings with the German Government.

First, there was no good-will towards England in Germany. We felt this all along, but the ill-will was even stronger than we realized. Consider the revelation of it in Bülow's Memorandum, written when he was on a visit to England in 1899. A translation was published in *The Times* of June 28, 1924. Here is the concluding passage of it:

> On the whole, it is certain that opinion in England is far less anti-German than opinion in Germany is anti-English; therefore those Englishmen like Chirol and Saunders (the Berlin Correspondent of *The Times*) are the most dangerous for us, since they know from their own observations the depth and bitterness of German antipathy against England.

The influence of men like Chirol and Saunders did indeed affect English opinion, but it was discounted by many people as being inspired by prejudice. We now know that the line they took sprang from knowledge. Sir Valentine Chirol still lives to appreciate the compliment Count Bülow paid him, and to enjoy our esteem; but a good many of his countrymen owe some apology to the memory of Mr. George Saunders for having underrated his sincerity and his knowledge.

Some German civilians in high places did not share this anti-English feeling; they saw that the growth of German naval competition must prevent a *rapprochement* and eventually imperil good relations between Britain and Germany. For that reason they deplored the German naval policy, and some of them tried to arrest it; but they were always overborne by the naval or military element. The fact is, that in dealing with Chancellors and Secretaries for Foreign Affairs at Berlin, we could make no progress, because we were not dealing with the men who really directed policy. The last and decisive word was with some military or naval person.

A summary of the *Memoirs* of Kiderlen Waechter, the Secretary of State for Foreign Affairs at Berlin in 1912, was published in *The Times* of July 3, 1924. It shows clearly how the civilians, even when they held a strong and definite view, could not carry a policy. Kiderlen Waechter was no sentimental pacifist, but we learn from his narrative how opposed he was to the prevailing naval policy, how powerless the civilian was, and how the Emperor sided with Admiral von Tirpitz. The civilians were quite right in their estimate of the barrier that the growth of German naval power must be to cordial relations. It forced our hands here: we had to build ships to meet it, and to tell Parliament frankly that we were doing this and why we were doing it. The Germans went on saying that their ship-building had no relation to ours; but this did not lessen distrust, and we know now (if we did not know then) that it was not true. Our offers to come to an agreement to stop naval competition came to nothing. Memoirs like those of Kiderlen Waechter explain why they failed. We may wonder now whether our offers to limit naval expenditure were not taken by men like Tirpitz as signs of weariness on our part; if so, these offers may have encouraged the hope of overtaking us and so have positively increased the competition.

Another difficulty was the inveterate tendency in Berlin to invent some hidden motive for whatever a British Government did. The ostensible motive was assumed not to be the real one; therefore some other had to be looked for, imagined, and supposed to be found. An appalling instance of this is revealed in the German Official Documents recently published.

In 1895 Lord Salisbury was so shocked by the Armenian massacres that he doubted whether Turkey must not break up. He spoke to the German Ambassador in London about it. Count Hatzfeldt recommended that his Government should enter into the discussion desired by Lord Salisbury, for, he said: "Lord Salisbury had spoken with the same confidence and frankness as in former days." This was what Holstein, the very able if not the directing mind of the Foreign Office at Berlin, wrote upon the proposal:

All the proposals of the English Minister, in my opinion, have no object except to alleviate the uncomfortable position in which England at the moment finds herself with regard to the French and Russians on account of Egypt, by creating complications in Asia Minor and the Balkans in which all the Continental Powers, even ourselves, would be entangled sooner than England.[1]

Bülow wrote, in the memorandum quoted above, that, according to German ideas, English politicians were somewhat naïve. Amongst other characteristics that he re-

[1] *Die Grosse Politik,* 1871-1914, vol. x, p. 19.

marked in them he notes, "They find it difficult to credit really bad intentions in others." German officials erred in the other direction, that of being too prone to credit others with really bad intentions.

These were the conditions that made it impossible for British and German minds to have real contact. We were thinking of an agreement to restrain the increasing burden of naval competition; Germany was thinking of some agreement to ensure that Britain should be neutral, if or when a great European war came. The only thing that would have been worth talking about was an agreement to work together to make war in Europe impossible. If Germany had made a fresh appeal to us for such an agreement, there would have been a great response from public opinion, qualified by very strong opposition from those who would have seen in the German overture a design to separate us from France and Russia, to isolate us and make us dependent again, as before 1904, on Germany.

Such an appeal was never made, and it is not worth while to ask whether, if made to us, we should have trusted it or should have accepted it. Had we made it to Berlin and had it resulted in a conference between the Triple Alliance and Entente, it would have come to nothing. There would have been the usual manœuvring for position and for special advantages, and the notion of a great agreement to maintain peace would have perished, frost-bitten to death in the atmosphere of militarism. The only sound basis for such an agreement would have been a sense in the Great Powers that the common interest of all of them in peace was so great as to transcend the special interests of each, and a belief on the part of each that the other Powers felt this and could be trusted. Militarism did not believe this. It held the contrary view—that the opposing interests of nations are the dominant factors, and that their tendency to attack each other can only be kept in bounds by armaments; that peace can be secured not by justice, not by desire for it, not by agreements, but only by armed force.

If a great peace proposal had been made to Germany and she had opened her heart in replying to it, her answer surely must have been on these lines. For she was the centre of a militarist Continent, and was herself the very centre and admired pattern of that militarism by which the Continent was dominated.

More than one true thing may be said about the causes of the war, but the statement that comprises most truth is that militarism and the armaments inseparable from it made war inevitable. Armaments were intended to produce a sense of security in each nation—that was the justification put forward in defence of them. What they really did was to produce fear in everybody. Fear causes suspicion and hatred; it is hardly too much to say that, between nations, it stimulates all that is bad and depresses all that is good.

One nation increases its Army and makes strategic railways towards the frontiers of neighbouring countries. The second nation makes counter-strategic railways and increases its Army in reply. The first nation says this is very unreasonable, because its own military preparations were only precautions; the second nation says that its preparations also were only precautions, and points out, with some cogency, that the first nation began the competition; and so it goes on, till the whole Continent is an armed camp covered by strategic railways.

After 1870 Germany had no reason to be afraid, but she fortified herself with armaments and the Triple Alliance in order that she might never have reason to be afraid in future. France naturally was afraid after 1870, and she made her military preparations and the Dual Alliance (with Russia). Britain, with a very small Army and a very large Empire, became first uncomfortable and then (particularly when Germany began a big-fleet programme) afraid of isolation. She made the Anglo-Japanese Alliance, made up her quarrels with France and Russia, and entered into the Entente. Finally Germany became afraid that she would presently be afraid, and struck the blow, while she believed her power to be still invincible. Heaven alone knows the whole truth about human affairs, but I believe the above sketch to be as near to a true statement of the causes of war as an ordinary intelligence can get in a few sentences.

If it be so, it is a complete answer to those who say that if we had adopted conscription and built up a big Army we should have prevented the war. We should not thereby have prevented the war; we should have precipitated it sooner.

Let anyone who doubts this imagine himself a member of the Government formed in 1905. He first divines for himself that there will eventually be a European war precipitated by Germany and that Britain must at once prepare for it. No one in the Cabinet, and not many people outside it, share this opinion. He sets to work to convince his colleagues that Britain must adopt conscription and that an Expeditionary Force of at least 500,000 men with the appropriate equipment and reserves is necessary. Let us assume (though it was in fact impossible) that he succeeds in convincing the Cabinet and that they coax the House of Commons to vote any Estimates rising to at least £100,000,000 a year, that is, more than double what the House did actually vote. Let us assume (though this, too, would have been impossible) that the Government succeeds in getting a majority to vote these Estimates; it will only succeed in doing that by explaining very clearly why the huge estimates and this large force are required. It will not be enough to say vaguely that European armaments are such as to make war probable if not inevitable; the Government will have to tell the whole truth, for on less than that they cannot justify this enormous increase of Army Estimates. They will have to explain that a large British Army is needed as counterpoise to the German Army; that it is for the contingency of war with Germany that we are preparing.

This large Army will not be built up in a year. There will have to be a year of beginning and several years of making. Year by year the Army Estimates will have to be larger and larger; there will be protests from the section in the country that does not believe in the German peril and from the still larger section which thinks we should keep out of a continental war, even if it does come. This latter section will feel their sentiment reinforced by the burden of Army expenditure. Year by year, to overcome opposition to the growing Army Estimates, the Government will have to be more and more explicit in explaining that German armaments and policy make this large Army necessary, more and more emphatic in asserting the reality of a German peril. Does anybody imagine that year by year, with all this going on, Germany is going to sit passive, to watch it all, to wait till Britain has really got the Army big enough to make the defeat of Germany certain? The Germans were not so pacifist as that; they looked like striking at France in 1905, and again in 1911. They would surely have struck long before we had built up our Army on the continental scale, avowedly, as it must have been, for the contingency of defeating the German Army, and defeating it in co-operation with the French or the French and Russian Armies. For this prospect must have formed part of the avowed justification for Army Expenditure. An Expeditionary Force even of 500,000 men would have been of little use on the Continent by itself. It could be effective only as part of a great combination. Nobody can seriously maintain that Germany would have waited till such a British Army was ready. Those who maintain that Germany chose the time and struck the blow in 1914 must be the first to see that she would have regarded great military preparations in Britain as a justification and imperative reason for striking sooner.

A change of our army system to conscription would have involved a transition stage that would have offered a moment peculiarly favourable to Germany. A scheme was actually considered in the War Office by high military authority in years before the war. It was put aside as futile, because no political party was prepared to consider it, because the country would not have conscription; but it was not considered in principle to be impossible.

Some 200,000 men could have been conscripted each year for two years' service, followed by ten years in the Reserve; this would have been combined with a voluntary army of the smaller size required for service in India or elsewhere in the Empire as at present.

The provision of equipment, barracks, material of all sorts would have been necessary, and also expansion of the cadres of officers and non-commissioned officers to meet not only peace requirements but those of general mobilization. All this would have been costly and not easy, but it could have been done. It would, however, have involved a period of transition; and in this period, especially in the first six or seven years of it, our Army would not have been so well trained or so well fitted for serious war as it was under the existing voluntary system. Such a risk could only have been incurred when the chance of war was remote. Ought we to have offered Germany such an opportunity as the transition period would give her, coupling with that opportunity the threat to her of a future British Army large enough in combination to make her defeat certain? Ought we to have done this, when it was already doubtful at Algeciras in 1906, and again over Agadir in 1911, whether Germany had not already made up her mind to war? There can be but one answer. We should not have averted war, but have precipitated it.

This is written with special reference to the period from the end of 1905, for that is the period during which the Liberal Government was responsible, and of which I can write with knowledge. But much of what has been said is applicable to the years before 1905. If a British Army

on a continental scale were to be built up, the beginning
must have been made in the years after 1870, when the
prospect of European war was or seemed to be remote.
Even so, the thing would have led not to peace, but to war.
We should have been doing just what Germany was doing
after she launched her naval programme: we should have
been aiming at a large Army as well as a supreme Fleet.
Other nations would not have stood that; we should have
brought a European combination into existence against
us; it would have been we, and not Germany, who would
have been forcing the pace and inspiring the fear that
leads first to armaments and then to war. The facts are
that conscription and a great Army, in addition to a
supreme Navy, were politically impossible in Britain before the war. Nothing but prophetic insight into the
German peril would have made conscription politically
possible—an insight not confined to a few minds but one
that penetrated the hearts and beliefs of the people. Such
insight must have dated back, and become effective in preparation long before 1905, long before the German peril
was above the political horizon.[1]

It is futile to speculate upon whether the war would
have been short and successful if there had been a large
British Army ready for it. The war would have anticipated such an event; it would have come when conscription and a large Army ceased to be politically impossible
in Britain; that is to say, at the moment when we began
to change our military system.

Here it may be convenient, and not altogether irrele-

---

[1] The above is founded on a memorandum written by one of our ablest military authorities who was then advising the War Office.

vant, to narrate a personal matter. It was in May 1914 that serious trouble in my eyesight became definitely and certainly known.

During my first years of office, as Secretary of State, I had not attempted to get any exercise in London. The charge upon my time at the Foreign Office and the Cabinet was too exacting to permit the arrangements in advance and the consistent practice twice a week that are necessary to play so serious and severe a game as tennis with satisfaction. From the moment of entering office I had, therefore, ceased to play tennis at all. In the more recent years I had found squash rackets a useful and enjoyable means of getting exercise. A court would be engaged, and a game with a friend arranged at short notice. I had no proficiency, and had known little of the game before; but it is a game in which indifferent or at any rate only moderate players can get concentrated exercise. If the players are evenly matched, and each does his best, it is easy, in the comparatively short space of an hour, to get the concentrated sensation of having extended lungs and limbs and perspired to heart's content. In this way it is a very useful game for men in middle life, who have but short or uncertain periods of leisure in the week, and who wish to retain something of the vigour and activity of youth.

In the autumn of 1913 I began to find difficulty in seeing the ball at squash rackets; it was natural at first to attribute this to the impaired power of focusing, which is not unusual, and is probably in some degree inevitable as we grow older. But the difficulty increased rapidly. A few years before this there had been an indication that all was not well. In December 1910 my brother George had been at home and had gone with me to election meetings. As we drove about the country we had compared our sight on starry winter evenings. I had then found out that I could no longer see the small star, familiarly known as "the Wagoner" in the "Great Bear," or "Charles' Wain," as I suppose the constellation should be called to keep the simile. This failing, too, was put down to some normal or not very abnormal lessening of keenness of vision, perhaps due to the exceptional strain of work and office, and only temporary. But I had remembered that my grandfather, when out with me on winter evenings on the gravel path in front of the house at Fallodon, had in advanced old age been able to see "the Wagoner" and point it out to me. Even in 1910 this recollection caused me some uneasiness. We are, however, apt to dismiss from our minds unpleasant symptoms of bodily failure, till they become practically important. Anxiety about health may sometimes be premature and pusillanimous, but it may also be true that some people dismiss unpleasant symptoms from their minds because they are reluctant to be anxious—are indeed afraid to face anxiety. Some people who are really quite well off suffer from apprehension that they are becoming poor; "workhouse fever" is one name for this disorder. Others become bankrupt from not having had the courage to look into their affairs when they first began to fear that all was not going well.

Early in 1914 an oculist was consulted: he found the vision abnormally defective, and asked me what I smoked and how much. He, having ascertained that I smoked four times a day, generally one pipe on each occasion, sometimes a cigar instead of a pipe, said that this did not seem enough to cause the trouble, but that there was no doubt the cause was over-smoking, and that if I left it off the sight would be restored in about a month. I left off smoking forthwith for two months; after that the eyes were examined again. This time serious trouble was discovered, with which smoking had nothing to do, and the oculist expressed a wish for a consultation. It took place in May. After examining the eyes the two oculists withdrew to consult. When they returned they informed me that they were both absolutely agreed, and they wished first of all to tell me that I should never be quite blind, never have to be led about, should always be able to distinguish light from darkness. Their manner was serious, and it was evident that they were preparing me for bad news. I said, "You mean that I shall lose the power of reading?" They replied, "That is it." In their opinion there was nothing to be done: they suggested I might go away for six months' rest and country life, but they did not press it as urgent; it would not be a cure. They said that after such a serious statement from them it would be natural that I might wish for other opinions. In answer to my questions they told me the treatment that a German oculist would probably advise, but said it would in my case be entirely empirical. They did not discourage the project of going to Germany, and named a great German oculist.

At this time—it was in the month of May—the crisis of the Home Rule trouble was coming upon us; the prospect before the Government was full of difficulty. I felt that without urgent reason I could not leave the Cabinet at that moment, and the opinion of the oculist was that my case was not urgent, because nothing was hopeful, and the progress of the mischief would be slow. I decided to do nothing till the Session was over, and then to go to Germany to consult the oculist there, who had been recommended. But before the Session ended the war had come upon Europe.

A year later I consulted a third oculist in London. He considered it essential that I should rest the eyes completely for six weeks. I did so, and at the end of that interval he pronounced the trouble quiescent, and I returned to the Foreign Office. Except for that interruption failing sight did not interfere at all with work, till after I left office, for I retained the power of reading with average ease and rapidity till the summer of 1918. Then I ceased to be able to read, and for six months was dependent for all correspondence and news upon being read to aloud. Since then, by the use of peculiar glasses of very high power, I have been able to write and to read slowly and with effort; but it is impossible for me to distinguish faces at a distance of more than a few inches, to identify birds and flowers, or see the beauty of a landscape or a sunset. On the other hand, it is quite easy for me to walk except on rough ground, as quickly and independently as other people, and even to ride an ordinary bicycle at moderate pace, and in confidence that whatever meets me will observe the rule of the road. Minute and tiresome examinations have discovered no trace of the diseases with which eye trouble is often associated. The removal of a discreditable tooth in 1919 may have helped to arrest the increase of the trouble, and since 1918 there has been very little change; but what there has been is not for the better. Hope exists in trying various treatments that do not involve drugs or operations, and can certainly do no harm; but, so far, the words of one of the oculists have proved true: "Never believe anyone who tells you that you can be cured—because you cannot be cured; never believe anyone who tells you that you will go blind—because you won't."

CHAPTER XX

(1914)

SOME QUESTIONS OF STRATEGY

Churchill and the Fleet—Readiness of the Fleet—Decision not to Demobilize—The Expeditionary Force—Two Questions—Appointment of Kitchener as Secretary for War—Advantages and Drawbacks—Kitchener's Intuitions—An Inspirer of Public Confidence—Mistakes in Strategy—Side-shows—The Dardanelles—The Antwerp Expedition—The Help of the Dominions.

WHOEVER has read this detailed account of the period of political discussion and negotiation must have often had present to his mind the question, What, during these critical but doubtful days, was being done to prepare for the event of war? The answer is that everything, naval and military, that could be done in this critical week was being done.

On Saturday, July 25, Churchill came to me and said that the naval manœuvres, which that year were a trial mobilization, were just over. They were an annual event, and had been arranged and carried out without reference to any prospect of imminent war. At the moment when he was speaking to me the British Navy was on a war footing, was in fact mobilized. On Monday, in the ordinary course, the leave that was usual after manœuvres would begin, and the Navy would go to the opposite extreme of being demobilized. He said that to him the diplomatic situation seemed so ominous that he thought

THE RIGHT HON. WINSTON SPENCER CHURCHILL, P.C.

it well not to demobilize the Fleet, but to keep it mobilized.

He wanted to know, if I confirmed his view of the diplomatic situation. The answer, of course, was to confirm it, and to say that, from the Foreign Office point of view, the action Churchill intended to take was entirely justified. He acted accordingly. From that moment the Navy remained ready. It was an accident that the end of the naval manœuvres coincided with the diplomatic stage of a foreign crisis; the fact that full advantage was taken of this good fortune was due to the vigour and alertness of Churchill. What went on inside the Admiralty is not known to me, and I can only write of what came under my own observation, and this was the activity of the First Lord, from the moment he took up his office. Full measure of credit must be reserved for naval officers and the Board of Admiralty, but undoubtedly the country owes much also to Churchill for the great advantage that war found us with a strong Fleet in an exceptionally good state of preparation.

It is not my province, nor is it within my knowledge, to say what went on inside the War Office. What is certain and known is that, when the moment came to send the Expeditionary Force abroad, it was there, ready and equipped; and the transport arrangements were ready too, for the four divisions sent abroad went to France, not only in the time estimated as required for this operation, but in less than the time.

For the first time perhaps in our history war found us with all the forces, naval and military, that we were believed or supposed to have, actually there, ready and

mobile. Every critic, who wishes to be fair, should first
gauge this fact. In the sense of having ready, what the
Government said we had, what Parliament had been
asked to vote, and what the country had a right to expect
that we had, we were better prepared for war than we had
ever been. Whether we ought, or could have had something else, something that we had not aspired to and that
Parliament had not been asked to vote, is another matter,
and has been considered in a former chapter.

The use to be made of the Expeditionary Force was the
first doubtful point to be decided, and on this two separate
questions presented themselves.

1. Was it safe to send the whole force abroad at once
and leave Britain without any military force available for
action, pending mobilization of the Territorial Army?
On this point there was room for discussion, and there was
naturally some difference of opinion. The landing of
even a small German force, after the Expeditionary Force
had gone, and before the Territorial Army was ready,
might do irreparable damage. Under modern conditions,
things might be possible that in the Napoleonic Wars had
been impossible to the enemy. A great War Council was
held; of course soldiers like Sir John French and Sir
Douglas Haig, who were to take an active part in the
execution of military operations, were present, but not
these alone. Lord Roberts also attended it. As far as I
remember, the military authorities were not greatly
troubled about home defence; it was felt that the Navy,
strong and ready as in war, would be able to prevent
any hostile landing that would be serious. Without much
difficulty a decision was reached to send to France four

divisions of the Expeditionary Force immediately; the
other two divisions were to follow with no long delay.
This satisfied military opinion, and represented the general sense of civilian opinion.   Haldane alone among
civilians was, from the first, for giving authority at once
to send all six divisions to France in the shortest possible
time.[1]

2. There was also a second point of doubt, which,
though settled in the decision just recorded, required
separate consideration. This was not concerned at all
with the provision for home defence. It related solely to
the moment at which the British Force could be used best
and most effectively to help the French Army. It was
entirely a military point, and the civilians left the discussion of it to the soldiers, who were not quite unanimous
about it. It was suggested that the British Expeditionary
Force should be kept in reserve till the first shock of the
German onset was over. Then there would be a critical
moment at which the despatch of the British Force would
be not only effective but decisive; when it would really be
the knock-out blow. The plan suggested to my lay mind
a comparison with the battle of Waterloo; the French
Army would in this instance have played the part of the
British at Waterloo, and the British Force would have
turned the scale decisively, as the Prussians did in 1815.

This plan was based on the assumption that the French
Army even if unable to repel, would be able to withstand

[1] It was stated that Haldane put difficulty in the way of the despatch of the
Expeditionary Force. This is quite untrue. The report arose probably from his
giving an order inside the War Office that the Force was not to go without the
authority of the Government: a proper and necessary restriction which, if
disobeyed, would have meant chaos.

the first shock of the German attack. This may seem a strange miscalculation in the light of what actually happened; but it must be remembered that both British and French military opinion of the highest order hitherto held that the French Army and the British Expeditionary Force would together be able to resist successfully a German attack, even if France and Britain were alone and unsupported by Russia. I had in my own mind discounted some of this opinion. British and French military authorities knew very well that no more than the six divisions of the British Expeditionary Force were or could be available at the outbreak of war. Military authorities, generally speaking, were anxious that the whole force should be sent; they were, therefore, predisposed to persuade themselves and us that this force would be sufficient and effective; for this was an encouragement to send it. To say that it would not be enough was to suggest that it would be sacrificed to no purpose in failure. Military authority, therefore, was naturally predisposed to the belief that the Expeditionary Force would make the whole difference and would ensure success; and this at the time was a genuine and sincere opinion. But it was not inconsistent with this view—it was an inference from it—that the French Army alone would be able, for a time, to withstand the German attack. For now it was not a case of Britain and France alone; Russia was to be taken into account as an Ally, and the Germans, while assaulting France, must be prepared to resist a Russian attack.

I trust it has been made clear that this plan was not put forward with any idea of sparing the British Force, of sheltering it from exposure; it was, in fact, inspired by nothing but consideration for the most effective use of the British Army in the common cause of victory. The prevailing opinion, however, was that the British Force should be sent at once; the chances of modern war were too unknown, and the risks of an initial German success or of an irretrievable defeat of the French Army were too great to allow of any nice calculation. The wisest course was to minimize the risk by sending the British Force at once to take its place in the front line.

When the Council broke up I found myself next to French in the passage on the way out. What the actual words were that passed between us I cannot recall, but I said something about his feeling it a great moment. The impression his reply made is vivid still. It was that of a man strung to the highest pitch of hope and spirit in the face of a great enterprise for which his whole life had been an anticipation.

Those, if any there be, who think that such feeling in a soldier shows want of sympathy for his fellow-men, had better read Uncle Toby's reply to a similar reproach by Mr. Shandy.[1]

It was necessary to appoint a new Secretary of State for War. Seely had resigned after the Curragh trouble in Ireland a few weeks before. Asquith had himself then taken the War Office temporarily to avoid making a new appointment, till the internal trouble was over. In this he had been justified; his own personal qualities, and his position as Prime Minister, were especially suitable for calming those troubles. But now, with the advent of

---

[1] See chapter xxxii in *Life and Opinions of Tristram Shandy,* by Laurence Sterne.

war, a new appointment was necessary. Asquith's first thought was naturally to send Haldane back to the War Office. The soldiers had made the Expeditionary Force the fine thing it was, but the creation of the General Staff and the whole organization of the Army was due to Haldane, and he had the confidence of soldiers like French and Haig, who were to have the chief commands in the field. From that point of view it was not only an obvious, but an ideal appointment. Haldane, however, had attracted much political animus. It was suggested that his known interest in German philosophy must make him pro-German; his work at the War Office, though well known to and admired by his colleagues and by the soldiers who had worked with, or under him, was not in the knowledge of, or at any rate not present to, the public mind. Kitchener, a popular hero, was in England, taking his leave from Egypt. An outcry arose, inspired partly by distrust of Haldane and made violent by desire to see Kitchener at the War Office. It was decided that he, and not Haldane, should be the Secretary of State for War. As will be shown directly, this decision was on the whole the better one; indeed, it was in the circumstances inevitable. But the public little knew the disadvantages that had to be set against the advantage of it. Kitchener knew nothing about the organization of the War Office, or of the Army at home; his knowledge of the personal value of the younger men was necessarily less than that of soldiers who had held home commands. He knew nothing of the Territorial Army, and grievously under-estimated its value. "A Town Clerk's Army," was his estimate of it.   In all this there was great disadvantage and much loss.

On the other hand, Kitchener foresaw, to an extent that no one else did at first, the need for raising a great Army, larger than anything that had yet been contemplated.   He based this demand for men on the opinion that the war would last for three years.   That seemed to most of us unlikely, if not incredible.   We thought only of a war of movement, that would bring a military decision one way or the other in less than three years; it also seemed to many of us that the terrific output of men and treasure that modern conditions made possible would bring exhaustion to every belligerent in much less than three years. Kitchener had more foresight than most of us in this matter, and announced to the Cabinet that he proposed at once to raise a million men.   As we walked away from the Cabinet a colleague asked me what I thought of this proposal.   I replied that I believed the war would be over before a million new men could be trained and equipped, but that, if this expectation were wrong, the million men should of course be sent abroad to take part in the war.   It was therefore clear that we should all agree to what Kitchener wanted.   Kitchener's foresight was amply justified by events, but it was never disclosed how or by what process of reasoning he made this forecast of the length of the war.   It was the deadlock of trench warfare that made the forecast come true, and indeed more than true, for the war lasted over four years.

The natural inference is that Kitchener foresaw trench warfare.   This, however, he did not foresee.   When the opposing armies had dug themselves in from Switzerland to the sea, no one was more perplexed than Kitchener. "I don't know what is to be done," he said to me more than once; "this isn't *war*." He must have reached his conclusion about the duration of the war by some flash of instinct, rather than by reasoning. If it were so, it did not make the conclusion less valuable to the country, and it made it more and not less individual to himself. He proceeded to appeal for the men by voluntary enlistment. "I don't want conscription yet. When I do want it, I will ask for it." That was his formula in the Government for the earlier part of the war. And he got the men. That is the great justification of his appointment. Conscription in the early days of the war was impossible; public opinion was not ready for it; it would have been resisted. Voluntary enlistment gave the country a good start in good-will and enthusiasm; conscription would have given a bad start. There would have been division of opinion, much resentment; the country might even have foundered in political difficulties. Kitchener brought to his Government a great asset of public confidence. Men believed that what he wanted was really necessary, and they responded; they trusted him, and came forward to serve under him. In war, if something clearly wrong or unwise is demanded, it is necessary to the utmost to resist public clamour; but it is also necessary to do what will inspire public confidence. The appointment of Kitchener had serious disadvantages and drawbacks, but it had also great advantages. He under-rated the value of the Territorial Army, and of an able General Staff at the War Office; but he set to work from the first to build up a really great Army, and he put heart into the country.

This narrative will contain little about military or naval operations. The history of these can be, has already been, and will still further be, much better told by others than by me. I do not remember that I initiated anything naval or military. It is a commonplace of history that amateur strategists are dangerous in time of war. I had no qualities that inclined me to become one, and if I had had, I hope I should have resisted the inclination. But the position of a civilian in a War Council, who feels that, from lack of military knowledge and training, this limitation is imposed upon him, is not glorious. He knows that credit is not due to him for successful strategy, and yet he must feel some responsibility for mistakes in which he has acquiesced.

The part of a civilian Government is to see that the highest professional posts in the Admiralty and the War Office, and the chief commands in the Army and Navy, are filled by soldiers and sailors best qualified for them; and that these are supported in the use of the armed forces. At the outbreak of the war there was no question about this. The military and naval officers of most known competence were in the highest posts or were appointed to the chief commands. The disposition of the Fleet and the use of the Expeditionary Force were in accord with the plans carefully prepared by the best naval and military authority, and for this the British Government was in August 1914 open to no reproach and is entitled to credit. As war proceeds new plans have to be made and new military and naval decisions taken to meet new developments. For these the Government cannot divest itself of responsibility, and its proper course is to ascertain what is the best naval and military opinion. In this we got presently on to debatable and difficult ground in military matters. We could always get Kitchener's opinion, but we did not insist on having before us the ascertained consensus of military opinion, as we should have done, if there had been a civilian instead of a Field-Marshal as Secretary of State for War. There was a natural tendency to yield to Kitchener's opinion as that of a soldier; on the other hand, there was a disposition in critical moments to attach less weight to it than we should have done if it had been presented to us as that of an able General Staff or of those in high commands. We might assume that his view was that of a General Staff, and represented a consensus of military opinion; but we did not know what this was as certainly as we must have known it if there had been a civilian at the head of the War Office. The ideal Minister for War is one who knows and observes his own limitations, who sets himself with ability to discern to organize the best military opinion, to focus and support it, and who by experience and training knows how to manage a Cabinet. Had such a Minister been appointed in 1914 some of the mistakes made in the earlier stages of the war would have been avoided. This reflection is made with consideration for the future, but let something else also be remembered in this and all other reflections on the conduct of the war. We can see in the light of after-events the mistakes that actually were made; we do not know the mistakes that might or would have been made by the Cabinet, had some-one other than Kitchener been at the War Office.

The chief mistakes in strategy may, in my opinion, be

Photograph by Messrs. Bourne & Shepherd, India

THE RIGHT HON. EARL KITCHENER OF KHARTOUM

summarized in two words: "Side-shows." In justice to
Kitchener it must be recorded that he disliked them all,
and my own particular regret is that I did not resolutely
support every resistance he made to them. But all of
them could not be avoided. The defence of Egypt and the
Suez Canal, for instance, was essential, and in justice not
only to Kitchener but to the Cabinet it must be stated that
sometimes concessions in strategy that we thought undesirable *had* to be made to Allies; though sometimes it
was they who reluctantly yielded to our initiative. Due
weight should be given to this qualification; but even
so, it seems to me to be a true criticism that we did not
sufficiently concentrate attention on the one cardinal
point: that it was the German Army which had to be
beaten, and that this could be done only on the Western
front. For us to attempt it anywhere else was to give
the Germans the advantage of interior and safe lines of
communication compared with our own. Had this been
grasped continuously as the central fact of the war, the
side-shows—Gallipoli, Bagdad, Salonika—would either
never have been undertaken or would have been kept
within smaller dimensions.

It may be urged that, but for such diversions as these,
the Germans would have brought Turks or Bulgarians to
fight on the Western front. It is doubtful if the Germans
could have done this. The Turks and Bulgarians had
other objectives of their own, such as Egypt and Macedonia, and if Bulgaria had conquered Macedonia, it was
by no means certain that the Bulgarian Army would have
done more than occupy what it had conquered. Even if
it be granted that there was risk of Germany getting help

in this way, it remains true that the side-shows, with their long line of sea communication on which every transport, every supply had to run the gauntlet of submarines, entailed an enormous strain and wastage that more than counter-balanced the advantage to be gained from them. Even if the Turks and Bulgarians had to be fought somewhere, surely we could have fought them to best advantage on ground where our own line of communication was shortest and most secure—that is to say, on the Western front. Instead of this, we sent forces that might have been kept for the West to meet Turks and Bulgarians at points where we had the disadvantage in lines of communication.

Various suggestions are made as to how the war could have been finished in shorter time. The suggestions that the war might have been won sooner if the strength spent on side-shows had been concentrated directly on the German Army at the Western front is at least worth considering. The moral for civilians in the future is to ascertain what the best and most responsible military opinion holds to be the central and cardinal point of the war, and, having ascertained it, to keep within the narrowest bounds everything that will divert strength from that point.

The highest military authority cannot be divided. The Government must choose someone to command. If they cease to trust him, they must change him; if military opinion be incompetent and wrong, no Government can save the country from defeat. The only hope, and that not an impossible one, is that the enemy Government or military authorities may be still more incompetent. In this war I believe the best and preponderating military opinion would have been as I have stated it; and, had it been so concentrated as to impress itself on the Cabinet, it would have been irresistible; for I think Kitchener's own views were such as would have been confirmed by it, and his authority with the Cabinet would then have been reinforced and more strenuously exerted. As it was, various suggestions as to military operations in different parts of the world were discussed too much as isolated questions, when the primary consideration ought to have been their conformity with or departure from a central scheme of military strategy. This criticism applies to Allied Governments as well as to our own.

After a year's experience of war the Cabinet began to insist upon having a real General Staff at the War Office. Kitchener yielded to Cabinet pressure and to the growing public anxiety about the conduct of the war. Finally towards the end of 1915 Sir William Robertson was appointed with a definite position as Chief of the General Staff. Thenceforward we had co-ordinated military opinion before us on matters of strategy. Kitchener loyally accepted the decision. In reality it greatly strengthened his hands, and there was no reason to suppose that his opinion differed from that of the General Staff. But he still seemed not to feel the necessity of having both a Secretary of State for War and a Chief of the Staff at the War Office. It was as if he could not see that there was room and scope for both. He gave the impression of feeling almost superseded. A few months later it was thought that his personality and authority would be invaluable in a visit to Russia to encourage the Tsar and the Russian authorities and to co-ordinate Allied strategy there. He undertook this difficult task willingly, as if he felt that it would give him new scope and that he would be of more use there than at home. The visit might have proved of inestimable value to Russia and to the Allies: the disaster to the *Hampshire,* in which Kitchener started for Russia, was one of the serious tragedies of the war.

With two operations only will I deal separately, and that merely to supplement what has been or may still be written of them by others.

1. THE DARDANELLES

My recollection is very clear that the attack on the Dardanelles was agreed to on the express condition that it should be a naval operation only; it was under no circumstances to involve the use of troops. The British and French armies were at death's grip with the Germans on the Western front, the situation there was still critical for the Allies, and it was important that there should be no diversion of force to other parts of the world, except under pressure of absolute necessity.

If the attack on the Dardanelles did not succeed, it was to be treated as a naval demonstration and abandoned. It was on this condition only that Kitchener agreed to it.

The first attack appeared to have a great success, and the importance of the operation was at once boomed in a way that made it impossible to treat it thereafter as nothing more than a naval demonstration. Had there been the ultimate success, which the first success seemed to assure, no embarrassment would have followed; but there came a check and loss of ships in the subsequent operation, and it was reluctantly decided that the forts could not be taken without the use of troops. We stood publicly committed to the attack on the Dardanelles, as a serious effort from which we could not withdraw, except by admission of a serious defeat. Kitchener was asked to provide troops for land operations in Gallipoli to support the fleet. This was the very thing that he had expressly stipulated that he should not be called upon to do[1]; but, in face of what had happened, he could not now refuse. His subsequent part in the Gallipoli campaign has been criticized. With that I do not feel competent to deal; but, in fairness to his memory, it should be remembered that, in being committed to land operations at all in connexion with the Dardanelles, he was the victim of circumstances that were beyond his control and against which he had endeavoured to guard. When at length the decision to abandon Gallipoli had to be taken, Kitchener was the most tragic figure of us all. He, like the rest of us, anticipated that the withdrawal of the troops could not be accomplished without catastrophe. The first part would get safely away, but the last detachments would not. "Distress" would not be the right word to apply to Kitchener in these dark days at the end. Distress suggests a breakdown, and this was never true of him. But he felt his responsibility to the Army, and he suffered intensely. Happily all the troops got away safely.

The brunt of the criticism fell at the time on Churchill,

---

[1] It is said that the operation on the Dardanelles should have been planned from the first as a joint military and naval operation. It will be apparent, from what has been said here, that if this had been proposed the operation would never have been agreed to.

who was naturally assumed to be the author of the whole affair, though all of us who consented to it originally shared the responsibility. We were told afterwards that the condition in the Turkish forts was such that if the attack by the ships had been pressed even for one day more, at the outset, it would have succeeded as an entirely naval operation. The real defence of it is that it very nearly did succeed as planned.

There were diplomatic objections to the attempt to force the Dardanelles. These will be dealt with when the narrative passes to the diplomatic side of events. It will be enough to say here that I must take the responsibility for not having urged them beforehand as a reason for not undertaking the affair at all.

2. ANTWERP

It has seemed right, in fairness to Kitchener, to give my recollection of the origin and beginning of the Dardanelles operations. The same will now be done respecting Churchill's expedition to Antwerp, because this should be given in fairness to him. It is also one of those incidents that stand out in my mind with dramatic clearness, and which for that reason are worth recounting in detail.

I was still in Haldane's house in Queen Anne's Gate, my own household being at Fallodon, whither I had of course been unable to follow it. It was now midnight on October 2, and I was just going to bed, when a message was brought to me that the Private Secretary at the Foreign Office wanted to speak to me on the telephone. I went to it and there heard that a telegram from Belgium was being deciphered, saying that the Belgians had decided to abandon Antwerp immediately. The news was quite unexpected, and was a great blow. I replied that I would go to the Foreign Office at once, and in a few minutes I was there. Churchill had already left the Admiralty *en route* for Dunkirk on some naval business; but he had only just started, and it was arranged that he should be intercepted with the news. The deciphering of the telegram was completed. I read it, put it in my pocket, and went at once to Kitchener (who was then living in Carlton House Gardens), leaving word that Churchill was to be told where I had gone.

Kitchener had gone to bed; there had not been time yet for his copy of the telegram to get to him. Presently he came down in a dressing-gown, and I gave him the telegram. It was as much a surprise and shock to him as it had been to me. We agreed to wait for Churchill, and I do not remember that much passed between us in the interval. In no very long time Churchill entered with Prince Louis of Battenberg, then First Sea Lord. Churchill's mind was already made up. Immediately he entered the room he said the abandonment of Antwerp *must* be stopped, and announced that he was going there at once to stop it.

I said something cautious, deprecating the enterprise, not because it seemed foolhardy or undesirable in itself. On the contrary, anything that would avert the fall of Antwerp was worth much risk; and if, as seemed possible, the proposed abandonment of so important a place was due to panic, the energy, resource, and courage of Churchill might save the situation. But the risk of having

the First Lord of the Admiralty shut up in Antwerp was
startling.   Kitchener   reserved   his   opinion,   while
Churchill developed his plan.   Shortly stated, it was
this.   The Germans were not attacking Antwerp in force.
One big gun was the sole trouble.   This was knocking out,
one after the other, forts that had been deemed, and that
were,   before   any   such   gun   had   been   invented,   im-
pregnable.   The German Field Force supporting this gun
was not strong; the assumption was that the Germans
could not easily or quickly strengthen it; if two allied
divisions could be spared, the German force could be
driven off and Antwerp would be saved.   What was essential, therefore, was to delay the abandonment of Antwerp.   This Churchill felt sure he could do by his
presence there, if there was the prospect of relief by two
Allied divisions; it was a matter of a very few days.   Such
was the situation and its prospects, as it presented itself to
us at that midnight consultation.

Churchill and Kitchener proceeded to discuss the possibility of using two Allied divisions for this purpose.   The
British 7th Division was not yet in the battle-line; there
was time to divert it to Antwerp.   Kitchener could answer
for that.   He could not be sure whether the French would
or could send a French division to join ours.   He thought
it not impossible that this could be done; he was ready to
ask the French to do it; the risk of their not being able
to do so was serious, but it had to be taken, for Churchill's
departure could not wait till enquiry had been made of
the French and an answer received from them; if he went
at all he must go at once.

Finally Kitchener gave an opinion in favour of his going, and then I acquiesced. The First Sea Lord would, of course, remain to deal with whatever might arise at the Admiralty. Churchill started off again, but this time not for Dunkirk, but for Antwerp. The sequel is well known, and can be better described by others. Churchill did delay the fall of Antwerp, but a French division could not be spared, and Antwerp was occupied by the Germans.

The action has been much criticized. I am not competent to pass a military judgment upon it, but, as I acquiesced in it and was one of the four persons present, it is right that I should give my independent recollection of the circumstances in which the decision for Churchill to go to Antwerp was taken. It was indeed his own idea and initiative, but it was part of a concerted plan, and not the mere madcap exploit of a passion for adventure, which it was for some time afterwards assumed to be.

Little has been said about the Dominions, because communication with them was not carried on through the Foreign Office. The part they took in the war, the numbers that they sent, the sacrifices that they made, are on record. The material value of their help is universally recognized; their deeds, notably in Gallipoli, are famous. What cannot be illustrated by figures, or measured by narratives of military exploits, is the immense moral value of their support. Promptly, spontaneously, without consultation or persuasion they gave their help. The effect on the fighting line, it was known, could not be immediate; the contingents from the Dominions must take some time to arrive, to be organized, to be trained; but the moral effect was instantaneous. The shock of being suddenly at war had disclosed no faltering or faintness of heart in

Britain itself. On the contrary, it evoked an independent and vigorous moral. This is true. But the news from the Dominions carried it still higher. Those who have watched the sea under the impulse of a great wave, urged to a mark further than the tide has yet reached, know how another wave, following while the first is still flowing, carries the flood forward beyond the limit of anticipation. They know how essential it is to this result that the second wave should rise and follow quickly upon the first. This simile may serve to illustrate something of the effect upon us at home of the prompt support of the Dominions. It is not easy to express in words influences such as this, that are intangible, though potent and pervading. One recollection may serve as an example. Shortly after the outbreak of war I met Albert Grey—the late Earl Grey—in St. James's Park. We walked on together. I found him in the highest spirits. It was not because he liked war: he was a man who desired and loved human happiness, and hated all that clouded it. It was not because nice calculations of strength or blind confidence made him feel sure of victory. He spoke not at all of war or of the chances of war, but solely of the splendid spirit of the British Commonwealth of Nations. By this he was uplifted, so that he said he rejoiced in having lived to see this day. It was the vision of the people of Britain and of the Dominions combined in one high resolve and effort that inspired him and raised his own spirits to a height of enthusiasm and confidence.

This chapter on the war has been concerned with military matters only. It contains some observations that may be of use to civilians, who in future may find themselves

10, Downing Street,
Whitehall. S.W.

Tel. to Sir G. Buchanan.

Private & Urgent

News just received that cruiser Hampshire on way to Archangel has been sunk with Lord Kitchener on board. Rumoured that nearly all the party going to Russia on board. It is feared that nearly all lives are lost. You should inform M.F.A.

E. G.

LORD GREY'S TELEGRAM TO SIR GEORGE BUCHANAN

members of a war council, and a few points on which it seemed desirable to supplement what has been or can be written by others. What follows now will be concerned with the diplomatic side of the war, in which the Secretary for Foreign Affairs had necessarily special knowledge and responsibility.

CHAPTER XXI

(1910-1914)

AMERICA AND THE WAR

British Relations with the United States—Affinities and Estrangements
—Anti-British Elements in America—Recent Ambassadors—
—Whitelaw Reid and Bryce—Roosevelt's Visit to England in
1910—His Speech about Egypt—A Walk with him in the New
Forest—His Knowledge—Woodrow Wilson and the Panama
Tolls—Walter Page—Conversations about Mexico—Villa and
Huerta—Page's View of the War—His Support and Encourage-
ment.

RELATIONS with the United States differ from
those of Great Britain with any other country.
The two countries have one language in common,
and the jurisprudence of both is founded upon the common law of England. The American Constitution was
drawn up and made by men of British race, whose
descendants form a large part of the present population
of the United States and are still proud of their race and
conscious of the kinship in blood and the common origin
and traditions. The whole people are attached to democratic Government and human freedom. There is a land
frontier of some 3,000 miles with the Dominion of
Canada, one of the most important parts of the British
Empire, and the relations between the United States and
Canada are such that not a regiment or a single soldier
is on guard to protect that frontier against aggression.
In all the relations of separate countries with each other

the world has known nothing so exemplary, so confident of peace as those between the United States and Canada. There is material here for many speeches based on the assumption that the relations of Britain and the United States must be more sympathetic and intimate and secure than those of any two foreign countries; and many such speeches are made.

On the other hand, there are some less agreeable influences, which do not find expression, when British and Americans meet and wish to be civil to each other.

The sense of common race and origin is closely associated with the historical memory of bitter war. Americans do not always seem to realize that those who left Britain to escape from King and prelates were not the only British of their generations who loved liberty. Others stayed behind, and in time there was established in Britain a democracy as free as that founded in the New World on the other side of the Atlantic. Successive generations in Britain have been brought up to regard the separation of the American Colonies as the work of a narrow-minded King, who has been dead for a hundred years, and the outcome of a political system that seems to us to-day as antiquated and intolerable as it does to people in the United States. But, while this change has taken place here, it seems at times as if Americans, who do not know the Britain of to-day, thought of us still in terms of the eighteenth century. Hence, even amongst Americans of British stock there may be the historical feeling of resentment, as well as the sense of kinship.

The British Empire also includes countries inhabited by other races, an inheritance from previous generations.

The problem of governing lands inhabited by different races with an Oriental and not a Western civilization presents features that are alien to the experience of the United States; this may tend to make British policy seem unsympathetic to American ideas; for their own experience of Empire in the Philippines is too limited and recent to have affected the consciousness of so great a country and so many tens of millions as the people of the United States.

To this may be added that the different conditions of Britain and the United States have necessarily caused some divergence in politics, perspective, and customs, and that each is apt to dislike or even despise what it does not understand in the other, because it is not itself familiar with it.

Besides all this, there is the fact that a large number of Americans are not of British race at all, and that certain of these, more particularly Irish and German, have strong Anti-British sympathies. The result has been a certain intimacy, if it may be called so, of attraction and repulsion, which has made the relations between Britain and the United States at once more easy and more difficult, more cordial and more intractable, than those between any two other countries.

In the years from 1905 to 1912 there was not much in the handling of public affairs between the Government of the United States and ourselves that retains sufficient interest to be described here. My recollection of that time is of persons rather than of affairs. The participation of the United States and the influence of President Roosevelt in the Algeciras Conference were important;

but it was not upon us or with us that this influence was exercised, nor did it come within our knowledge at the time. What I knew of it afterwards came not officially, but in private talk with Roosevelt, when he had left office some years later.   Indeed, the whole of this chapter will be concerned greatly with persons, in the earlier years because personal relations were more interesting than public relations, and in the later years because the public matters, then of supreme interest, were transacted with me and through the important personalities of Mr. Walter H. Page and Colonel Edward M. House.

In my first years of office Mr. Whitelaw Reid was Ambassador in London. His courteous and kindly manner, and the friendly sense of good-will that he brought with him, made every visit of his to the Foreign Office a pleasure to the Secretary for Foreign Affairs. It was difficult to remember that one was talking to the Ambassador of another country. New York is not farther in distance and not much farther in time from London than it is from San Francisco, and Mr. and Mrs. Whitelaw Reid were well known in England, and formed part of social life in London and its neighbourhood. There was in those years no clash of policies to throw the character of an Ambassador into strong relief; he lived among us as a friend, and his death was felt by the many friends that he and Mrs. Reid had in England as a personal loss and sorrow.

At Washington the personal position of Mr. Bryce was less that of an Ambassador than of a distinguished man of letters and knowledge, who, amongst other literary achievements, had written a classic work on the American

Constitution. He must have done much to submerge difference of country in a feeling of the brotherhood of letters. Probably no Ambassador was ever so qualified as Bryce, by a combination of great intellectual gifts and natural simplicity, to bring out the points of resemblance and sympathy between the two countries, and to recommend them to Americans.

With Whitelaw Reid in London, Bryce at Washington, and President Taft at the White House, and no serious troubles arising between the respective countries, it may be imagined that the British Foreign Office enjoyed a genial period as far as the United States were concerned.

It is therefore easy to understand how, in recalling those years, the visit of Theodore Roosevelt to England in 1910 stands out as a point of special interest.

While Roosevelt was still President, Bryce had written to me to say that after Roosevelt's term of office was over he intended to travel, and among other places to visit England. He had not heard the songs of British birds, and would time his visit so as to be in England at the time of the singing of birds. He would like it to be arranged that someone, who knew the songs of birds, should spend a day walking with him and naming the songs as they were heard. In youth I had spent much time in identifying the songs of different species; hearing and recognizing them had been a pleasure kept up every year, and all the common songs were very familiar to me. I therefore replied that I should be glad to do this service, and probably I named May as the best month for the purpose. Roosevelt left the White House in 1909 and travelled on a big game expedition in British East Africa, eventually passing through the Soudan and so by Egypt to Europe. He had a royal progress; the newspapers were full of it, Europe resounded with it; the birds were singing, though I doubted whether their songs would be heard. But the thing had been in Roosevelt's plans, and he had not forgotten it, and while he was still on the Continent, Arthur Lee, who was to be his host in England, had a message desiring him to arrange a time for the bird walk with me. The programme for Roosevelt was already very full, and, but for Roosevelt's thoroughness, the walk would have been squeezed out. It required a whole day to be set apart for it, and the last day of his visit was the only opportunity. That postponed the walk till well into June, but the weather was good singing weather, grey and moist, and not hot and dry, and the birds sang well. This part of the story has been described in an address given at Harvard, Roosevelt's own University, in 1919, and must not be repeated here; but there are other aspects of the visit that are also of interest.

Soon after his arrival Whitelaw Reid brought him to see me at the Foreign Office. Roosevelt was to be received at the Guildhall; a speech was expected of him; he wished me to know beforehand what he was going to say; he produced the MS. or type and read it to me. It expressed enthusiastic praise of the work of Britain in the Soudan and Egypt—praise so unstinted and thorough and strong that I listened to it with a glow of satisfaction. It was the finest tribute ever paid by a citizen of one country to the work of another; and it came from the most world-renowned citizen of the United States in praise of British work in governing an Oriental country, that sort of work of which Americans were apt to be most critical, and on which they looked most askance. The tribute was of real value to us as well as very pleasant to hear. Then came one note of criticism. Roosevelt had evidently come in contact with people who thought that, since Cromer had left Egypt, the British purpose was faltering and the grasp relaxing. He uttered a note not only of encouragement but of warning.

"Get on with the good work; but if you are not going to get on with it, if you are going to let it drop, then get out"—that was the gist of it.

When the reading was finished, Roosevelt asked me if there was anything to which I took exception. It would have been a poor and paltry thing to say that we appreciated the praise, but resented the criticism; to ask him to let the tribute stand, but to leave out the advice. I had no hesitation in deciding that the speech as a whole was so valuable to us, that I would ask for no alteration and accept it as it was. How much more worth while it would be to have such a eulogy of British work in Egypt and the Soudan than the usual polite commonplaces, carrying no conviction and with no force and drive behind them! If there were people who, after lapping up the praise, were going to be annoyed by the advice, let them be annoyed; they deserved to be.

So the speech was delivered [1] as read to me beforehand. Cromer, who was present, was well pleased with it; but there was some criticism to the effect that it was not Roosevelt's business to give advice. The answer was

[1] May 31, 1910.

easy—it was not his business to praise either. If we were glad that he went out of his way to do the one, we ought not to resent the other.

The advice itself was wholesome, and goes to the very root of the British position in Africa and Asia. We stay in certain parts of those continents because we can do certain things, efficient administration free from corruption, preservation of order, development of the country, etc., better than these would be done without us. Let us be sure that we are doing these things, that we mean to go on doing them; that is our justification for staying in the country; if we are not doing that, or do not mean to go on doing it, we had better come out. Let there be a decision one way or the other, firm in our minds and known to the world.

Since Roosevelt spoke we have decided to get out of Egypt and not to get out of the Soudan. If we are to maintain and continue to do the work in the Soudan that Roosevelt praised so highly we must make our purpose and intention to do this in the Soudan as clear as we have made it that we are not going on with the work in Egypt.

During the walk with Roosevelt and the evening after it at the inn in the New Forest, our attention was given largely to birds, but the talk also ranged over other subjects. Roosevelt's spirit was much troubled by what was happening in his own country since he left office. This concerned internal policy and administration in the United States, of which I had not knowledge sufficient to form an opinion. The purport of what Roosevelt said is given here as he spoke it, without any comment of mine.

He spoke of Taft and of their work together with very live affection; he had wished Taft to succeed him, had supported him, made way for him. How could he now break with Taft and attack him? Roosevelt spoke of this prospect in a way that left no doubt of sincerity and poignancy of feeling. On the other hand, how could he sit still and see all his own work being undone and the policies in which he believed being ruined? Roosevelt had come to no decision then, but there was evidence of strong internal combustion of spirit. Such spirits as his, however, are not consumed in this process; the result is energy, decision, and action. What it was eventually in this instance is well known.

The popular impression of Roosevelt conveyed by the Press was that of a very important and striking personality; but it was nevertheless in one respect very inadequate. He was renowned as a man of action; public opinion was fascinated by this quality, and it was not so generally recognized that he was also remarkable as a man of reading and knowledge. The student is often a contrast to the man of action, and it is rare to find the two capacities possessed in a very high degree and combined in one person. The man of great knowledge is apt to be so balanced in mind as to be sometimes hesitating in opinion; and when he expresses an opinion he will take time to avoid over-emphasis of one point, to qualify, or to give finish and literary form of expression; he eschews the rough-and-ready style. Roosevelt could be rough, and he was always ready, and his manner in controversy was that of a fighter. There was not much of the patience of Job, there was a great deal of the war-horse rejoicing

in his strength and saying "Ha, ho" among the trumpets.
So perhaps it came to be overlooked that he had great
knowledge; sometimes it was even assumed that the rush
of his life had left no time to acquire it.   This was the
reverse of the truth.   His knowledge of birds, though a
small instance, was very remarkable.   With few excep-
tions, the birds of the North American States are different
from ours; there are more thrushes and larks, for example,
in the United States than in Britain, but the species there
are not the same as ours.   For example, they are without
the skylark.   Of all the songs that Roosevelt and I heard
in the one afternoon and evening of our walk, there was
only one song, that of the golden-crested wren, that he
recognized as being practically the same as the song of
an American bird, and when I consulted the late Mr.
Ogilvie Grant afterwards, he told me that the resemblance
in this instance was correct, and that it was the only one
we could have heard in that walk.   Our time was short,
and the number of varieties of birds heard or seen was not
remarkable; but it amounted to between forty and fifty
different species, and there was not one of which Roosevelt did not know the general character and classification.
This is the sort of thing that went on throughout the walk.
I would say:
    "Do you hear that?"
    "Yes, what bird is it?"
    "A black-cap."
    "So that's the song of the black-cap."
    It was not necessary for him to see the bird; he knew
already what sort of bird it was, and what it was like.
    I was told, when I was in the United States a year

afterwards, by one of the greatest authorities on natural history, that Roosevelt was the only amateur he had known who could hold his own in talk with real experts on the subject of mammals. Those competent to appreciate found the same revelation of his knowledge in history. He had a store of knowledge, remarkable both for range and volume, and his power of acquiring it quickly in a life of such constant and strenuous activity must have been extraordinary. But in controversy he would take a short cut to his point.

I once heard him asked whether it would be possible in the United States to pass into law a Budget with changes in taxation corresponding to those proposed in Lloyd George's Budget in 1909. The answer was not a learned exposition of the limitations of the American Constitution; it was simply this: "It would depend upon whether a Judge of the Supreme Court came down heads or tails."

Speculation as to how the European War would have been affected had Roosevelt been President of the United States in 1914 must be left to those who knew the United States and knew him intimately.

In 1912 Woodrow Wilson was elected President, and in 1913 he had to deal with the controversial question of Panama Canal Tolls. The United States had made the Canal with their own money and skill and enterprise. A demand arose that their own shipping should have the benefit in preferential dues. Why should the shipping of the nationalities that had contributed nothing to make the Canal have the full use and benefit of it on just the same terms as ships of the United States? The answer

WALTER HINES PAGE
American Ambassador in London, 1913-1918

was that the United States had bound itself by treaty with Britain not to give preferential dues on its own ships in the event of the Canal being made.

In each generation a country already great inherits a reputation for a lifetime. It is trustee of that reputation; it must hand this on to posterity preserved, diminished, or enhanced. Historians will judge it afterwards by moral as well as material standards. Nothing ensures for it more certainly a high place in history than a record that, where honour and interest appeared to be in conflict, honour was preferred to self-interest. The present generation in the United States has in this respect a position of unusually clear responsibility and opportunity. It is more free than any other nation in the world to choose for itself what its decision shall be in any controversy with another nation. It has no rival in the American Continents. With the not vital or very important exception of the Philippines, its territory is secure from serious attack by any other Power. It is so strong potentially in all resources necessary for war, so self-contained financially and commercially, that its decisions in policy are beyond question of being influenced by outside pressure. President Wilson's decision in this matter of the Panama tolls was an independent and unqualified example of putting the sanctity of a treaty above immediate self-interest. As such it was noted at the time and ought still to be remembered.

After the death of Whitelaw Reid and the election of Woodrow Wilson as President, Walter Hines Page came as American Ambassador to Britain. It was understood, at the time, that he came as the personal friend possessing the confidence of President Wilson.   That was his credential to public opinion here, to which he was otherwise unknown.   He was received with all cordiality, but nobody could foresee the immense importance of his appointment.   To have realized this it would have been necessary to have the most intimate knowledge of the man as well as prophetic foresight of the war.

Our first diplomatic relations were concerned with Mexico.   The long rule of President Diaz was over, and the state of anarchy and confusion that was bound to ensue upon the withdrawal of that remarkable figure and strong hand had succeeded.   Huerta had seized the central authority and proclaimed himself President, but his authority was challenged by other personalities and their followers.   We had no intention of interfering or attempting to influence the situation.   All we could do was to wait for Mexicans to settle their own Government; to appeal to the central authority, when there was one in a position to protect long-established and legitimate British commercial interests, or to leave it to those interests to make the best arrangements they could on the spot, when there was no authority with which diplomacy could deal.

President Wilson's policy, as explained to me by Page, was to bring about a better state of affairs in Mexico. The precedent of Cuba was quoted.   That island had fallen into disorder; the United States had gone into it more than once and brought about the establishment of order and properly constituted government.   If that broke down again, the United States would intervene again, till Cuba realized that she must govern herself well. This was the policy to be applied to Mexico. Diaz had kept order, but his rule had been a tyranny; and, that being over, the time had come to secure the establishment of civilized government of approved modern pattern. The policy was altruistic; it was not being pushed for material interests; it was a policy of using the influence of the United States to lift a backward neighbour on to a higher plane. This account does not purport to give the words of Page himself, but to give the policy as I understood it from his statement. It appealed to him as a policy with an ideal.

Our conversations about Mexico were not always very sympathetic. I made it quite clear that we should look passively on with acquiescence in whatever policy the United States thought fit to pursue about Mexico, but I could not be enthusiastic about the prospect. The first practical step in the policy of President Wilson was to get rid of Huerta; it was said that there were moral blemishes on Huerta's character. It was no concern of mine to defend Huerta; but I could not be enthusiastic when I heard that General Villa, one of Huerta's chief opponents, was spoken of as the "Sword of Revolution" in Mexico. Villa had shot a British subject in cold blood, and it was impossible to feel that morality was really to be secured by substituting him or his like for Huerta. In fact, I could not see a moral opening to be made in Mexico by backing one set of the contending factions against another; and I had the impression that Page felt me unresponsive. It must not be supposed that he was suggesting British co-operation. That would have been quite contrary to the settled policy of the United

States; but he wanted us to know what the policy was, and that we should not get in the way of it by backing Huerta. It was clear that, as the United States Government had made up their minds to eliminate Huerta, he would have to go. He could not stand against that influence, as well as against his enemies in Mexico.

I accepted the situation, and Page accepted my assurances that we were not interfering to support Huerta; but Page believed that British commercial interests were doing so. Whatever they were doing was entirely unknown to me, and I was prepared to look to the United States Government to see fair play for British interests, if and when it took a position of responsibility; but till that time came the very fact that the British Government could not interfere in the Mexican revolution or protect its commercial interests made it only fair that these interests should make what terms they could with whoever on the spot could protect them or might destroy them. Page saw an ideal in the Mexican policy of President Wilson. I was ready to sympathize with the ideal, and to believe in the moral purpose of the policy; but I did not believe that morally there was much to choose between Huerta and his opponents. That was the difference between us. Had I realized then, as I came to know afterwards, how devotedly Page cared for an ideal of right in public affairs, how indifferent he was to anything else but that, I should have been less reserved and more frank in our Mexican conversations. The time was near when, in the stress and extremity of war, all reserve was to be stripped from me, and the whole mind of each was to be clear to the other.

Page was of authentic British stock, but he came to London absolutely and entirely American. He had not by previous association got any British-tinted spectacles through which to view us. His outlook, his sympathies, his ideals were American, and by these he formed his opinion of Britain and Europe. He believed in a certain type of civilization and world ideal for which the United States stood and for which its influence was making. When the war came he saw in it a struggle to the death between the forces in Europe that made for the American ideal and the forces that would destroy it and replace it by something that was to him detestable. It was therefore a supreme issue of right against wrong. To many people the violation of Belgium was a shock and offence, a cruel wrong done to a small and unoffending country. To Page, it was more than that; it was something that shook the foundations of everything that made the world tolerable and progress possible. His own country was not in any present danger, as Britain was; that left his mind more free to comprehend, his vision more clear to see, the greatness of the issue. As the war went on, I became more and more absorbed by the danger to Britain; he grew more anxious too, but it was for the danger to his world ideals, lest his own country should stand passive, while these went under.

From the first he considered that the United States could be brought into the war early on the side of the Allies if the issue were rightly presented to it and a great appeal made by the President. Whether he was right in that opinion does not matter now. What does matter is that his record stands, and will stand as a conspicuous example of the highest type of patriotism—that patriotism which is not only love of one's country, but belief in it.

The forces that made for dangerous trouble between Britain and the United States were often formidable in the first two years of the war. Page was earnest and active, in advice to us and by all persuasion and influence that he could use at Washington, to counteract and foil these forces. The comfort, support, and encouragement that his presence was to the Secretary for Foreign Affairs in London may be imagined, but cannot be overestimated.

CHAPTER XXII

(1914-1916)

AMERICA AND THE WAR (*continued*)

The Japanese Alliance and American Interests—Questions of Contraband—The Declaration of London—The Blockade of Germany—Delicate and Uncertain Ground—The List of Contraband—Reasons for not Including Cotton—Difficulties about Copper—The Objection to Orders in Council—The Case of the *Dacia*—Russia and Sweden—The Omission of Cotton Justified—Opinion in the United States—A Fair Field for Diplomacy—German Propaganda—American Visits to Europe.

LET me now deal specifically with some of the questions which arose between us and America as the war proceeded.

In the early days the Japanese Alliance was a matter of some embarrassment and even of anxiety. Japan was ready to take her part in the war as our Ally; the Far East and the whole of the Pacific Ocean lay open to her and were her natural sphere of operations. But the prospect of unlimited Japanese action was repugnant to Australia and New Zealand. They already regarded Germany, her position, and transactions in the Pacific with misgiving; they would have viewed the substitution of Japan for Germany with positive alarm. Equally important, the effect of Japanese action on public opinion in the United States might be disastrous; it might even make American sentiment definitely antagonistic to us. It was unthinkable that we should not have the most scrupulous care for the interest and the feelings of British Dominions that were taking their part in the war, ready to face danger and to make sacrifices with so much patriotism. We dared not risk offending the United States. We had, therefore, to explain to Japan that her help would be welcome, but that her action must be limited and her prospective acquisition of German territory must not extend beyond certain bounds. To explain to an Ally that her help will be welcome, but that you hope it will not be made inconvenient, is a proceeding that is neither agreeable nor gracious. It was, however, not only politic, but essential for us and for the Allies.

The Anglo-Japanese Alliance is ended; it has been superseded by the Washington Agreement, to which the United States as well as we are a party with Japan; but for all the eleven years when I was Secretary of State at the Foreign Office Japan was our Ally. In all that period the obligations that the Alliance might entail upon us, the advantages that Japan might claim from it, were never unfairly exploited by her. We found in the Japanese Government and its Ambassadors honourable and loyal Allies. They understood, as in the case of the Bryan Peace Treaty with the United States, the difficulty in which we sometimes found ourselves, and they smoothed the path.

In the Great War they took some advantage of the opportunity to strengthen their position with China in East Asia. Europe was prostrated in war, the attention and at last the energy of the United States were absorbed in it. The opportunity for Japan was immense and unique. What Western nation with a population feeling the need

for territorial outlets would have used such an opportunity with more or even with as much restraint?

The problems that may cause difficulties between Japan
on the one hand and America or British Dominions on the
other, are well known; they are very real and there are
some points in them that are fixed and insuperable; but it
is right, and may be helpful, that those who are preoccupied with these matters should bear in mind that the Government of Japan was for us for many, many years a fair,
honourable and loyal Ally, and that, thanks to its forbearance, no serious friction arose between us and the United
States on Pacific questions during the war.

The most difficult and dangerous controversy with the
United States was over questions of contraband and the
consequent interference with neutral trade; but, before
approaching it, let me say a word about the Declaration
of London.

That Declaration had never been ratified, and its rules
played little part in the war.[1] It had not been the work of
the Foreign Office alone: the Admiralty had been represented in the negotiations in which it was drawn up.   I
had, however, promoted and supported it and was the
Minister specially responsible for it.   The Declaration
passed the House of Commons, but its rejection by the
House of Lords prevented its ratification.   Had it been

---

[1] On August 20, 1914, the British Government announced by proclamation that
"it would act in accordance with the provisions of the Convention known as the
Declaration of London, so far as may be practicable," but with modifications
which, in the opinion of the State Department at Washington, largely nullified
the original Declaration.   Very critical questions arose with the United States,
and on October 29, 1914, a second order was issued, the principal effect of which
was to withdraw the general application of the doctrine of "continuous voyage"
to conditional contraband (mainly food) with the result of permitting some of

in full force its rules would have hampered us in some respects, particularly in the list of contraband, at the outset of the war; and those who opposed and defeated it are entitled on this account to take credit for their action. Whether, if the Declaration had been ratified and observed as a whole by the belligerents, the balance of advantage and disadvantage would have been in our favour or not is a different question, and one less easy to answer. If it had prevented the submarine war on merchant vessels, it would have saved us from our greatest peril in the war. To this it may be replied that, but for the German submarine war on merchant vessels, the United States would not have come in on the side of the Allies.

The question is not worth pursuing: if the Declaration had been ratified, it would have been broken. The same ruthless spirit that introduced the use of poison-gas, an offence not only against rules of war but against all humane considerations, would have made short work of the Declaration of London.

One lesson from the experience of the war is, that we should not bind ourselves to observe any rules of war, unless those who sign them with us undertake to uphold them by force, if need be, against an enemy who breaks them. We kept the rule against the use of poison-gas till the Germans broke it, and when they did break it we had

---

this to pass through neutral ports into Germany. This was, however, subsequently supplemented and to a considerable extent superseded by the "Reprisal Order" of March 11, 1915, which gave power to stop all goods of whatever description, destined for Germany, leaving the Declaration of London in being only in so far as it governed the decision whether conditional contraband could be condemned as prize.

For the diplomatic history of this matter see *The Life and Letters of Walter H. Page,* vol. i, chap. xii.

neither gas nor protection against gas ready. The rule was nothing but a disadvantage to us, for its violation by the Germans brought no help to us. To bind ourselves by rules which we intend to keep and others intend to break is unreasonable, so long as those who break them can do it with impunity.

To return to the question of contraband, blockade of Germany was essential to the victory of the Allies, but the ill-will of the United States meant their certain defeat. After Paris had been saved by the battle of the Marne, the Allies could do no more than hold their own against Germany; sometimes they did not even do that. Germany and Austria were self-supporting in the huge supply of munitions. The Allies soon became dependent for an adequate supply on the United States. If we quarrelled with the United States we could not get that supply. It was better therefore to carry on the war without blockade, if need be, than to incur a break with the United States about contraband and thereby deprive the Allies of the resources necessary to carry on the war at all or with any chance of success. The object of diplomacy, therefore, was to secure the maximum of blockade that could be enforced without a rupture with the United States.

This was very delicate and uncertain ground. International law has always been elastic; neutrals and belligerents with inferior sea-power always contended for rules of contraband and blockade that would involve the very minimum of interference with trade. Germany and the neutrals were therefore at the same point of view in this matter. A belligerent with superior sea-power always contended for an interpretation of international law that would justify the maximum of interference with goods that might conceivably reach the enemy. Britain and the Allies, having superior sea power, naturally took the latter view. The British contention had not always been the same. When we were a neutral we had, in the interest of our commerce, disputed the maximum right of interference claimed by belligerents, as in war between France and China in 1885, when the French declared rice to be contraband of war. One general principle was admitted —goods were of three kinds:

1. Articles that were free and not to be interfered with even when consigned to enemy ports, unless these ports were included in an effective blockade, and the definition of what constituted effective blockade under modern conditions left room for argument.

2. Articles in the list of conditional contraband; these were only to be stopped if found to be destined for the armed forces of an enemy.

3. Articles in the list of absolute contraband; these might be seized wherever found on the high seas if they were destined for the enemy country at all.

It was evident that the first step was to put on the list of absolute contraband all the articles that were essential for armies under modern conditions; the second and more important step was to get the United States to accept that list. The United States is mentioned above all others, because that country was the only neutral that could effectively dispute the list, and because all other neutral States would presumably accept what the United States agreed to. We were at once on debatable ground, but were obliged to put on the list of absolute contraband articles that had in previous wars been held to be free, or, at most, conditional contraband. There were articles that in old days had been of little or no use to armies, but were now essential to them. Would the United States dispute our right to put some of these on the list? They might do so on the ground that they were articles of general use for general commercial as well as for military purposes, and ought therefore not to be in the same category as munitions of war.

It would be politic for us not to make the list too large at first; to put in it only things that were really vital to Germany for the war. The three most important novel additions would be copper, rubber, and cotton. It was felt that to include cotton would certainly provoke a challenge from the United States and would impair the prospect of her agreeing to a list that included copper and rubber. We decided to concentrate on getting copper and rubber included, and we secured this most important point. We got a list of absolute contraband that was not seriously challenged. But there was much more difficulty to come. We were now entitled to seize such things as copper and rubber in any ship on the high seas, if they were consigned to a German port. This alone was of little use. Germany could import goods as easily through Dutch, Danish, or Swedish ports as through her own, and in Sweden especially there were people disposed to make Sweden a source of supply for Germany. It was therefore as essential to Britain and the Allies to seize copper or rubber going to a Swedish or neutral port as when going to a German port.

It was on this point that controversy arose with the

United States. The very fact that the United Sates was
in a sense the trustee for the right of weaker neutrals made
its Government disposed to champion those rights. Was
a peaceful Swede desiring copper for innocent purposes
to have it stopped? On the other hand, was the British
Navy to let copper pass under its very guns to a Swede
who was importing it for the German Government and
going to send it straight to Germany to be made into
munitions to kill British soldiers? The argument between
these two opposite points of view was long, voluminous,
and extensive. It was published, and anyone who has
enough curiosity and time may read it.

The Navy acted and the Foreign Office had to find the
argument to support the action; it was anxious work.
British action provoked American argument; that was
met by British counter-argument. British action preceded
British argument; the risk was that action might follow
American argument. In all this Page's advice and suggestion were of the greatest value in warning us when
to be careful or encouraging us when we could safely
be firm.

One incident in particular remains in my memory.
Page came to see me at the Foreign Office one day and
produced a long despatch from Washington contesting
our claim to act as we were doing in stopping contraband
going to neutral ports. "I am instructed," he said, "to
read this despatch to you." He read, and I listened. He
then said: "I have now read the despatch, but I do not
agree with it; let us consider how it should be answered!"
On other occasions he would urge us to find means of
avoiding provocation of American feeling; for instance,

he urged us to find some way of acting other than by Orders in Council, which since 1812 had had such odious associations for the United States. He knew that these were only a matter of form, and that there was nothing in them intrinsically offensive to the United States, but the name was hateful in America. Unfortunately Orders in Council were formalities essential to make our action legal in British Courts of Law and we could not do without them.

The Germans were naturally active and ingenious in devising means to exploit and cultivate this ground, so fertile for quarrel between Britain and the United States; and they had plenty of clever agents and friends in America to help them. A ship would be chartered with contraband; the name of the ship and its intended voyage would be carefully revealed; American attention would be drawn to it; American feeling would be instigated to the point of readiness to resent British interference with it. The ship would then start; if we interfered with it, we ran the risk of provoking an outburst of opinion in America that might be formidable; if we allowed it to pass, we stultified our own action in other similar cases and admitted that our blockade was ineffective or non-existent. The *Dacia* was an example of this. Everybody knew what the *Dacia* was, when she was to sail, and where she was going. She was an open challenge to our blockade which we were bound to take up. Page suggested that the French Navy instead of the British should intercept the *Dacia*. This was done, and there was not a murmur in America. We used to hear it said, in days when Bryce was Ambassador at Washington, that he was the most popular European in America since Lafayette; but it was the memory of Lafayette that persisted through the war. France was the historical friend, and Britain the historical enemy.

It was possible, in notorious cases such as that of the *Dacia*, for French action to disarm American resentment and to counter German manœuvres; but, in the nature of things, the bulk of the blockade and contraband operations had to be carried out by the British Navy, which was not only the larger, but the best equipped for this purpose. The burden of defending it fell upon British diplomacy, i.e. the Foreign Office; the Board of Trade, which controlled British exports, and the Admiralty devised or executed the measures we took. The Secretary for Foreign Affairs was bombarded with the protests from neutrals that ensued. Much of his time was spent in reconciling neutral countries to what we were doing, justifying British action, or promising enquiry, as the merits of each protest might seem to require. In the interest of the Allies, and of Britain in particular, it was desirable not to lose the good-will of neutrals; but the task of soothing and reconciling them was difficult and thankless. The stopping of contraband was bound to cause annoyance to neutral trade and shipping, and yet it had to be maintained.

The United States was the formidable and vital difficulty, but it was not the only one. Sweden was a difficulty. It soon became evident that Germany intended Sweden to become a main channel of supply; copper was going to Sweden that was, in fact, imported by Germany. We decided that all copper for Swedish ports must be stopped,

unless Sweden would agree to prohibit and would effectively prohibit, the export of copper from Sweden to
Germany. Whether such a measure had any precedent
in international law I do not know, but unless the United
States, which was a great source of supply of copper,
interfered, we could and should enforce our decision.
Sweden must either go without copper or prohibit its
export. She preferred the latter course.

One day, the Swedish Minister came to protest to me
that the British Navy had stopped a cargo of copper for
Sweden, in spite of the fact that the Swedish Government
had prohibited the export, and had now proceeded to
prohibit the export of statues of Hindenburg. I was not
familiar with the executive details of blockade, which
only came to me when they led to international complications. I did not see at first what statues of Hindenburg
had to do with the matter; then I understood. Sweden
had prohibited the export of copper, but had not simultaneously prohibited the exports of works of art, and
under this heading masses of copper were made up and
exported as statues of Hindenburg. Our agents had found
it out, and we had of course required it to be stopped.

After the Russian disaster in 1915 there was a period
when the Russian Government was in real fear of Sweden.
The intervention of Sweden against Russia might have
threatened Petrograd itself and have given the finishing
touch that would have knocked Russia out of the war.
Sazonof, at any rate, thought so, and I remember being
urged by him at least once to be very careful not to irritate
Sweden by too much interference with her trade, lest the
consequences should be embarrassing, or even disastrous,

to Russia. A British submarine operating in the Baltic, but dependent on a Russian base, captured a Swedish vessel loaded with contraband for Germany. The Russian Government urged us to release the vessel, so afraid were they at that moment of offending Sweden. The Russian request was most embarrassing to us. There was no doubt that the vessel and her cargo would be condemned as lawful prize by a British Prize Court. Our whole transactions with neutrals were founded on the contention that vessels captured by our Navy were brought before a Prize Court and that British Courts dealt with them impartially according to international law. If we released this vessel against all evidence, the character of British Prize Courts was vitiated; the precedent would be quoted against us in future cases of the same kind. As the only way out of the difficulty, I suggested that, as the Swedish ship was taken to a Russian port, it should be handed over to the Russians. Whatever they did could not be quoted as precedent for British Prize Courts. This course was followed, and my recollection is that the Russians released the vessel. The Russians were sore enough at the inability of the French and British armies to relieve them of the pressure of the German army upon them; they insisted that we should not, by what they considered untimely and impolitic interference with Swedish commerce, expose them to the risk of an attack by Sweden. We did not, so far as I remember, alter our own practice in dealing with goods consigned to Sweden, but it added perceptibly to the difficulty of the work of the Foreign Office that we had sometimes to consider the susceptibility not only of neutrals, but also of an Ally in dealing with contraband.

The question of cotton needs a little more explanation. It was important enough to be considered separately by the Cabinet in the early stage of the war. I thought it inadvisable to make it contraband. One reason has already been given, but there was more than that to be taken into account.

The cotton-growing States of America were hard hit in 1914 by the outbreak of the war. Their trade was temporarily disorganized, if not altogether suspended. That was not the fault of Britain; it was due to the war. But, if cotton were made contraband, this would be regarded as a fresh blow dealt mainly by Britain to an important industry of the United States, when it was already in distress. The attitude of the United States was going to be important and might be vital in the war; there were already materials enough for friction between us and the United States; the fomenting of these was the trump card of German diplomacy. My opinion was very decidedly that there was far more to be lost than to be gained by making cotton contraband in the first year of the war. The Cabinet took this view; it was right, even more right than we knew at the time.[1]

After the war, when I went to America in 1919, an American of very high position in the business world, and friendly to us, volunteered the remark that it was very fortunate that we did not declare cotton contraband in 1914. I said that I had felt this at the time, but I was not quite sure what the consequence would have been; my fear was that the United States would begin convoying merchant ships possibly to enemy, certainly to neutral,

[1] See infra, letter from Theodore Roosevelt, pp. 145-8.

ports; in this event we must have let the convoys pass, which means giving up our blockade and the stopping of supplies to Germany, for convoying, once begun, would not have been limited to cotton, but would have covered other things in which American trade was interested. Our only alternative would have been to stop the convoys by firing on the American ships of war that accompanied them; this meant war with the United States. My friend said that was not the danger to us that he thought the most likely. What he thought would have happened was an embargo on all export of munitions of war. Even as it was, there had been risk of this; the pacifist feeling in the United States was pressing for it; this section of opinion regarded the European war as a detestable thing in which American citizens should have no part, and which they should not help to keep alive by feeding any country engaged in it with munitions. All the pro-German element was pressing for an embargo, because the Allies needed American munitions and Germany did not; the anti-British element was strong on the same side. Had we exasperated the cotton States by making cotton contraband, this "block" of political influence would have gone to swell the body of opinion pressing for an embargo, and the thing which was already an appreciable risk might have become a certainty.

Another American friend, with unsurpassed knowledge of the feeling in executive and political circles at Washington at the time, has since told me that he thinks the United States would have resorted to convoy.

Later on, cotton was made contraband with a guarantee

of a minimum price—that was when the trade had recovered and the cotton States were not in acute distress. The Germans at once found a substitute. Had we made it contraband in 1914 we should have run all the risk I have described, and gained nothing.

In all this discussion of contraband with the United States we were like men who had to steer a ship through an uncharted sea, perilous with shoals and rocks and treacherous currents. We kept on our course and came safely through, but we had to feel our way and often to go slow. It is to be hoped that those who think we ought to have gone straight ahead on higher speed may never have to make that voyage.[1]

After the United States came into the war all these difficulties disappeared. There was no longer need to prove that goods going to a neutral port were intended for Germany; the prohibition to export copper or other contraband from neutral countries into Germany was no longer accepted as satisfactory. Neutral countries able or likely to supply Germany were rationed; their own need was assessed, and they were allowed to have so much and no more, in order that they might have none to spare for Germany. That was a blockade such as the world had never known, but it was possible only because the United States was not criticizing but co-operating. I was out

---

[1] It is known now that in Germany, during the autumn and winter of 1916, the military and naval authorities pressed for unlimited submarine warfare in disregard of all considerations of international law or diplomatic expediency. They carried the day. Their action brought the United States into the war and ended in the defeat of Germany. If the British Government had been overborne by those who wished us, in matters of contraband, to set aside all legal and diplomatic considerations the result might well have been the defeat of Britain and the Allies.

of office then, and I read one day in a newspaper that
people in America were saying, "We can't think why this
was not done before." The reason was, that the point
of view of the United States had changed from that of a
neutral to that of a belligerent with superior sea-power.
In matters of blockade and contraband the point of view
makes the whole difference. It always has done so to
Britain; it did so in 1917 to America.

There was another and larger aspect of the diplomatic
field in the first years of the war, which much concerned
the Secretary for Foreign Affairs in London and the
British Ambassador in Washington. The United States
was the only country whose attitude and policy could not
be influenced by the military course of the war. Whatever division of sympathy there might be in different
sections of its people—some pro-British, some pro-German, all well disposed to France, all with an antipathy
to Russian Tsardom—there was probably a widespread
consciousness or subconsciousness that a German victory
would mean a Prussianized Europe, and that this would
be inimical to American ideals of world polity. German
victories, therefore, would not predispose American opinion to side with Germany against the Allies. With America, diplomacy did in consequence have a fair field and
counted for something either to alienate or attract. The
Germans were quick to see the importance of this field;
they sent their cleverest agents to America, and there was
a real diplomatic struggle between the diplomacy of the
Allies and that of the Central Powers. It was on Britain
that Germans concentrated, and the attack was twofold:

   1. To represent Britain as the cause of the war. This

we left the White Paper to answer—that paper had been issued in great haste with the sole object of laying the facts before Parliament, when Parliament was asked to vote money for the war; but it was a full disclosure of our action in the critical days before the war; nothing important had been concealed, and there was nothing important left to reveal.

2. The second point of attack was that Britain was the one and only Power that was adamant against peace, determined to force the war relentlessly to the point of crushing Germany.

The Agreement signed with France and Russia on September 5, 1914, was represented as evidence of British policy to bind her Allies to keep up to the mark. The fact was that this Agreement had arisen from the desire of the Allies to make sure that we should continue with them in the war. But for us to explain this would have been an attempt to divert upon our Allies the odium that it was sought to cast upon us, and perhaps to suggest to them that we were lukewarm about the Agreement itself. This would have been both impolitic and untrue.

The three following documents will exemplify what was going on:

Sir Edward Grey to Sir C. Spring-Rice

FOREIGN OFFICE,
September 9, 1914.

SIR,—The American Ambassador showed me to-day a communication that he had had from Mr. Bryan. It was to the effect that Mr. Straus and Mr. Speyer had been talking with the German Ambassador, who had said that, though he was without instructions, he thought that Germany might be disposed to end the war by mediation. This had been repeated to Mr. Bryan, who had spoken to the German Ambassador, and had heard the same from him. Mr. Bryan had taken the matter up, and was asking direct whether the German Emperor would accept mediation if the other parties who were at war would do the same.

The American Ambassador said to me that this information gave him a little concern. He feared that, coming after the declaration that we had signed last week with France and Russia about carrying on the war in common, the peace parties in the United States might be given the impression that Germany was in favour of peace, and that the responsibility for continuing the war was on others.

I said that the agreement that we had made with France and Russia was an obvious one; when three countries were at war on the same side one of them could not honourably make special terms for itself and leave the others in the lurch. As to mediation, I was favourable to it in principle, but the real question was: on what terms could the war be ended? If the United States could devise anything that would bring this war to an end and prevent another such war being forced on Europe I should welcome the proposal.

The Ambassador said that before the war began I had made suggestions for avoiding it, and these suggestions had been refused.

I said that this was so, but since the war began there were two further considerations to be borne in mind: we were fighting to save the rest of Europe from being dominated by Prussian militarism; Germany had prepared to the day for this war, and we could not again have a great military Power in the middle of Europe preparing war in this way and forcing it upon us; and the second thing was that cruel wrong had been done to Belgium, for which there should be some compensation. I had no indication whatever that Germany was prepared to make any reparation to Belgium, and, while repeating that in principle I was favourable to mediation, I could see nothing to do but to wait for the reply of the German Emperor to the question that Mr. Bryan had put to him, and for the United States to ascertain on what terms Germany would make peace if the Emperor's reply was favourable to mediation.

The Ambassador made it quite clear that he regarded what the German Ambassador had said as a move in the game. He agreed with what I had said respecting terms of peace, and that there seemed no prospect at present of Germany being prepared to accept them.—I am, etc.,

E. GREY.

Sir C. Spring-Rice to Sir Edward Grey
(Received September 18)

WASHINGTON,
September 17, 1914.

German Ambassador has stated in Press that Germany is anxious for peace on basis of *status quo,* and desires no new territory, but that England has declared intention of fighting to a finish for her selfish purposes, and is consequently responsible for further bloodshed.

French Ambassador and I have stated that Allies have made no conditions nor heard of any.

A newspaper campaign will probably be conducted with a view to gaining sympathy of the United States Government on the ground that we are refusing pacific overtures of Germany. It is undesirable that British newspapers should advocate extreme conditions of peace, such as destruction of German fleet, etc., which provide German Embassy with useful material.

Sir Edward Grey to Sir C. Spring-Rice

FOREIGN OFFICE,
September 18, 1914.

Your telegram of September 17: Mediation.

Germany has planned this war and chosen the time for forcing it upon Europe. No one but Germany was in the same state of preparation.

We want in future to live free from the menace of this happening again.

Treitschke and other writers of repute and popularity in Germany have openly declared that to crush Great Britain and destroy the British Empire must be the objective for Germany.

We want to be sure that this idea is abandoned. A cruel wrong has been done to Belgium—an unprovoked attack aggravated by the wanton destruction of Louvain and other wholesale vandalism.

What reparation is Germany to make to Belgium for this? If Germany really desires mediation of United States she should state conditions of peace that deal with these points. We have no indication that she is ready to consider them.

At present we have neither heard of nor stated any conditions of peace, and there is nothing to show the German Ambassador's suggestions, vague as they are, to be either authoritative or sincere.

This is the line I should take in dealing with the German Ambassador's publications, but I leave it to your discretion whether it is desirable to inspire any counter-statements.

The Secretary for Foreign Affairs had to exercise himself on the same ground in many interviews in the Foreign Office in London. Americans came over to Europe to explore the ground to see what opportunities there were of making peace. To examine the mentality of the combatants, they went to Berlin, and were received by the Chancellor, or by high officials. Each was presented with the view that Germany was prepared for peace on moderate terms, but that it was the Allies, perhaps Britain especially, that were the obstacle to a reasonable peace. These Americans came to see me in London, and I did my best to put the situation in what I thought its true light. It was an immense relief not to have to do this with the American Ambassador, as well as with unofficial persons; it was a still greater relief to feel sure that if Page's own countrymen were interviewing him as well as myself, they were getting from him a view of the merits of the war that was favourable to the Allies.

SIR CECIL SPRING-RICE
British Ambassador in Washington, 1913-1918

CHAPTER XXIII

(1914-1916)

NEGOTIATIONS WITH COLONEL HOUSE

Colonel House, the Friend and Confidant of Wilson—Informal Conversations—House's Great Qualities—His View of the War—Stalemate and what next?—The Memorandum of 1916—What President Wilson was prepared to do—Communication to the French—A Projected Mission to Petrograd—Provisions for Absence—A Memorandum for the Cabinet—What might have been.

IT is now time to give some account of negotiations with the man who, during all the time that I was in office, was more in the confidence of President Wilson than anyone else known to me, Colonel Edward M. House. We had met pleasantly enough once or twice on his visits to London before the war. He came to London in the early weeks of the war as President Wilson's friend and confidant. No official business was transacted through House; that was all done through Page. The relations with House were therefore quite informal; there was no question of our conversations being turned into official despatches and explained in the State Department by the British Ambassador at Washington. Whatever I said to House, or he to me, was private and informal, to be repeated direct to President Wilson as House might think fit, sure not to be misunderstood, and not to be in any way binding except when it was written down and agreed between us, as a definite expression of view.

When House came to London after the outbreak of war our conversations almost at once became not only friendly but intimate. I found combined in him in a rare degree the qualities of wisdom and sympathy. In the stress of war it was at once a relief, a delight, and an advantage to be able to talk with him freely. His criticism or comment was valuable, his suggestions were fertile, and these were all conveyed with a sympathy that made it pleasant to listen to them. After a day that began about seven in the morning I broke off work by seven in the evening, and took things easily at my house for an hour before dinner. It was arranged that in this hour House should come whenever he wanted to have a talk. In this way we had many conversations that ranged over a large field of human affairs. I possess no records of these; they were for the most part too informal to be recorded, but in 1916 House and I drew up together one document that was one of the only two papers, private or official, that I deliberately took home with me when I left the Foreign Office and London towards the end of that year. It is printed in this chapter.

In the absence of records made at the time, no attempt will be made to give House's views in the form or in the language that he expressed them. What follows will give the impression conveyed to me by him, reproduced in my own way.

House left me in no doubt from the first that he held German militarism responsible for the war, and that he regarded the struggle as one between democracy and something that was undemocratic and antipathetic to American ideals. It was not necessary to spend much time in putting our case to him. He had a way of saying "I know it" in a tone and manner that carried conviction both of his sympathy with, and understanding of, what was said to him. I felt sure that he did not differ much from Page in his view of the merits of the war; where he differed from Page was in his view of what President Wilson could or ought to try to do. House considered that the United States could not be brought into the war in the early days; immediately after the sinking of the *Lusitania* he thought this might have been possible, but, with the exception of that passing moment, he considered that an attempt to bring the United States into the war would be premature and unsuccessful. His mind was always practical. He was not less studious of the means by which an end was to be accomplished than he was of the end itself. In this awful calamity of war the end to be sought and worked for was a just, fair, and reasonable peace. He was in Europe to study the situation, to investigate the means by which such a peace could be brought about, and to inform and advise his friend at the White House thereon.

House followed public affairs with the close attention and informed himself about them with the industry and zeal of a man who lives for a public career. Yet a public career was what House desired to avoid for himself; his mind therefore worked with all the keenness of one who feels the spur of ambition, but with the free impartiality of one whose ambition is quite impersonal. He longed to get good accomplished, and was content that others should have the credit. His judgment of men and things was both keen and detached. Believing that to work for the entry of the United States into the war was not yet practical politics, he set himself to consider how the influence of the United States could be used most effectively to bring about a good peace. A rapid and complete victory of Germany or of the Allies would give the least opening for the intervention of the United States; prolonged deadlock and stalemate might make the influence of the United States, exercised diplomatically with the whole of American sentiment behind it, decisive and paramount. After the battle of the Marne stalemate seemed much more probable than complete victory. House thought stalemate the most likely contingency, and worked earnestly and continuously so to prepare the way as to make it certain that the United States would exercise its influence effectively in a good peace; and the essential point in his mind was that everything should be ready for the first opportunity, that it should be decided what peace terms President Wilson would consider to be fair and to what length he would go to secure them, if he were assured that one side of the belligerents would accept them. House agreed that the moment for President Wilson to propose a Conference had not yet come, but it would come, if either side were ready to accept a Conference and the terms for which the President would help with the whole force of American opinion behind him.

In February 1916 House drafted with me a memorandum to define as precisely as could be done in advance the action that President Wilson would be prepared to take, and the terms of peace that he would use all the influence of this country to secure. A copy was left with me, and House took the memorandum to Washington to get the text confirmed by the President. From Washington he cabled confirming it, with the alteration of only one word. The following is the final form of the document as authorized by President Wilson:—

Memorandum

(*Confidential*)

Colonel House told me that President Wilson was ready, on hearing from France and England that the moment was opportune, to propose that a Conference should be summoned to put an end to the war. Should the Allies accept this proposal, and should Germany refuse it, the United States would probably enter the war against Germany.

Colonel House expressed the opinion that, if such a Conference met, it would secure peace on terms not unfavourable to the Allies; and, if it failed to secure peace, the United States would leave the Conference as a belligerent on the side of the Allies, if Germany was unreasonable. Colonel House expressed an opinion decidedly favourable to the restoration of Belgium, the transfer of Alsace and Lorraine to France, and the acquisition by Russia of an outlet to the sea, though he thought that the loss of territory incurred by Germany in one place would have to be compensated to her by concessions to her in other places outside Europe. If the Allies delayed accepting the offer of President Wilson, and if, later on, the course of the war was so unfavourable to them that the intervention of the United States would not be effective, the United States would probably disinterest themselves in Europe and look to their own protection in their own way.

I said that I felt the statement, coming from the President of the United States, to be a matter of such importance that I must inform the Prime Minister and my colleagues; but that I could say nothing until it had received their consideration. The British Government could, under no circumstances, accept or make any proposal except in consultation and agreement with the Allies. I thought that the Cabinet would probably feel that the present situation would not justify them in approaching their Allies on this subject at the present moment; but, as Colonel House had had an intimate conversation with M. Briand and M. Jules Cambon in Paris, I should think it right to tell M. Briand privately, through the French Ambassador in London, what Colonel House had said to us; and I should, of course, whenever there was an opportunity, be ready to talk the matter over with M. Briand, if he desired it.

(Initialled) E. G.

FOREIGN OFFICE,
February 22, 1916.

At present there was no use to be made of it. We believed and the French believed, that defeat of the German armies was the only sure overthrow of Prussian militarism, and to the French the recovery of the lost provinces of 1870 had become an object to be fought for. Before 1914 France had given up the idea of going to war to recover them, but, once war was forced upon her, she was determined to fight on to win them. Both France and Russia had up to this time suffered more heavily in the war than we had. We could never be the first to recommend peace to them. We still had large reserves of men to train, group, and bring into action. We were bound to go on till we had used all our yet undeveloped strength to support our Allies, and in the effort to defeat Germany. We all felt that we could take no initiative in the American direction. But things had looked very bad at the end of 1915; the Russian losses in men, guns, and material had been crushing; according to their own account they had only 700,000 rifles left. A Russian recovery seemed doubtful, Serbia was overrun, and her army a refugee outside her own territory. Roumania and Greece dared not stir, the prospect of the Germans being unable to hold and of the Allied armies ever being able to break through on the Western front was very dubious, and certainly remote. To attempt to transfer the main theatre of war anywhere else was to substitute for the short channel crossing a line of sea communication of huge length exposed to the risk of submarines; to operate from unsatisfactory bases such as Salonika; to make it easy for the Germans to use Turks or Bulgarians in the main theatre of war; and, in short, to give Germany every advantage in communications, for hers would be comparatively short and quite safe. The chances seemed that things might get worse rather than better in 1916. If this happened it would be most valuable to bear in mind what sort of a peace could be obtained by the mediation and influence of the United States, and also to know that these would be forthcoming.

The communication to the French was a matter of extreme delicacy. If nothing was said to them, and if things took a sudden turn for the worse, I should be open to the gravest reproach; the French would say with justice that they ought to have been told that this means of terminating the war had been open to the Allies. The imputation would be that I had kept the knowledge of it from them, lest they should be disposed to take advantage of the opportunity offered by it. The memorandum was in effect an offer by President Wilson to end the war on the terms described, and, if Germany refused, then to bring the United States into the war against her. If we ignored President Wilson's offer, the Allies might forfeit his sympathy, and for that we alone should be held responsible, if the French had not known of what had passed between House and ourselves.

On the other hand, to recommend the memorandum to the French was to suggest that we were weakening and to undermine their confidence in our determination to support them. Furthermore, to have made such a recommendation without the approval of the Cabinet or at least the War Committee would have been disloyal to colleagues; and the War Committee, with my full concurrence, had decided not to take the matter up. I therefore let M. Briand, then French Prime Minister, know of it without recommending it.

About this time the Germans began the tremendous attempt to deal a knock-out blow at Verdun. For some weeks all attention was concentrated on the splendid resistance and terrible sacrifice made by the French Army. Then came the counter-offensives by French and British armies and the hopes founded on them, and on the temporarily successful Brusiloff offensive in the East, and the entry of Roumania into the war on the side of the Allies.

When these hopes had died away and the news of things in Russia was bad, it was decided that a British Mission to Petrograd was desirable to strengthen Russian solidarity with the Allies.

I was to go there and to be absent from London for at least a month. The prospect of the war had again become dark. To military uncertainties had been added the menace of submarine warfare on merchant vessels. This was getting serious, and we could not calculate what the development of it might be.

I considered that, in my absence, my colleagues should have the House Memorandum before them to consider, if unforeseen emergency should require it.

For this purpose I wrote this covering paper to be sent to the Cabinet with the Memorandum:

I shall be absent for a month; it is impossible to foresee what may happen in this time, and I wish before I go to leave with my colleagues some reflections on the situation.

Nothing but the defeat of Germany can make a satisfactory end to this war and secure future peace. To that all our efforts must be given, and to effect it the nation must submit to organization and sacrifice, as Germany and some of our Allies, at any rate, France, do already submit. I know my colleagues are impressed with the necessity of this, and are working at it; and I have no special knowledge that entitles me to give advice about it. I only state it to record that in my opinion, as I believe in theirs, this is the question of first importance.

We must, however, be careful in stating our determination to continue the war to make it clear that our object is not to force, but to support our Allies. Increasing mischief is being made between us and our Allies by German propaganda. This propaganda represents the war as one of rivalry between Great Britain and Germany; it insinuates that France, Russia, and Belgium could have satisfactory terms of peace now, and that they are continuing the war in the interest of Great Britain to effect the ruin of Germany, which is not necessary for the safety of the Allies, but which alone will satisfy Great Britain.

It is just possible that this insidious misrepresentation, false though it be, may create in France, Russia, Italy, and Belgium a dangerous peace movement—a movement positively unfriendly to us.

It would be well if we could all, Ministers and Press alike, strike one note, that of determination to help the Allies who have suffered the most grievous wrong, to secure the liberation of their territory, reparation for wrong done, and the advantages necessary for their future security. We should emphasize the impossibility and disgrace of thinking of peace till the Allies are secure, but should let it be understood that it is for them whose territory is occupied by the enemy, whose population has been, and is being so grossly ill-treated, rather than for us, to say when it is opportune to speak of peace. Till that time comes, we use all our efforts and make every sacrifice to defeat the enemy in the common cause, and have no other thought but this.

What I fear most is that one of the Great Allies when told, as they ought to be told now, that our support in shipping and finance, one or both, has to be curtailed in a few months, will abandon hope of ultimate victory, and demand that the war be wound up on the best terms available. If either France or Russia came to this decision it is probable that the other would follow suit, Italy would drop out, and we should be left the option of entering peace negotiations, or continuing the war alone.

I do not say that this contingency is probable, but it is possible, and if it happens I think the Cabinet should have before it the record of what passed with Colonel House in February 1916. I annex the record.

This record was drawn up in agreement with Colonel House; after his return to Washington, it was confirmed through him by President Wilson.

A copy was sent through the French Ambassador to M. Briand with an intimation that I did not propose to raise the question with M. Briand unless he wished to discuss it with me. He has not, so far, mentioned it to me, and the French line has been that mediation is not desired.

The War Committee were informed of what had passed with Colonel House, and we were unanimously of opinion that the time had not come to discuss peace, and such communication as there has been with Colonel House since has been on that basis.

At the time the conversations with him took place it was assumed by him that Germany would not consent to peace negotiations such as he indicated, except under pressure. It is supposed now at Washington that Germany is ready, and even anxious, to have peace negotiations. In the absence of any communication from us or the French Government, and after speeches made here and at Paris, it continues to be assumed that we are opposed to them.

Whether the disposition of President Wilson is still the same as it was in February I do not know, for I have made no enquiry. If the Great Allies desired to begin peace negotiations, and if we decided to join them in this rather than to continue the war alone, then I think we should contend for President Wilson's intervention in the negotiations. His influence would be exercised whole-heartedly on behalf of Belgium, at any rate: a point on which we cannot yield without sacrifice not only of interest but of honour, but also a point on which Germany would make specious efforts, by tempting offers, to separate our Allies from us.

I hope it will be clearly understood that I am not raising the question of mediation now; that I am submitting this paper to my colleagues only because I shall be absent, and out of touch with them for so long,

COLONEL EDWARD M. HOUSE

and that I do not urge them to give attention to it, unless one of the contingencies contemplated as possible arises before I return.

Defeat of Germany is, and will continue to be, the only satisfactory end of the war.

But we cannot force the Great Allies to continue the war against their will, or beyond their strength. And if their action makes peace inevitable before Germany is defeated, then I would submit that the intervention of President Wilson—(if it is still available in the spirit described)—should be seriously considered.

Shortly after this was written the Asquith Coalition Government resigned; I was out of office, and my visit to Russia was cancelled. My last act was to put my successor at the Foreign Office in possession of a copy of the House Memorandum, and the paper I had intended to send with it to the Cabinet, in case the course of events should make it desirable for the new Government to consider them.

My impression now is that, for reasons that I did not know at the time, the Memorandum was already out of date. What these reasons were I can only infer from what has since been disclosed in Germany.

The reader has perhaps asked himself what was passing all the time between President Wilson and the German Government. London was not the only place that House visited during the war; he went not only to Paris, but also to Berlin, and had intimate conversations there. This was public knowledge, and House himself had spoken to me often of his visit both to Berlin and Paris. President Wilson's object was to secure a peace which he considered would make a just end to the war, and be the beginning of enduring peace. He might invite the opinion of the Allies first, but he would explore the mind of Germany too. His whole policy was founded on the assumption that the war was a stalemate, and that the most useful rôle of the United States was to promote an honourable end without a crushing victory. If either side, even Germany, were to agree with him in this, he would use the influence of the United States to bring the other side into line. His suggestion of mediation could not be confined to one side.

I have written hitherto as if President Wilson's move was on the side of the Allies. I regarded it as such, because it seemed to me certain that Germany would refuse anything like the terms suggested. The German people had been led to expect a victorious war; they had been told, and believed, that they were winning; Berlin had been beflagged again and again in honour of victories. The American terms were, it is true, not the terms that the Allies would regard as those of victory, but for Germany they were the terms of positive defeat. Germany was to repair the wrong done to Belgium, and she was to get nothing, unless it were some colonial concession from France in return for some concession to France in the matter of Alsace and Lorraine. It seemed to me inconceivable that Prussian militarism could look at such terms, while it was still undefeated and hoping for victory.

It appears from recent German disclosures that in the autumn of 1916, if not before, the German Government became aware of the intention of President Wilson to approach them, and that they eventually countered this by an intimation to him of their terms of peace that may well have made him despair of anything like a just peace

being secured except by the use of force.[1] If so, the
House Memorandum, by the time I sent it to Balfour,
had ceased to have importance for President Wilson, who
knew now that even such terms as he thought just could
not be obtained from Germany except by force; and that,
if the United States was to take any part in securing them,
it must be by the use of force. The German defiance in
the submarine warfare precipitated war between
America and Germany, but the German manner of
countering his mediation policy must surely have turned
President Wilson's thoughts in the direction of war.

How does it all look now? In the light of after-events,
it is clear that Germany missed a great opportunity of
peace. If she had accepted the Wilson policy, and was
ready to agree to a Conference, the Allies could not have
refused. They were dependent on American supplies;
they could not have risked the ill-will of the Government of the United States, still less a *rapprochement* between the United States and Germany. Germans have
only to reflect upon the peace that they might have had
in 1916 compared with the peace of 1919.

Did the Allies also miss an opportunity? The notion
would have been scouted when the Treaty of Versailles
was signed; judged by that, and in the light of victory,
the terms of the House Memorandum seem preposterously
inadequate. But now, some years after the mighty peace
of 1919, the condition of Europe is sufficiently disappointing to make it interesting to imagine what the course of

[1] See despatch from von Bethmann-Hollweg to Ambassador Count Bernstorff,
Supplement to Minutes of Second Sub-committee to inquire into the responsibility
for the war. *Official German Documents,* Carnegie Endowment Translation,
Vol. II, 1048-50.

events might conceivably have been if the Allies and Germany in 1916 had told President Wilson that they were ready for the Conference he was prepared to summon.

If Germany had refused the Conference, or refused to settle on the terms foreshadowed, the United States would have joined the Allies some months sooner than she did. This would have been a gain to the Allies.

If Germany, rather than face this contingency, had settled on the Wilson terms of 1916—what then? The terms were such as must have demonstrated the stultification and failure of Prussian militarism. Granted that militarists are incorrigible and would have desired to prepare a new war, would the German people have been so disillusioned about war as to depose militarism from control? Or would they simply have resented the Wilson intervention as having deprived them of victory and have supported Kaiserdom and militarism in future plans to gain it?

All depends on the answer to these questions, and we can never know certainly which answer would have been true.

But, if a Wilson peace in 1916 had brought real disillusionment about militarism, it would have been far better than what actually happened.

Two years of war, in which expenditure of life and national strength and treasure were at their maximum, would have been avoided. European markets and trade might have recovered quickly, for the impoverishment and exhaustion would have been much less. The future peace of Europe, with the unsevered co-operation of the United States, might have been safer than it is to-day.

Prosperity and security might be to-day more fair in prospect for us all than the victory of 1918 and the treaties of 1919 have made them; and there would have been a peace with no noxious secret ideas of *revanche*.

So disappointing have events been since 1919, so dark are the troubles still, that we are tempted to find some relief in building castles in the air; and, if the future is too clouded for this, we build them in the past.

CHAPTER XXIV

(1912-1915)

A CORRESPONDENCE WITH ROOSEVELT

A Tribute to Roosevelt's Courage—His Answer—The Panama Canal Tolls—The Abyss of War—If Roosevelt had been President—Speaking out—Three Objects of the War—America and Contraband—Roosevelt's Advice—A pro-German Senator and his Opinions.

I HAVE several times, in the previous narrative, referred to my relations with Theodore Roosevelt, which began with his visit to the Foreign Office and our walk together in the New Forest in 1910. From that time onwards I was in frequent correspondence with him, and this seems a fitting place to publish some of the letters that passed between us. His personality appears in everything that he wrote and gave a human interest to our correspondence. The letters printed here all have relation to matters mentioned in other chapters; but to insert each in the place for which in time and substance it is most relevant would break the sequence both of the narrative and of the correspondence. They are, therefore, printed all together, with such of my own as will enable them to be understood.

From Sir Edward Grey to Mr. Roosevelt
October 24, 1912.

MY DEAR ROOSEVELT,[1]—I must send a line to say with what con-

---

[1] Letter written on receipt of the news that Mr. Roosevelt had been fired at and wounded on his way to a public meeting, which he insisted on addressing in spite of his wound.

cern and sympathy I heard the news of your being wounded—
I might add also with what relief and admiration I heard the full news,
for the news that the wound was not dangerous, and that you had had
courage and endurance sufficient to make a speech after it, were all part
of the first news.

My thoughts went back to our bird walk; indeed, I often think of
that with pleasure, and great desire to do something of the same kind
with you again.

Soon I suppose that I must be free; for this Government has lasted
so long that a change cannot be very far off, though the means of
bringing it about are not yet apparent.

You apparently may be in for another spell of office, though here
we know little of the chances in the Presidential contest, and I can't
in an official position comment upon the issues.

The account of your wound stirs me with a curiosity to know
whether, if the experience had been mine, I should have had the nerve
to make the speech, and whether my body would have proved as healthy.
You have a great gift, moral and physical, of stimulating other people,
and I never hear of you without wishing to see you again.—Yours
sincerely,

EDWARD GREY.

From Mr. Roosevelt to Sir Edward Grey
THE OUTLOOK,
287 FOURTH AVENUE, NEW YORK,
November 15, 1912.

MY DEAR GREY,—I greatly appreciate your letter. I am glad
you sometimes think of our bird walk, because it was one of the incidents
I shall always remember. I cannot help hoping that sometime I shall
have the chance to get you over here and repay in kind.

I regret that you think your Government may soon come to an end.
As for the political fight here, I did not believe we would win, and
I can say quite honestly that I have little or no personal regret in the
outcome. But I do feel sorry from the broader standpoint. Nine-tenths
of wisdom is being wise in time, and, if a country lets the time for
wise action pass, it may bitterly repent when, a generation later, it
strives under disheartening difficulties to do what could have been
done so easily if attempted at the right moment. We Progressives
were fighting for elementary social and industrial justice, and we had

with us the great majority of the practical idealists of the country. But we had against us both the old political organizations, and 99 per cent. at the very least of the corporate wealth of the country, and therefore the great majority of the newspapers. Moreover, we were not able to reach the hearts of the materialists, or to stir the imagination of the well-meaning, somewhat sodden men who lack wisdom and prefer to travel in a groove. We were fought by the Socialists as bitterly as by the representatives of the two old parties, and this for the very reason that we stand equally against government by a plutocracy and government by a mob. There is something to be said for government by a great aristocracy which has furnished leaders to the nation in peace and war for generations; even a democrat like myself must admit this. But there is absolutely nothing to be said for government by a plutocracy, for government by men very powerful in certain lines and gifted with the "money touch," but with ideals which in their essence are merely those of so many glorified pawnbrokers.

I am a little amused, my dear fellow, at your saying that the account of the shooting stirred you with a curiosity to know whether, if the experience had been yours, you would "have had the nerve to make the speech," and whether your "body would have proved as healthy." I can answer both questions with absolute certainty. Your nerve would not have been affected by the least, you would have made the speech as a matter of course; and your body would have proved *more* healthy. You would have shown the absolute coolness and courage and lack of thought of self that your brother showed when mauled by the lion. Modern civilization is undoubtedly somewhat soft, and the average political orator or party leader, the average broker or banker or factory owner, at least when he is past middle age, is apt to be soft—I mean both mentally and physically—and such a man accepts being shot as a frightful and unheard-of calamity, and feels very sorry for himself and thinks only of himself, and not of the work on which he is engaged or of his duty to others, or indeed of his real self-respect. But a good soldier or sailor, or, for the matter of that, even a civilian accustomed to hard and hazardous pursuits, a deep-sea fisherman, or railwayman, or cowboy, or lumber-jack, or miner, would normally act as I acted without thinking anything about it. I believe half the men in my regiment at the least would have acted just as I acted. Think how many Bulgars during the last month have acted in just the same fashion and never even had their names mentioned in bulletins! Recently

John Murray sent me *The Life of Sir Harry Smith,* and I was reading his experiences in the Peninsular War, and his account of the many officers who continued to perform their duties with bullets in them, it being often many hours before a surgeon could attend to them. Why, even in our little San Juan fight there were thirteen men of my regiment who, after being shot, continued in the fight.

Now I wish to rank myself with such men as Harry Smith and his comrades in the Peninsular War, and with the men in my regiment, and I expect to be judged by their standards, and not by the standards of that particular kind of money-maker whose soul had grown hard while his body had grown soft; that is, who is morally ruthless to others and physically timid about himself.

I doubt if any man has had a greater volume of obloquy poured upon him than I have had during the past nine months, and I have been assailed with an injustice so gross as to be fairly humorous. But there is a good deal in Emerson's law of compensation, and to offset this I have been praised in connexion with the shooting with quite as extravagant a disregard of my deserts. The bullet passed through the manuscript of my speech and my iron spectacle case, and only went three or four inches into the chest, breaking a rib and lodging against it. I never saw my assailant, as it was dark, and he was mixed with the dense crowd beside the automobile, and, as I was standing unsteadily, I half fell back for a second. As I stood up I coughed, and at once put my hand to my lips to see if there was any blood. There was none; so that, as the bullet was in the chest, I felt the chances were twenty to one that it was not fatal. I would not have objected to the man's being killed at the very instant, but I did not deem it wise or proper that he should be killed before my eyes if I was going to recover; so I immediately stopped my men who had begun to worry him, and had him brought to me so that I might see if I recognized him; but I did not. There was then a perfectly obvious duty, which was to go on and make my speech. In the very unlikely event of the wound being mortal I wished to die with my boots on, so to speak. It has always seemed to me that the best way to die would be in doing something that ought to be done, whether leading a regiment or doing anything else. Moreover, I felt that under such circumstances it would be very difficult for people to disbelieve in my sincerity, and that therefore they would be apt to accept at its face value the speech I wished to make, and which represented my deepest and earnest convictions. If, on the other hand, as I deemed overwhelmingly probable, the wound should turn out to be slight, it was still likely that I would have little further chance to speak during the campaign, and therefore it behoved me to go while I had the chance, and make a speech to which under the circumstances it was at least possible that the country would pay some heed. This is all there was to the incident.

I am sorry Bryce is going. I am glad Cecil Spring-Rice is to succeed him. I had a delightful letter from Trevelyan the other day.— With all good wishes, faithfully yours,

THEODORE ROOSEVELT.

From Mr. Roosevelt to Sir Edward Grey
THE OUTLOOK,
287 FOURTH AVENUE, NEW YORK,
January 9, 1913.

OFFICE OF THEODORE ROOSEVELT.

MY DEAR GREY,—For fear you might think I agree with my fellow editors of *The Outlook* on the matter of arbitrating the canal tolls,[1] I write to say that this is not so. In the next issue of *The Outlook* I have a letter on the subject, and I shall take the liberty of sending you a copy. I believe we should arbitrate the matter.

I heard of you through Miss Asquith, who was here the other day.

Well, I hope the Bulgarians come out ahead in the Balkans business!

Wishing you all success through the New Year.—Very faithfully yours,

THEODORE ROOSEVELT.

From Sir E. Grey to Mr. Roosevelt
FOREIGN OFFICE, LONDON,
January 29, 1913.

MY DEAR ROOSEVELT,—I have read with much appreciation your article about Arbitration.

It is very healthy that a stand should be made for the principle of maintaining an existing Arbitration Treaty. If this question of Panama is not settled by diplomatic means, and Arbitration is refused, it will be a tremendous set-back to the cause of Arbitration in the whole world.

[1] See supra, Vol II, p. 97.

Knox's reply to us is now being considered here, and our reply to it will have to come before the Cabinet, so I cannot discuss what it is likely to be.

One point, however, occurs to me with reference to what you say about coast-wise shipping. In principle, the matter seems very simple, as you treat it. Foreign ships are excluded from taking part in American coast-wise trade. They were so excluded before the Hay-Pauncefote Treaty was made, and therefore to exempt them from tolls can be no injury to foreign shipping, if the foreign shipping does not in consequence have to pay higher tolls for the upkeep of the Canal than it would have to pay if tolls were levied on coast-wise shipping. But I am told that it would be impossible, in practice, to prevent coast-wise shipping from competing with foreign shipping in trade which is not coast-wise. For instance, a ship going from New York to San Francisco, may, when she passes through the Panama Canal, have some cargo on board for foreign ports; or, again, a ship, having gone through the Canal with coast-wise cargo only, may for her return voyage call at Central or South American ports for foreign cargo, and be able to take it at cheaper freights because her outward voyage through the Canal has been free of toll.—Yours sincerely,

EDWARD GREY.

From Sir E. Grey to Mr. Roosevelt

28 QUEEN ANNE'S GATE, LONDON, S.W.,
September 10, 1914.

MY DEAR ROOSEVELT,—J. M. Barrie and A. E. W. Mason, some of whose books you have no doubt read, are going to the United States. Their object is, as I understand, not to make speeches or give lectures, but to meet people, particularly those connected with Universities, and explain the British case as regards this war and our view of the issues involved.

In case you have not met them before, I wish to tell you that I am sure you would like them, and find them interesting. I have asked Spring-Rice to give them letters of introduction to you.

This war is a terrible thing. It is as if we had fallen into an abyss where the barbarous ages had been buried and were in them again.

If the Germans win Prussian militarism will dominate the whole of Europe, with the exception of Russia, who will remain a Power in the East of Europe and in Asia. The ideals of right and wrong, and good faith in treaties, and other things that make for humanity and civilization, will all be subordinated in the whole of Western Europe to a rule of force, under the iron standard that what makes for German power is right, and everything else is to be crushed.

In this war Germany has the great advantage of having planned for it and chosen the time when she would force it upon Europe. She is therefore absolutely prepared at every point. France and England, being democratic countries and not desiring war, never can prepare for war in the same way. We were too conscious of the innocence of our own intentions to make preparations equal to those that have been made by a country that not only prepares for war, but plans it and chooses the moment. Russia is, of course, a much less highly organized State than Germany, and her policy and her preparations are always in a sort of loose, half-baked condition. Poor Belgium, till the ultimatum from Germany reached her, never believed that her neutrality would be violated; and the way in which she has preferred to risk ruin and destruction of every sort, rather than allow herself to be trampled upon unresistingly, is very fine.—Yours sincerely,

E. GREY.

From Mr. Roosevelt to Sir E. Grey

THIRTY EAST FORTY-SECOND STREET,
NEW YORK CITY,
October 3, 1914.

MY DEAR GREY,—I have just received your letter, and have immediately asked Barrie and Mason to lunch with me.

I have just written an article for *The Outlook,* and a series of articles for various daily papers upon the war, in which, while I did my best not to be in any way offensive to Germany, I emphatically backed the position that England, and specifically you, have taken. I have been in a very difficult position. I am in opposition to the Administration, and to say how I myself would have acted, when I am not in power and when the action I would have taken is the reverse of that which the present Administration takes, would do harm and not good. This is especially so because the bulk of our people do not understand foreign politics and have no idea about any impending military danger. When I was President, I really succeeded in educating them to a fairly good understanding of these matters, and I believe that if I had been President at the outset of this war they would have acquiesced in my taking the stand I most assuredly would have taken as the head of a signatory nation of the Hague Treaties in reference to the violation of Belgium's neutrality. But, of course, I should not have taken such a stand if I had not been prepared to back it up to the end, no matter what course it necessitated; and it would be utterly silly to advocate the Administration taking such a position unless I knew that the Administration would proceed to back up its position. In my articles I spoke very plainly, but I believe with proper reserve and courtesy. I do not know whether they have reached England or not, but they certainly reached Germany, for the *Cologne Gazette* assailed me for them. Doubtless Spring-Rice will send them to you if you care to see them. —Very sincerely yours,

THEODORE ROOSEVELT.

From Sir E. Grey to Mr. Roosevelt

33 ECCLESTON SQUARE, LONDON, S.W.,
Tuesday, October 20, 1914.

MY DEAR ROOSEVELT,—Thank you for your letter.

I saw, from one or two articles, the line that you were taking in *The Outlook,* and Springy has now sent me some more, which I hope to read.

Your idea, that the United States might have come forward on the eve of the outbreak of war to uphold Treaty rights, makes me glow at the thought of what might have been achieved. I see all the difficulty there would have been in getting American public opinion to endorse such action. The line that the present United States Government have taken is, of course, the natural and expected one. But, if the United States had taken action, they might possibly have stopped the war. I say "possibly," because the accumulated evidence of the enormous preparation of Germany, her confidence, and her intention, makes me doubt whether anything could have stopped her at the last moment. But, if the United States had stopped the war, they would have broken militarism without a war. It would have been made clear that it was not worth while to maintain these enormous armaments, if, when an attempt was made to use them for aggressive purposes, the world was brought out against them. The result might have been an agreement between France, Germany, Russia, and England that none of them would attack another; that they would keep their armaments within certain bounds; that, on any dispute arising on this or any other question between any of them, it would be referred to arbitration, possibly the arbitration of the United States; and that, if any one Power refused arbitration the others would all join forces against it.

We had, I thought, during the Balkan crisis of a year ago or so, made some progress towards getting the European groups of Powers together. We got on very well with Germany at that time, because the Prussian military party did not think the time for war had come, and left the civil element alone.

Now, I can see nothing for it but to fight on till we can get a peace that will secure us against Prussian militarism. Once freed of that, Germany will have nothing to fear, because we shall have no more to fear from her.

I still think it possible that the United States Government may play a great part in the making of the peace at the end of this war, and in securing permanent peace afterwards. But it has, of course, become a point of honour for us that there should be reasonable redress to Belgium for what she has suffered. Germany will not look at this till she is beaten, and we cannot give up contending for it while we are unbeaten.—Yours sincerely,

E. GREY.

From Mr. Roosevelt to Sir E. Grey

THIRTY EAST FORTY-SECOND STREET,
NEW YORK CITY,
November 11, 1914.

MY DEAR GREY,—I enclose you something I have just written, as in it I spoke much more openly than I felt at liberty to speak prior to the elections, for anything I said before the elections would have been attributed to political purposes on my part.

I entirely agree with you in what you say, that you must fight on as things are now, and that there must be reasonable redress to Belgium for what she has suffered.

I sincerely regret to say that I have lost all my German friends by what I have written, and you who are in politics know that even an ex-politician does not particularly enjoy incurring enmities when to do so gives him personally absolutely nothing in return. But in this case I felt that I could not follow any other course than that which I actually did follow, that I owed it to my country and that I owed it too to the world, no matter how little influence I possessed, to exert whatever it was in favour of what I deemed vital justice.—Sincerely yours,

THEODORE ROOSEVELT.

From Sir E. Grey to Mr. Roosevelt
33 ECCLESTON SQUARE, LONDON, S.W.,
Friday, December 18, 1914.

MY DEAR ROOSEVELT,—I have read with much interest your article about a *Posse Comitatus* of neutral countries.

Personally, I should welcome such an organization. I hope that one result of this war may be to bring home to neutral countries the interest they have in preventing war. They all know now the suffering that war entails to the whole world. Some day, when we ourselves are again a neutral country, I think that we should welcome any proposals in the direction you suggest.

Meanwhile, we have to fight on for three objects:

(1) To save the British Empire and all that makes life at home here worth living.—It is clear enough now to us that the real objective of the Prussian military party has been domination; that we have been the great obstacle in the way of this; and that Prussian domination would mean the negation of our liberty and national life as an independent State.

(2) To get Belgium restored to her people, with redress of the wrong that has been done to her.—I hear that the Germans are putting it about that Belgium was in some plot with us. That has been sufficiently disproved by the documents that the Belgian Government have published, as well as by those that we have published:

(3) To secure that the Prussian military party, who prepared and planned this war, shall not in future dominate the policy of Germany.— This, I suppose, can be secured only when the German people realize that they have been deceived and misled by the Yunkers, and when they turn themselves into a democratic State. It is a difficult thing to arrange, but until it is secured Europe cannot be free from the terrific burden of expenditure on armaments: we should have to continue prepared, in future, for attack, and on a larger scale than heretofore.

We are, of course, bound mutually with France and Russia not to put forward terms of peace except by mutual agreement. We have not yet discussed terms of peace, and France and Russia will no doubt have their own conditions to make. But the three objects that I have mentioned are those that I believe this country wishes to get: to save ourselves, to obtain redress for Belgium, and to be secure in future against a policy of premeditated and prepared aggression.

It is in securing this third object that I think neutral nations may very well take a hand; if not in the actual terms of peace, then by entering into some agreement such as you have sketched, to which all the Great Powers would be parties, and which would, of course, give security to Germany as much as to anyone else.

My own views as to Hague Conventions and international treaties have suffered a good deal of evaporation in the heat of this struggle. I am disposed to think that all the Hague Conventions that have so far been made had better be abrogated, and new ones signed only on the condition that those becoming parties to them bind themselves to uphold them by force if need be.—Yours sincerely,

E. GREY.

From Mr. Roosevelt to Sir Edward Grey

30 EAST 42ND STREET,
NEW YORK CITY,
January 22, 1915.

MY DEAR GREY,—Through Spring-Rice I am sending you this letter. If you choose to show it to your colleagues in the Cabinet you are welcome to do so. But I need hardly say that, outside of such action, it is strictly confidential—not from reasons personal to you or me, but because of what I have at heart in writing.

You probably know my general attitude toward this war, as set forth in the little volume I have just published. (It would be entirely unnecessary for you to read this volume. It is addressed to and intended for my own countrymen.)

To me the crux of the situation has been Belgium. If England or France had acted toward Belgium as Germany has acted I should have opposed them, exactly as I now oppose Germany. I have emphatically approved your action as a model for what should be done by those who believe that treaties should be observed in good faith and that there is such a thing as international morality. I take this position as an American who is no more an Englishman than he is a German, who endeavours loyally to serve the interests of his own country, but who also endeavours to do what he can for justice and decency as regards mankind at large and who therefore feels obliged to judge all other nations by their conduct on any given occasion.

I do not think you need to have me show a precedent for writing you; but, if you do, I shall ask you to turn to young Trevelyan's *Life of John Bright,* pages 314 to 316. Bright was writing to Sumner at the time, when the bulk of the leading English politicians, from Palmerston and Derby to Gladstone and the editor of *The Times,* were more or less openly hostile to the cause of the American Union and the freeing of the slaves. Bright's letters were written to Sumner in order that they could be read aloud by Lincoln to his Cabinet, which was actually done. He was afraid the United States would drift into war with England. His letters run in part as follows:

"You know that I write to you with as much earnest wish for your national welfare as if I were a native and resident of your country. I need not tell you, who are much better acquainted with modern history than I am, that nations drift into wars. I fervently hope that you may act firmly and courteously (towards England). Any moderate course you may take will meet with great support here. I have no doubt you will be able to produce strong cases from English practice in support of your actions, but I doubt if any number of these will change opinion here. You must put the matter in such a shape as to save your honour and to put our Government in the wrong if they refuse your propositions. *At all hazards you must not let this matter grow to a war with England, even if you are right and we are wrong.*[1] War will be fatal to your idea of restoring the Union. I am not now considering its effects here; but I am looking alone to your great country, and I implore you, not on any feeling that nothing can be conceded and that England is arrogant and seeking a quarrel, not to play the game of every enemy of your country. Nations in great crises and difficulties have often done that which in their prosperous and powerful hour they would not have done; and they have done it without humiliation and disgrace. You may disappoint your enemies by the moderation and reasonableness of your conduct; and every honest and good man in England will applaud your wisdom. If you are resolved to succeed against the South, have no war with England. Make every concession that can be made. Do not hesitate to tell the

[1] The italics are mine. I am as little in sympathy with Wilson and Bryan in their attitude now, as Bright was in sympathy with the Palmerston-Derby view of our Civil War in '61-'65.

world that you will even consider what two years ago no power would have asked of you rather than give another nation a pretence for assisting your enemies. It is your interest to baffle your enemies even by any concession which is not disgraceful."

America then acted along the lines John Bright advised. I do not know whether his advice carried any weight. I have not the slightest idea whether you may not resent my giving advice; but I assure you that it is given with as much friendliness and disinterestedness as fifty odd years ago John Bright gave his to Sumner and Lincoln, and with as sincere a purpose to serve what I believe to be the cause of justice and morality; and with reversal of names the advice I am giving is the same as John Bright gave; and my reasons are the same.

There have been fluctuations in American opinion about the war. The actions of the German Zeppelins have revived the feeling in favour of the Allies. But I believe that for a couple of months preceding this action there had been a distinct lessening of the feeling for the Allies and a growth of pro-German feeling. I do not think that this was the case among the people who are best informed; but I do think it was the case among the mass of not very well-informed people, who have little to go upon except what they read in the newspapers or see at cinematograph shows. There were several causes for this change. There has been a very striking contrast between the lavish attentions showered on American war correspondents by the German military authorities and the blank refusal to have anything whatever to do with them by the British and French Governments. Our best war correspondent, on the whole, is probably Frederick Palmer. He is favourable to the Allies. But it was the Germans, and not the Allies, who did everything for him. They did not change his attitude; but they unquestionably did change the attitude of many other good men. The only real war news written by Americans who are known to and trusted by the American public comes from the German side; as a result of this, the sympathizers with the cause of the Allies can hear nothing whatever about the trials and achievements of the British and French armies. These correspondents inform me that it is not the generals at the front who raise the objections but the Home Governments, and in consequence they get the chance to write for their fellow-countrymen what happens from the German side, and they are not given a chance from the side of the Allies. I do not find that the permission granted them by the Germans has interfered with the efficiency of German military operations; and it has certainly helped the Germans in American public opinion. It may be that your people do not believe that American public opinion is of sufficient value to be taken into account; but, if you think that it should be taken into account, then it is worth your while considering whether much of your censorship work and much of your refusal to allow correspondents at the front has not been damaging to your cause from the standpoint of the effect on public opinion without any corresponding military gains. I realize perfectly that it would be criminal to permit correspondents to act as they acted as late as our own Spanish War; but, as a layman, I feel sure that there has been a good deal of work of the kind of which I have spoken in the way of censorship and refusing the correspondents permission to go to the front which has not been of the slightest military service to you and which has had a very real effect in preventing any rallying of public opinion to you.

I have also written to Spring-Rice a letter of which I shall ask him to send you a copy, which I should like you to consider in connexion with this letter I am writing to you and as part of it.

Now, as to the question of contraband. You know that I am as little in sympathy with President Wilson and Secretary Bryan as regards their attitude in international matters as John Bright was in sympathy with Lords Palmerston and Derby and Mr. Gladstone in their attitude toward the American Republic when it was at war fifty years ago. But they speak for the country; and I have no influence whatever in shaping public action, and, as I have reason to believe, very little influence indeed in shaping public opinion. My advice, therefore, must be taken or rejected by you purely with reference to what you think it is worth.

President Wilson is certainly not desirous of war with anybody. But he is very obstinate, and he takes the professorial view of international matters. I need not point out to you that it is often pacificists who, halting and stumbling and not knowing whither they are going, finally drift helplessly into a war, which they have rendered inevitable, without the slightest idea that they were doing so. A century ago this was what happened to the United States under Presidents Jefferson and Madison—although at that time the attitude of both England and France rendered war with one of them, and ought to have rendered war with both of them, inevitable on our part. I do not know if you have seen the letter I wrote to Spring-Rice on this question a couple of weeks ago. I presume he has sent it to you, or, if not, that he will send it together with this letter. I regard the proposed purchase by the Administration of German ships as entirely improper. I am supporting the Republicans in their opposition to the measure. I regard some of the actions of the Administration in, for instance, refusing to make public the manifests in advance and the like as improper. I think Great Britain is now showing great courtesy and forbearance. I believe that she has done things to our ships that ought not to have been done, but I am not aware that she is now doing them. I am not discussing this question from the standpoint of right. I am discussing it from the standpoint of expediency, in the interest of Great Britain. Our trade, under existing circumstances, is of vastly more service to you and France than to Germany. I think I under-estimate the case when I say it is ten times as valuable to the Allies as to Germany. There are circumstances under which it might become not merely valuable but vital. I am not a naval man, I do not know what the possibilities of the submarine are. But they have accomplished some notable feats; and if they should now begin to destroy ships carrying foodstuffs to Great Britain, the effect might be not merely serious but appalling. Under such conditions, it would be of the utmost consequence to England to have accepted the most extreme view the United States could advance as to her right to ship cargoes unmolested. Even although this possibility, which I do not regard as more than a very remote possibility, is in reality wholly impossible, it yet remains true that the trade in contraband is overwhelmingly to the advantage of England, France, and Russia, because of your command of the seas. You assume that this command gives you the right to make the advantage still more overwhelming. I ask you merely to take careful thought, so that you shall not excite our Government, even wrongfully, to act in such a way that it would diminish or altogether abolish the great advantage you now have . . . The German-Americans wish to put a stop to all exportation of contraband because such action would result to the benefit of Germany. The pacificists are inclined to fall in with the suggestion, because they feebly believe it would be in the interest of "Peace"—just as they are inclined heartily to favour any peace proposal, even though it should leave Belgium in Germany's hands and pave the way for certain renewal of the war.

Now, in all this I cannot advise you in detail. Many different cases come up; and the circumstances vary completely from case to case. I very earnestly hope that you will ostentatiously show every possible consideration to the American Flag and the American position and that, wherever possible, you will yield the point, even though you think you are right, rather than increase friction with this country and make our well-meaning but not well-informed people feel a sense of irritation and grow to regard England as trying to wrong America and being with difficulty prevented by the patriotic activities of the American Administration, the American Government. Exactly how far you can go in any given case, I cannot say. But where it is so very important for you that there should be no American hostility, I hope you will not only avoid doubtful action but will not insist on your rights, even when these rights are clear, unless you are convinced that the gain to you will more than off-set causing an irritation in this country which might have effects that I will not even contemplate, because they would cause me real horror.

I have publicly taken the position that, inasmuch as we did not stand up for Belgium's rights, it is a base and ignoble thing to take any action for our own moneyed interests as regards neutral affairs which may bring us into collision with the warring powers; but I need not say to you that in countries like England and the United States, although in times when there is no strain, everybody is willing to applaud the most foolish pacificist utterance, yet under strain there is always a tendency to assert the overwhelmingly superior claim of pure self-interest, untinged by any regard for international morality. I am as wholly hostile to the one tendency as to the other; but it is the part of wisdom to recognize that these tendencies exist.

I make no apology to you for writing; for I am certain that you understand the spirit in which I write and the reason for my doing so; and you are under no obligation to pay a moment's heed to what I have written or to answer the letter.—Yours very truly,

THEODORE ROOSEVELT.

SIR EDWARD GREY.

From Mr. Roosevelt to Sir E. Grey
THIRTY EAST FORTY-SECOND STREET,
NEW YORK CITY,
February 1, 1915.

MY DEAR GREY,—Just after having sent you my long letter, I receive yours of December 18. I only hope, by the way, that the feats of the submarines in sinking incoming merchant vessels, which have occurred since I wrote you, will not justify the fear I had in my mind and which partly influenced me in writing you.

As you read what I wrote in the *Posse Comitatus* article, I have taken the liberty of sending you a small book I have written called *America and the World War.*

I entirely agree with the three objects which you say you have to fight on for. As for the third, I also agree that probably the movement must come from within Germany itself. I do not know how it can be secured; but some such agreement as that I have sketched in outline would be one of the methods for securing it.

I am very much pleased at what you say as to the evaporation of your former views about Hague Conventions and international treaties. I have been frantically denounced by the pacifists because I would not enter into these treaties. But the reason was simply that I would not enter into any treaty I did not intend to keep and think we could keep. I regard with horror the fact that this Government has not protested under the Hague Conventions as to the outrageous wrongs inflicted upon Belgium. (*I* would have made the protest effective!) I agree absolutely with you that no treaty of the kind should hereafter ever be made unless the Powers signing it bind themselves to uphold its terms by force if necessary.

Well, I wish I were able to do something more efficient than merely talk. May all good fortune come to your country and to you.—Faithfully yours,

THEODORE ROOSEVELT.

From Sir E. Grey to Mr. Roosevelt

33 ECCLESTON SQUARE, LONDON, S.W.,
Saturday, March 13, 1915.

MY DEAR ROOSEVELT,—I have had no time to answer your letters, but I am very glad to get them.

We do what we can to avoid provoking neutrals, and especially the United States; but, with German submarines round our coast, torpedoing merchant vessels and drowning merchant seamen, people here will not stand letting goods go past our doors to Germany. The Germans began their game of sinking unarmed ships before we detained the cargo of the *Wilhelmina;* and we now find that at least two neutral merchant ships, one American and the other Dutch, bound for un-

Photograph by Henri Manuel

PRESIDENT ROOSEVELT

defended British ports and laden with grain, which they were bringing in the ordinary way for the civil population, were sunk by German cruisers before ever we detained the *Wilhelmina* with her foodstuffs for Germany.

As Senator —— brought me a letter from you, I was very glad to see him, and I enjoyed my talk with him. I heard that he was very pro-German, and I knew that he had been in Germany and had been very well entertained there, so I did not ask him anything about Germany, assuming that he would naturally not like to give away information to Germany's enemies; and also that, if he was pro-German, he would not wish to express his feelings to me.

One or two of his questions made me rather indignant. I told him that the German Minister in Peking had announced that, after this war, Germany was to be the mistress of Europe; and I said that what Germany wanted was to dominate the whole of the West of Europe. He asked whether it would matter if Germany did so, assuming that she did not annex any territory? It seemed a quite new idea to him when I explained that it would mean that we should no longer have independence, but should be obliged, in every question that arose, to do what Germany told us; to go out of Egypt if she chose; to arrange our tariffs to suit her; and generally to give way to her in everything. I said that, if there were a German domination, people like myself would certainly either perish or leave Europe. It seems to me really extraordinary that this point of view should appear new to him. What would the United States think, if they were in a position of political inferiority to another country?

He also repeated to me the German view that it was our business to have prevented Russia from going to war. This made me indignant. Last July, we asked Germany to accept a fair and honourable Conference, such as the one that had settled the Balkan Crisis not long before, or any similar means of settling the dispute between Austria and Serbia. We got Russia to accept that method unconditionally, and we refused to promise Russia in advance any support if she did go to war. But the Germans contend that we ought to have gone to Russia and told her that the "shining armour" was out, as it was in 1909, and that she must submit to another diplomatic humiliation, such as she had submitted to then: a thing that no great nation could stand twice, especially after it had been rubbed into them as it was by the Kaiser's speech in Vienna in 1909.

These things made me speak rather warmly, but I liked my talk with Senator ——, because he was alive and good-humoured.

If all goes well, and I survive this war, I shall take a long leave of public life, though I don't suppose I shall put a new river on the map.[1]—Yours sincerely,

EDWARD GREY.

[1] This refers to Roosevelt's own phrase describing his discovery of a river in South America.

CHAPTER XXV

(1914)

ALLIED DIPLOMACY IN WAR

A Tangled Skein—Impossibility of Consistent Policy—Three Partners and a Fourth—The Deciding Factors Military—Mistakes Fatal and Otherwise—Possible Issues to the War—Inter-Allied Agreement—Objects of Allied Diplomacy—The Neutral States—Four Categories—Different Methods—The Case of Turkey—A Twofold Objective—The Complication of the Battleships—Efforts to Gain Time—A Tribute to Louis Mallet—The Status of Egypt during the War.

IT is certainly difficult, it may prove to be impossible, to give a clear and connected account of Allied diplomacy in the war. Indeed the skein of "Allied" diplomacy was so tangled and confused that to unravel it and show it as a consistent whole is not possible. British diplomacy had necessarily to be one thread in this skein; sometimes it was almost lost as a separate thread, at other times it can be traced by itself. The mass of despatches and telegrams that constitutes the round of Allied diplomacy makes heavy reading. In the nature of things it could not be otherwise. From the first there were three great Allies who had in all diplomacy to act together—Britain, France, and Russia. After Italy entered the war a fourth was added, but in the first year of the war there were three; it was not till some time after her declaration of war with Austria that Italy was also at war with Germany, and a complete partner in Allied diplomacy.

The first step to the understanding of Allied diplomacy is to realize that consistent policy was impossible. Circumstances were always changing. A diplomacy that was suitable when the Allied armies were having success was hopelessly unsuitable when Germany seemed to be winning. Diplomacy had to adapt itself to what happened at the battle front, and in the adaptations the Allied Foreign Ministers sometimes got out of diplomatic step with each other. Sometimes there was a tendency in one quarter to make diplomacy more active, when the Allies were having military reverses; as if a more copious use of words in the form of threats or promises could compensate for the effect of defeats on the battle-field.

Imagine three Foreign Ministers in different parts of Europe, each representing a country with some sense of values peculiar to itself, with some special interest of its own. Then take into account the fact, inevitable in human nature, that the three were men of different temperament and intellectual outlook. Such differences between individuals there must always be, but in ordinary days of peace there is time to adjust, to make allowances, to understand. In war there is little or no time for this process; and in war fierce differences of temperament or outlook that might ordinarily have been suppressed were thrown into relief. In a crisis each Minister had his own suggestion to make for immediate action at some neutral capital. It was no uncommon situation for three different suggestions to be made. Of these his own suggestion would seem the best to the Minister who made it; to act on one or either of the others might seem a fatal error. Meanwhile, joint diplomatic action would be urgent, and none could be taken till all three Allied Ambassadors or Ministers at any foreign capital had received identic instructions. It may be imagined how busy the telegraph was and often how futile. It is not easy to see how this could have been avoided. If only two countries were engaged in war it would be possible for one of the two Foreign Ministers to agree that the main direction of diplomacy should be in the hands of the other; this would not in practice be probable, but it is conceivably possible, on the assumption that one of the Ministers might be wise enough to see that a second best diplomacy consistently followed and rapidly applied in war is better than the best policy delayed and compromised. But when three Ministers are concerned, the same two cannot be expected always to yield to the third.

Anyone who has read thus far may well ask how it was that Allied diplomacy, or rather want of diplomacy, did not lose the war. There are three observations to be made in reply to this very natural question.

(1) As far as Europe was concerned diplomacy in the war counted for little. When it appeared to fail most, it was when the Allies were having military reverses; when it seemed to succeed, it was because the Allies were having military success or because the military achievements of Germany were falling short of the expectations that had been formed of her invincibility. Thus, when Bulgaria joined Germany in 1915, it was considered a failure of Allied diplomacy; it was really due to the effect on Bulgarian policy of the terrible disasters to the

Russian Army in the summer of 1915 and to the British failure at the Dardanelles.

When Roumania joined the Allies in 1916 it was hailed as an Allied diplomatic success: there were, we read at the time, demonstrations against the German Foreign Office on account of its supposed diplomatic failure. The deciding factor in the entry of Roumania on the side of the Allies was not diplomacy at all; it may be found in the great success of the Russian Army under Brusiloff against the Austrians. If diplomacy could do little in Europe to win the war, it happily could do little to lose it. German military success, when it existed, made Allied diplomacy fruitless and would have made it so, however perfect. On the other hand, German military failure rendered even gross diplomatic errors, if such there were, unimportant.

(2) There was one mistake in diplomacy that, if it had been made, would have been fatal to the cause of the Allies. It was carefully avoided. This cardinal mistake would have been a breach with the United States, not necessarily a rupture, but a state of things that would have provoked American interference with the blockade, or led to an embargo on exports of munitions from the United States.

(3) Germany, on the other hand, did make this cardinal mistake. The answer, therefore, to the question why Allied diplomacy did not lose the war is that, in Europe, diplomacy counted for little, and that outside Europe, German diplomacy was worse than that of the Allies. These remarks apply to the dealing of the Allies with other nations; that is, to their external diplomacy. In

their dealings with each other, that is, in their internal diplomacy, they were successful. By good will and mutual concessions they avoided the fatal danger of falling apart.

In August 1914 we were in the war, but without the obligation of Allies. There was no agreement, verbal or signed, and none was necessary to make us loyal partners in war. There could have been no question of our backing out at the expense of our partners; no question of our entering upon any negotiations behind their backs or without their knowledge. But if a chance of stopping the war on fair terms had come, we were in a specially strong position to urge upon France and Russia that advantage should be taken of the opportunity. I was not without hope, though it was very faint indeed, that such an end might be yet possible and Europe be saved from the awful disaster of a protracted war. This depended entirely on the course of the war in the first few weeks, and there was only one hypothesis on which it would be possible, and that I feared was a very unlikely one. No such opportunity would come if Germany gained initial success, and that was the contingency that I apprehended. Such a success would not be in accordance with what British or French military authorities had told us, but it has been explained in a previous chapter why I had discounted the military opinion as being too sanguine. I feared and expected a great German success in France, and I felt on the outbreak of war that the only thing for us to do was to use all our strength, to strain every nerve, to fight strenuously, desperately if need be, to help the French to stop the German attack.

If that attack were successful we must be in for a long struggle—unless, indeed, there were a rapid German victory, but that was hardly possible. Britain, France, and Russia could not all be knocked out in a moment; even if Paris fell, the French armies would still be on the Loire, and the whole strength of Russia and Britain could yet remain and be brought to bear on Germany and Austria.

Another contingency, unhappily far less probable than the first, was that the British and French Armies might, as military opinion hoped, hold the German Army on the Western front. Then Britain and France must wait for the result of the Russian advance on the East. If that were successful the war must go on, till Germany was defeated; but if there were stalemate on both Western and Eastern fronts there would be a pause, in which the voice of reason might be heard. Germany would then have lost the hope of victory; the war in which she had counted on speedy defeat of France and Russia would on her part have been a failure; her fatal belief that she was invincible and irresistible would have been shattered. On the other hand, the Allies might reflect that, to resist a German attack was one thing, to advance and to conquer Germany another and very different thing. It might seem preferable to make peace on terms that, though short of victory for the Allies, would be anything but victorious terms for Germany. In such a situation the influence of the United States would be invaluable. The following record of a conversation with the American Ambassador illustrates what was in my mind in the first few days of the war.

Sir Edward Grey to Mr. Barclay

FOREIGN OFFICE,

August 7, 1914.

SIR,—I explained to the United States Ambassador to-day how strongly I felt now that, even if we had decided last Monday (3rd instant) to be neutral in the present European war, we could not have maintained that decision in face of the appeal made to us from Belgium to defend her, the address of the King of the Belgians to his people, and the fight that Belgium was now making against the Germans who had invaded her territory. One could not help asking indignantly why the Belgians should be killed. They were rivals to no one, they were inoffensive, they provoked no one, their neutrality was guaranteed, so that they were entitled to expect protection, and now the Germans had marched into their country and were shooting them down when they defended themselves. It was a most ruthless act on the part of Germany. We had been drawn into the war. We had no objective of our own in it, nothing that we particularly sought or had entered the war to obtain for ourselves. At the first moment, therefore, that it could be stopped honourably on fair terms we should like it to be stopped. Of course, if the Germans won easily against the French they would listen to nothing. If, on the other hand, the French and Russians won easily, they would insist that Germany should receive a lesson. What terms of peace would be fair would depend upon how things went. Perhaps the struggle might be more or less even, in which case there might be an opportunity for mediation, when both sides began to feel exhausted and neither was predominant. I knew that President Wilson wished to mediate, and, whenever there appeared a fair opportunity of stopping the war by mediation, we should, I felt sure, throw our influence on the side of it, and, having taken part in the war, our influence would be stronger than if we had stood outside. —I am, etc.,

E. GREY.

An early opportunity of expressing this view to the Ambassador was taken in order that the appeal might, if necessary, be made to the United States Government later on with the best effect. If it were made as something we had had in mind from the beginning, it would come with much better grace, and more force, than if it seemed to be something suggested to us by some unforeseen emergency or disappointment. The initial German success, the retreat from Mons, the German conduct in Belgium and the occupied districts put an end to any possibility of peace for many a long day to come. The German victories had to be turned into a defeat before there could be any prospect of fair or honourable terms of peace. In a few weeks France and Belgium had suffered terribly in lives and devastated territory; after that it could not be for us to suggest peace till they desired it; at any rate, not till we had suffered as much as they.

Early in September it was proposed that we should sign an Agreement with France and Russia binding all three countries to make war together and not to make peace except in common. The proposal did not come from us; it was made to us presumably because France and Russia felt that they would be more comfortable, and feel more sure of us, if we were bound to them, as they were already bound to each other, by the long-established Franco-Russian Alliance. After the Agreement of September 4 was signed the terms of the Franco-Russian Alliance, of which we had no previous knowledge, were communicated to us. There was, however, no surprise in them; they were what the terms of any comprehensive but defensive alliance would be assumed to be. We, of course, agreed without question and immediately to sign the Agreement of September 4; the first effect of it was to reassure and satisfy France and Russia; in a short time, when the extraordinary and sustained hatred of Germany against Britain became manifest, it was our turn to be comforted by the thought that we had Allies pledged to stand by us.

Enough has been said already to show that Allied diplomacy, and of course my own conduct in it, was not above criticism; and that it did indeed offer plenty of legitimate targets in which it was easy for critics to make bull's-eyes. Therefore a word of comment on the critics is now not unreasonable or out of place. There has been a tendency to judge diplomacy in war by the same standards as diplomacy in peace; to make insufficient allowance for the fact that in war words count only so far as they are backed by force and victories. Up to the end of 1916 (and even after that, but it is only with the war till December 1916 that this book is concerned) Allied diplomacy had little enough of this backing. Even the battle of the Marne was, to outside opinion, rather the saving of Paris than a great victory; an arrest of the German advance rather than a turning of the tide in favour of the latter. Then followed the first battle of Ypres, in which the Franco-British line was brought near to another catastrophe. In 1915 there were no Allied successes of magnitude sufficient to counteract the deplorable impression made by the huge Russian disasters. In 1916 the Germans failed at Verdun, but the French suffered heavily, and the year was rather one of German failure than of Allied success, except the Brusiloff offensive. This brought the Roumanians in. Even the gaps in the Austrian line made by Brusiloff were completely stopped in a short time. The task of Allied diplomacy in Europe during this part of the war was indeed uphill and thankless work.

To judge Allied diplomacy fairly it is right, first of all, to ask what were the chief objects that it ought, after the outbreak of war, to have set itself to achieve. What were these objects? This is the question that a fair critic should first set himself to answer. The first object undoubtedly was to preserve solidarity among the great Allies. This was completely and successfully achieved; had it not been, the war would have been lost. It needed constant care and mutual concessions and sacrifices, in view both of strategy and policy. Some of the things done have been condemned, as if they stood alone and were gratuitous actions done on their own merits, when they were, in fact, done solely because they were essential to prevent Allied disruption. The whole series of secret treaties is in this category. We made no secret treaty in time of peace after 1905, and indeed none for many years before that. In 1914 to 1916 we made or were parties to several secret treaties. To those who denounce secret treaties the just reply is: "You are quite right: in time of peace all secret treaties are wrong and detestable; so is the use of poison-gas; but, in a great war, you will be driven in self-defence to the use of both." In saying this let me not be supposed to mean that the actual terms of all the secret treaties made in the war were condemnable. It is the secrecy, not necessarily the substance, that is comparable to poison-gas.

Let it be put, then, to the credit of Allied diplomacy that Allied solidarity was preserved; it was even strengthened in the first part of the war by Italy becoming a party

to it. In this capital and vital object the Allies succeeded. The mistakes by which Allied solidarity might
have been jeopardized and which were in fact avoided,
the measures that were essential to preserve it and which
were in fact taken, will appear as this narrative proceeds.

The next most important object of Allied diplomacy
was the relations with neutrals. This was a much less
simple matter. It was indeed so varied and so complex,
turning on so many different pivots, varying with the
course of the war, complicated now by one incident, now
by another, arising out of contraband, that any writer
may well despair of giving a connected account of it. It
may not be possible to do more than illustrate the difficulty and complexity by giving some account of Allied
dealings with individual neutrals. Almost each one of
them presented a different problem that required separate
treatment.

At the outbreak of war the neutral States might be
classed under four heads.

1. Those who were in sympathy favourable or not
markedly unfavourable to the Allies, but who were presumed to be determined to keep out of war, whatever
their feelings might be for one side or the other. These
were the real neutrals. No concessions or promises from
one side or the other were required to induce them to
remain neutral. Our only care was to avoid pushing the
interference with their trade that blockade demanded to
such a degree of provocation as would make any of them
inconveniently hostile. Spain, Norway, Denmark, Holland, and all the Central and South American States may
be taken as examples of this category.

2. The States who were at present neutral, but whose sympathies were either pro-German or adverse to one or other of the Allies. Turkey, Bulgaria, Sweden, were in this category.

3. The States which, though neutral at the beginning of the war, were favourable to the Allies and disposed to join them when it seemed from the point of view of these States to be opportune. Italy, Roumania, and Greece were in this category.

4. The United States must be counted in a category by itself. That country was so powerful that it could not be affected in its sympathy or policy by the course of the war. The United States was able to do whatever it felt to be right or desirable without fear of the consequences. It was a factor so potentially important that its attitude might be decisive in deciding the war in favour of either set of belligerents. I have dealt with that in the previous chapters.

Little need be said about our dealings with the States in category 1, though these were not without importance. Holland will serve as an illustration of how delicate some of the dealings with Germany's neighbours had to be. It was not long before I had to assure Holland that Britain would not violate her neutrality, so long as Germany did not do so. It was suggested, that it might, somehow, suit British operations in the war, the blockade for instance, to violate the neutrality of Holland. The need for giving such an assurance showed how the German violation of Belgium had lowered the whole standard of international morality; perhaps war tends to do this anyhow. War arouses the physical and moral

courage of individuals, and in that sense it may be said
to raise their morals; but it prompts nations to do what
they would not do in time of peace, and in this sense it
may be said to depress morals. Holland was reassured
as to our intention to respect her neutrality, and expressed
her satisfaction thereat. On the other hand, we could
not venture to encourage her to maintain her neutrality
by giving her an assurance that we would support her
in doing so against German pressure. To do that might
compromise her in the eyes of Germany. The Dutch
Minister in London gave us to understand that such an
assurance from us would be unwelcome. With the
example of Belgium before their eyes the small States,
who were neighbours of Germany, cannot have felt comfortable.

Diplomatic relations with the States in category 2
must now be described; these overlap and intertwine, but
in order to give any clear account of them it will be necessary to deal with each separately. Let Turkey be taken
first. We did not know at the time that Turkey already
had a secret treaty binding her to join Germany; in my
opinion, that makes little difference. There was always
a great power of inertia in the Turkish Government, and
if things had not gone well for Germany in the first year
of the war, and if the two German cruisers and their
crews had not got to Constantinople and stayed there,
the Turks might have been a long time before they acted
on that treaty, or might never have acted upon it at all.
Without knowing of the treaty, we knew well enough
that some of the most influential Turks were fanatically
pro-German, and we knew what the influence of Ger-

many was at Constantinople. Knowledge of the treaty would not have made much difference; we feared the worst, even without knowing of the treaty. I remember a conversation in the Foreign Office in which someone spoke of the Grand Vizier being opposed to Turkey's departing from neutrality. I replied that I believed this to be true, but that Enver Pasha wished to bring Turkey out on the side of Germany; and that nothing but the assassination of Enver would keep Turkey from joining Germany. I remember adding that, in times of crisis and violence in Turkey, there were apt to be two classes of persons—assassins and assassinated, and that the Grand Vizier was more likely than his opponent to belong to the latter class.

Such was the prospect regarding Turkey—a very dark one; but the task that was set for diplomacy was very clear.

Kitchener was insistent that Turkey must be kept neutral, or, at any rate, that Britain must not be involved in war with Turkey till after the Indian troops had got through the Suez Canal. We were, therefore, to delay the entry of Turkey into the war, irrespective of whether we could ultimately prevent it or not.

An Indian personage of very high position and influence in the Moslem world came to see me. He urged earnestly that Turkey should be kept out of the war: if we were at war with Turkey it might cause great trouble for Moslem British subjects and be a source of embarrassment both to them and to us. I replied that we all felt this, and desired not to be involved in war with Turkey, but that with the *Goeben* and *Breslau* and their full crews at Constantinople and the strong pro-German element there, I feared it would be impossible to prevent Turkey joining Germany. He saw the difficulty, and admitted the danger; he then urged that, if it was impossible to avoid war with Turkey, it should come in such a way as to make it clearly and unmistakably not our fault; that it should be evident that we had done all that was possible to avoid war. The objective before us was therefore twofold: (1) to delay the entry of Turkey into the war as long as we could, and at all costs till the Indian troops were safely through the Canal on their way to France; and (2) to make it clear, if the worst had to come, that it came by the unprovoked aggression of Turkey.

This task was difficult enough in itself—as will be apparent from what has been said already. But another difficulty was added. Two battle-ships were being built in Britain for the Turkish Government. They were nearly ready. The Admiralty commandeered them to add to the strength of the British Fleet. This was quite legal. All ships of war built for foreign countries in British yards were subject to the right of the British Government to take them in an emergency. If the ships were for a neutral country, full money compensation would of course be paid for them. But the Turks were very sore. They wanted the battle-ships, and the duty of Sir Louis Mallet, the British Ambassador at Constantinople, was on the one hand to do all he could to please the Turks and to effect the delay that Kitchener required, and on the other hand to explain to the Turks that they could not have their ships, a point on which the Admiralty was adamant. A perusal of the shoals of despatches and telegrams would show the poignancy of the situation in which Mallet was placed. In war, however, diplomacy is the handmaid of the necessities of the War Office and the Admiralty, and Mallet had to do his best to satisfy both.

Apart from this, everything conceivable was done to make it easy and even profitable for Turkey to remain neutral. A promise, in which France and Russia joined, was made to her to see that in any terms of peace at the end of the war her independence and integrity should be preserved. Nothing was asked from her in return, no help, no facilities for the Allies, open or covert, nothing except that she should remain neutral. The obligation of neutrality would, of course, require the repatriation of the belligerent German crews of the *Goeben* and *Breslau*. The following documents will illustrate sufficiently the line that we took.

Sir Edward Grey to Sir F. Bertie

FOREIGN OFFICE,

August 15, 1914.

SIR,—In speaking to the French and Russian Ambassadors to-day separately, I pointed out how desirable it was not to fasten any quarrel upon Turkey during the present war as long as she would remain neutral. It would be very embarrassing to us, both in India and in Egypt, if Turkey came out against us. If she did decide to side with Germany, of course there was no help for it; but we ought not to precipitate this.

If the first great battle which was approaching in Belgium did not go well for the Germans, it ought not to be difficult to keep Turkey neutral. I impressed upon the Ambassadors that the proper course was to make Turkey feel that, should she remain neutral, and should Germany and Austria be defeated, we would take care that the integrity of Turkish possessions as they now were would be preserved in any terms of peace affecting the Near East; but that, on the other hand, if Turkey sided with Germany and Austria, and they were defeated, of course we could not answer for what might be taken from Turkey in Asia Minor.—I am, etc.,

E. GREY.

Sir Edward Grey to Sir L. Mallet
FOREIGN OFFICE,
August 22, 1914.

We do not wish to repel Turkish desire for discussion, but the demands made are excessive.

You may, however, when your French and Russian colleagues are similarly instructed, say:

The three Allied Powers will jointly give a guarantee in writing that they will respect the independence and integrity of Turkey, and will engage that no conditions in the terms of peace at the end of this war shall prejudice this independence and integrity. They will also secure for Turkey economic advantages, such as the cession to Turkey of the German railway and other concessions.

As to the Capitulations, we will agree to withdraw our extra-territorial jurisdiction as soon as a scheme of judical administration is set up which will satisfy modern conditions.

In return, Turkey must repatriate at once the German officers and crews of all rating of the *Goeben* and *Breslau,* and give a written assurance that she will afford all facilities for peaceful and uninterrupted passage of merchant vessels, and that she will observe all the obligations of neutrality during the present war.

Besides this, every point of procedure was strained in favour of Turkey. Her conduct with regard to the crews of the *Goeben* and *Breslau,* which she would neither intern nor repatriate, was a breach of neutrality, and there were other things that gave reasonable cause for complaint. There was ample justification for an ultimatum to Turkey demanding compliance with the requirements of neutrality; but the Allies would do nothing to precipitate war or to give any pretext or occasion for war.

At last, on October 28, the Turkish Fleet, with the *Goeben* and *Breslau,* went out and attacked Russian ports and shipping in the Black Sea. Never was there a more wanton, gratuitous, and unprovoked attack by one country upon another. Russia had been genuinely anxious to avoid the complication of war with Turkey, and had joined in the offered guarantee. This should never be forgotten in considering the secret treaty about Constantinople that was made after Turkey attacked Russia. The plunder of Turkey was no part of the Russian view in entering the war. Turkey had a fair and genuine offer from the Allies, and she rejected it. Turkey alone was to blame for what followed.

By this time the Indian troops were through the Canal and the manner of Turkey's entry into the war made it clear that it was her own doing, and that the Allies and not Turkey were the injured party. These two objectives diplomacy had attained. Nevertheless, criticism, almost obloquy, was poured upon our diplomacy and especially and most unjustly on Mallet. It was said that we ought to have known that Turkey was sure to join Germany, and the futility of attempting to placate her was ridiculed. Something must be added here to try to do justice to Mallet's position. All the time he was carrying out the British and Allied policy at Constantinople, it was Germany and not the Allies, who was having the best of the war. Paris was nearly taken, the French Government had retired to Bordeaux, the German Army was entrenched far in French territory, and Brussels and

Antwerp were held.   Mallet at Constantinople, endeav-
ouring in face of this to keep Turkey neutral was like a
general with scant ammunition and no big guns, who is
ordered to hold a position against an enemy well equipped
with heavy artillery.   He doubts whether he can hold
the position, but is ordered to try as long as he can.
When eventually the position is taken by the enemy, it
can hardly be usual to abuse him for having tried to hold
the position at all.   Yet that would be approximately a
parallel to the treatment that Mallet received after he
left Constantinople.   When the Turks had joined the
enemy, there was no other post available for him, while
the Great War lasted.   After it was over he would in
the ordinary course have been appointed to another
Embassy, but in consequence of the attacks made upon
his conduct of affairs at Constantinople, he was passed
over and not employed again, and the country has been
deprived of the services of one of the ablest men in the
diplomatic service.   Let me here print a despatch which
I addressed to him in December 1914:

Sir Edward Grey to Sir L. Mallet
FOREIGN OFFICE,
December 4, 1914.

SIR,—I have received Your Excellency's despatch of the 20th ultimo,
in which you summarize the events since your return to your post on
August 16 last, until your departure on November 1.

I have read, with great appreciation and pleasure, of the invaluable
assistance rendered to Your Excellency in the difficult circumstances of
your departure by the United States Ambassador, and every member
of the United States Embassy, and I have already requested the United
States Government to convey to Mr. Morgenthau the most sincere
thanks of His Majesty's Government for the valuable services rendered

by His Excellency on that occasion and subsequently in helping the British community to leave Constantinople.

I have also been much gratified to receive Your Excellency's testimony of the cheerful courage of the British community in Turkey under exceptionally trying circumstances, and I have noted with great satisfaction Your Excellency's appreciation of the valuable services of the embassy and consulate staff, and of the members of His Majesty's Consular Service throughout the Ottoman Empire.

I desire also to convey to Your Excellency my high sense of the marked ability, patience, and discretion shown by Your Excellency in carrying out, in the face of great difficulties, the policy of His Majesty's Government. War was eventually forced by wanton and unprovoked hostilities of the Turkish Fleet under German inspiration and orders, but it was the desire of His Majesty's Government to avoid a rupture with Turkey; and Your Excellency rightly directed all your efforts to encourage those influences at Constantinople that were moderate and reasonable. To your efforts it was at any rate in some degree due that the inevitable catastrophe did not occur sooner.—I am, etc.,

E. GREY.

A word here may be added about Egypt, which presented a question of great difficulty after Turkey had entered the war. I do not recall with certainty the particular arguments that influenced us at this moment. One thing after another pressed for hasty but imperative decisions. But the facts were substantially these. The status of Egypt in relation to Turkey had not, so far as international law was concerned, been affected by the British occupation. Technically Egyptians became enemy subjects after the entry of Turkey into the war against us. Something had to be done to prevent legal complications. To annex Egypt would have been a complete solution of technical difficulties, but it would have been a great political blunder. It would have impaired the Moslem prestige and the character of Egypt as a

Moslem State; it would also have been construed by our Allies as a hasty grasping at the opportunity of war to improve our position and gain a separate British advantage. The result must have been to make our Allies suspicious, to offend the sentiment and hurt the feelings of Moslems in India, and probably to stir up trouble in Egypt itself. This was not the time when we could afford to run such risks. To declare a Protectorate was therefore the best solution for the moment, but it necessarily left serious questions to be settled afterwards.

CHAPTER XXVI

(1914-1915)

ALLIED DIPLOMACY IN WAR (*continued*)

Greece and Venizelos—A Proposed Balkan Confederation—The Greek Offer to Join the Allies in 1914—Reasons for Declining It—Complications with Russia—An Attractive Theory—Its Refutation—A Demand from Russia—The Conservative Party in Council—The Russian Secret Treaty—Further Efforts with Bulgaria—More Despatches.

I T will be convenient to next take the Allied relations with Greece. Greek offers to the Allies and Allied overtures to Greece went through so many phases that it is not easy to disentangle the confused record. It may be well to summarize the general trend of them.

In the early part of the war it was Greece who made offers to join the Allies. This was embarrassing to us, particularly before Turkey entered the war; but after the entry of Turkey the Russian sensitiveness about Constantinople made these Greek offers of help a very delicate matter.

Later on, when Russia was reassured about Constantinople and when Serbia was in dire straits, it was the Allies who were urging Greece to join them. If this general view is kept in mind it will explain what may seem to be inconsistencies in the narrative.

Greece has been named in the third category of neutrals, that of States disposed to join the Allies. Greece is there because of the personality of Venizelos, who throughout the war, no matter how bad the fortunes of the Allies sometimes appeared to be, remained from beginning to end a staunch friend. His support never wavered; but, though his influence in Greece was great, he was not all-powerful, and he was not always Prime Minister. There were other persons in Greece, notably King Constantine and his adherents, who had influence too. These other forces he regarded with the greatest distrust. How far this feeling was justified need not be considered here, but it is necessary to bear it in mind in order fully to understand Allied dealings with Greece in all their phases.

Very soon after the outbreak of war Venizelos launched the proposal of re-forming the Balkan *bloc,* or Confederation; it was now to include Roumania as well as Greece, Serbia, and Bulgaria. This Confederation would, of course, be in favour of the Allies and against Austria, for Serbia was already at war with Austria, and Roumania as well as Venizelos was favourable to the Allies. But to bring Bulgaria into it large concessions would be necessary, particularly from Greece and Serbia. Neither of these States was prepared to make concessions, and the proposal for a Confederation fell to the ground. We naturally expressed ourselves strongly in favour of it, but we had no power to induce Greeks or Serbians to make the concessions to Bulgaria that were necessary if the Confederation was to have any chance of being born alive. Venizelos then offered[1] that Greece should join the Allies. No one doubted the sincerity and good faith

[1] August 18, 1914.

of the offer. The Cabinet appreciated it, but, after consideration, decided that it would be impolitic to accept it. This was in accord with the advice I gave to the Cabinet, and for this I have never disclaimed and have always been ready to accept full responsibility. The wisdom of that advice has been severely impugned; I still think it was right, and that, had we accepted this or a subsequent Greek offer in the early days of the war, the consequences might have been very serious, perhaps fatal to the cause of the Allies. The consequences, in my opinion, would have been: the immediate entry of Turkey into the war on the side of Germany; the immediate or early entry of Bulgaria into the war against Serbia probably; the unsettlement of Russia's whole-heartedness in the war, at first possibly, later on certainly.

To explain this view it is necessary to describe the Balkan situation as it was after the Balkan War of 1912-13 and the Treaty of Bucharest, and as it still was in August 1914.

Turkey had, in 1912-13, lost large portions of territory in Europe and also some islands as the result of her defeat by the Balkan States. Bulgaria had in 1913, by the Treaty of Bucharest, been despoiled by Greece, Serbia, and Roumania of what she had hoped to gain by her share, a very large share, in the defeat of Turkey. She had even been deprived of any outlet to the Ægean. Turkey and Bulgaria were both very sore and indignant. Each was longing for a *revanche,* and it was against the same States that they both wanted their *revanche.* The outbreak of the Great War, therefore, found them both waiting for their opportunity and not at all indisposed to help each other to take advantage of it. Turkey was particularly concerned with some of the islands that now belonged to Greece; and when France and Britain were hard pressed, and even getting the worst of it in the war in the West, and when Russia was fully occupied with Germany and Austria on her side, it seemed quite possible, and even likely, that Turkey might make a spring on Greece even if Greece remained neutral. That this estimate of the situation was not fantastic or unreal is shown by the following documents:

Sir G. Buchanan to Sir Edward Grey
(Received September 7)

PETROGRAD,
September 6, 1914.

From a telegram received from the Russian Ambassador at Constantinople, of which contents will be communicated to you by the Russian Ambassador in London, it appears that Turkey will declare war on Greece if the latter refuses to make concessions about the islands. In that case Bulgaria is, in the opinion of Minister for Foreign Affairs, almost certain to join her unless Greece purchases her neutrality or support by territorial concessions.

His Excellency said that he had all along been pressing the necessity of this on Greece, as in present critical stage of the war Russia had no wish to face a war with Turkey as well. A Turco-Greek War would also paralyze Serbia at a moment when we needed her army for an attack on Austria. He was not, he said, going to allow Greece to drag Russia into a war with Turkey, and unless she listened to our advice he would disinterest himself in her altogether. In view of the large number of German troops which are being transferred from western to eastern theatre, Russia is calling up every available man from Asia and the Caucasus, and is only leaving one army corps in the latter. She would not, therefore, be in a position to give any support, nor would France or England be able to do so if war, as seems probable, be restricted to land.

Greece will therefore have to bear the brunt of the war single-handed unless she can square Bulgaria.

Sir L. Mallet to Sir Edward Grey
(Received September 7)

CONSTANTINOPLE,
September 6, 1914.

I had a long conversation with Minister of Interior yesterday. He assured me that there was no question of Turkey going to war, but when I pressed him about Greece, he admitted that, unless Turkish Government could get some real satisfaction about islands, by which I gathered he would be satisfied with regime at Samos, they would go to war on land. He spoke as if Bulgaria was with them, at any rate to the extent of allowing their troops to pass through Western Thrace without resistance. He said that Roumania would remain quite neutral, and would not move against Bulgaria to preserve Treaty of Bucharest, as greater interests were at stake.

I used every possible argument to dissuade Minister of the Interior from leaping on a military adventure, reminding him that Bulgaria was not to be trusted, and that in the end Turkey would inevitably pay. It was not likely that a war with Greece would long remain localized, and it seemed extremely probable that Turkey in the long run would find herself up against the Triple *Entente*. I told him His Majesty's Government regarded Turkish Fleet as annex of German Fleet, and that if it went out into the Ægean we should sink it. He quite realized this, and said that it had no intention of leaving Dardanelles.

I also told him that Admiral Kerr had hoisted his flag on *Averof* as Commander-in-Chief of Greek Fleet. He seemed surprised, and I reminded him that until Admiral Limpus had been set aside he was Commander-in-Chief of Turkish Fleet.

I went carefully over several infringements of neutrality of which they had been guilty. I said that so long as a single German officer, naval or military, remained here, I should consider Turkey as a German protectorate. I said that I had been informed that Turkish Government attached no importance to written declaration which I and my French and Russian colleagues had made them respecting their integrity. I was greatly surprised at this attitude, but personally somewhat relieved, as to guarantee integrity and independence of Turkey was like guaranteeing life of man who was determined to commit suicide.

We sincerely desired independence and integrity of Turkey, but he must not imagine that Great Britain was afraid of Turkey, or that we feared to face alternative if forced upon us.   Most ridiculous stories about insurrections in India and Egypt and approaching downfall of British Empire were being circulated broadcast, and were apparently believed by Minister of War.   I hoped that Minister of the Interior was not under those and similar dangerous illusions.

(It is only the first paragraph of this latter document that is relevant to the immediate point of discussion, but the whole quotation is given, as it is of interest as showing the general line taken by Mallet.)

This makes it abundantly clear that grave complications were bound to follow the entry of Greece into the war at this stage; that these complications were dreaded by Russia, and would have been most unwelcome to her. If they had come as a result of Britain and France having accepted the offer of Greece to enter the war, Russia would have held us responsible for placing her in the difficulties that she wished to avoid.   This would have happened at the very moment when the Franco-British Army was in a precarious position in France; when the only hope of holding out in the decisive theatre of the war was that Russia should press her advance on the eastern side and so lessen Germany's power to attack again on the West.   Let it never be forgotten that it was the energy and tremendous sacrifice with which Russia made this advance that saved the Allies in the autumn of 1914.   The first battle of Ypres was critical enough, as it was in spite of all that Russia was doing to draw German strength away to the East.   The whole-hearted effort and all the strength of Russia were needed in the early stages to save the Allies; and it was fortunate indeed that our diplomacy in those stages avoided any of the mistakes that would have made us responsible in Russian eyes for complications in the Balkans and Turkish regions that would have damped the spirit of Russia and diverted some of her strength.

Greece was not at all ready to make the concession that might placate Bulgaria. She was not going to risk war on the side of the Allies with a view to giving up territory. The consequences of accepting the Greek offer would have been to unite Turkey and Bulgaria even more actively; to annoy Russia; to precipitate the very thing that our diplomacy was charged by our military authority to delay, namely, war with Turkey. Even that is not all: Greece was regarded as the special enemy of Turkey, and if Greece had entered the war as our Ally, while Turkey was still neutral, we should have lost the very great advantage of demonstrating to the Moslem world that it was in truth Turkey who was the real and unprovoked aggressor. Against all these disadvantages, any help the Greek Army could have given us away from the main theatre of war would have been a mere feather-weight in the balance, and we should have been bound to help it, if it got into difficulties with the Turks, as post-war events have shown to be a not impossible contingency. Looking back on it all, it seems now that the decision we came to in this matter at this time was wise. People are apt to say that by deciding otherwise than we did at this, that, or the other critical moment me might have won the war sooner; it is more impressive still to think how easily we might have made some mistakes that would have lost the war altogether.

If it is asked how or why so many people, even some who approved of the refusal of the first Greek offer at the time, now hold an opinion contrary to the one expressed here, the answer, it seems to me, is "Gallipoli." Nothing so distorted perspective, disturbed impartial judgment, and impaired the sense of strategic values as the operations on Gallipoli. The strain, the effort, and the suffering of it so wrought upon our minds and feelings that it came to seem that anything that would have saved the failure and make a success at Gallipoli would have been worth any risk elsewhere. This view I believe to be quite unsound, and it becomes necessary now to examine the Dardanelles and Gallipoli operations from the diplomatic as well as the military point of view.

First, however, let one attractive theory be weighed. If Greece had entered the war as our Ally, it would have been possible to plan the Dardanelles operations from the first, not as a naval operation only, but as a joint naval and military operation to be carried out by the British Fleet and the Greek Army co-operating. For the success of this operation it is necessary to assume that neither the Turks nor their German advisers would have foreseen this as a probable Anglo-Greek operation, and that they would have taken no steps to anticipate it—a very large assumption. So much of the comment on the strategy of the war is based on the assumption that if we had done something other than we did the enemy would nevertheless have acted not otherwise than they eventually did. The probable assumption is exactly the contrary. In any case, combined Anglo-Greek operations with a Greek Army in the direction of Constantinople would have unsettled Russia at the later date[1] when a Greek offer was made to assist us in Gallipoli. King Constantine was to head the Greek Army; and, if the operations were successful, he would have entered Constantinople in triumph at the head of Greek troops. The effect on Russia would have been disastrous; there is no limit to the disaster that would have ensued. Even the authority of the Tsar and Sazonof and their loyalty to the Allies might not have sufficed to keep Russia in the war. We were wise enough to decline that Greek offer too. Solidarity with Russia in the first two years of the war was essential to avoid defeat in France, and the occupation of Constantinople by British ships and a Greek Army would have been no compensation for a German break through in the West and the capture of Paris or the Channel ports of France.

Even as it was, and even without the irritant to Russia of a Greek Army *en route* for Constantinople, the British operations against the Dardanelles came near to impairing our relations with Russia. When it was evident that these operations were serious and it was thought that they might succeed, we became aware of a very nasty reaction upon Russian opinion that might soon become dangerous. Whether this was fomented by Germany I cannot say; we always supposed that, among the variety of influences and opinions in Petrograd, there were some strings that Germany surreptitiously could pull. If so, the British attack on the Dardanelles gave her an opportunity of

[1] March 22, 1915.

Photograph by the James Press Agency

M. VENIZELOS

which she would naturally take advantage.   But even
without German prompting the disagreeable feeling
might have arisen in Russia spontaneously.   It was so
obvious when it came that I may justly be criticized for
having acquiesced in the attack on the Dardanelles, without giving a warning of what we should have to reckon
with diplomatically at Petrograd.

The construction put upon our operations at the Dardanelles was shortly this.   It had always been British policy
to keep Russia out of Constantinople and the Straits; we
fought for that object in the Crimean War of the fifties,
and it was our main policy under Beaconsfield in the
seventies of the nineteenth century; of course it was our
policy still.   Britain was now going to occupy Constantinople in order that when Britain and France had been
enabled, by Russia's help, to win the war, Russia should
not have Constantinople at the peace.   If this were not
so, why were British forces being sent to the Dardanelles
at a time when the French and British Armies were being
so hard pressed in France that the Russian Armies were
making unheard of sacrifices to save them?   This imputation of motive to us was absolutely without foundation,
but it must, in the light of our past policy, have presented
itself naturally to the Russian mind.   How were we to
undo the mischief, to dispel the suspicion?   The thing
gathered force at Petrograd.   Sazonof was represented
as a tool of British policy; we were told that his position
was being undermined; we believed that next after that
of the Tsar himself, it was the loyalty of Sazonof to the
Allies that was the pivot of Russian policy.   At last there
came a definite demand from Petrograd for an agreement

promising Constantinople to Russia, with an intimation that this was absolutely necessary to save Sazonof's position and policy and to prevent serious mischief. This was not bluff; there was real danger.

A rumour that we should object began to creep about. We felt that, with the light of past history making the rumour seem probable, we must counteract it at once; not only by denying the rumour, but by giving our positive consent. It was such an important step in policy, such a grave commitment, that the leaders of the Conservative Party were taken into council. We sat together in consultation upon it; the force of circumstances was irresistible. It was agreed that the promise of Constantinople to Russia must be made; but neither we nor the French liked the thing. I felt personally that, after all Russia had done in the common cause, the risks she had taken and the losses she had incurred in pressing her advance in the East to relieve us in the West, we must in justice agree to her access to Constantinople. As we had been the protagonists against that in the past, so we should now be the first to concede it. But, when the present is thick with dark uncertainties, we naturally shrink from making very clear and definite engagements about what is far ahead; also it was not very pleasant to promise what at the time was not ours to give nor Russia's to take. The French agreed; the thing was done. It would be going too far to say that, but for the Dardanelles expedition, Russia would never have made the demand. I think that in the end it must have come, but the attack on the Dardanelles undoubtedly strengthened and quickened it.

That is how and why this secret treaty was made—the one that would have been the most important of all if Russia had not subsequently cancelled it by breaking her agreement with her Allies of September 1914 and making peace without them.

At the time I shared to the full the hope that the attempt on the Dardanelles would succeed as a naval operation only, and I was a willing party to it in the expectation that its success and the arrival of British ships of war at Constantinople would have caused the collapse of Turkey. That this would have been the result seems less certain now. The Turks might have set up their Government elsewhere, as they did later on at Angora: in that event the task of holding Constantinople would have involved a strain upon troops that Britain and France could not spare. Russia would, no doubt, have claimed that Russian troops should be used, and her attention might have been diverted from the Austrian and German eastern front at a time when it was essential to her safety and that of the Allies that her whole strength should be concentrated on that front.

The entry of Turkey caused new complications—we had, for instance, now to reckon certainly with an attack on Egypt—but it also cleared away some complications. The objection that Greece's entry into the war might precipitate a conflict with Turkey and affect the feeling of our own Moslems no longer existed. The way was clear for Greece to take part in the war by assisting Serbia or helping us in Egypt or in any way that would not arouse Russian susceptibilities about Constantinople. The Allies were also free to make promises about future division of Turkish territory in any way that would help them in the war. Turkey, by her rejection of our most fair offer of her integrity and by the gross outrage of her attack on Russia, had forfeited all claim to consideration and richly deserved whatever consequences might follow.

The Allies had now to concentrate upon the attitude of Bulgaria, which was all-important. About this I have already spoken. Apprehension of what Bulgaria would do weighed upon both Greece and Roumania. Both were favourable to the Allies, but each feared that a movement on its own first might bring Bulgaria out against it. The Allies could afford no protection to either against this contingency—they had no troops to spare. Serbia was in dire need in her war with Austria and an attack upon her by Bulgaria would be crushing. It was therefore vital to assure the neutrality of Bulgaria. The prospect was not hopeful. Bulgaria wanted very large concessions at the expense particularly of Greece and Serbia.

Germany had presumably made large offers to Bulgaria; she was free to promise anything that Bulgaria wished about Serbia, for Serbia was enemy territory. The Allies could offer nothing of Roumanian or Greek territory, for these countries were their friends, and the Allies were rather under obligation to them for their friendly attitude than they to the Allies. Serbia, on the other hand, was under obligation to the Allies. They were not responsible for Serbia being at war, and were giving her what help they could. Indeed, the very life of Serbia depended on the victory of the Allies. But this hardly gave the Allies a right to promise Serbian

territory to Bulgaria.   The utmost they could say was
that if, as the result of an Allied victory, Serbia got new
and large gains of territory, the Allies would use their
influence to get for Bulgaria the territory that in 1912
Serbia had agreed to be Bulgaria's share in Macedonia.

All that the Allies were now free to offer was the territory in Thrace that had been left to Turkey.   Unfortunately, this was not what Bulgaria most wanted.   What
she did want was a port on the Ægean and her claims
in Macedonia; and these (since the Balkan War) concerned Turkey not at all, and only Greece and Serbia.
This was the insuperable handicap of Allied diplomacy
in dealing with Bulgaria.

Nevertheless, we had to do our best and to persuade
ourselves that the attempt was worth making.   Bulgaria
still announced her intention to remain neutral.   To confirm this intention, and if possible to get Bulgaria to join
a Balkan *bloc,* was the object.   The following documents
will illustrate the line taken after Turkey came into the
war:

Sir Edward Grey to Sir H. Bax-Ironside

FOREIGN OFFICE,

November 13, 1914.

SIR,—The Bulgarian Minister came to see me to-day, and gave me
complete assurances that Bulgaria would maintain an attitude of neutrality.

I said that at the beginning of the present war we had promised
to respect the integrity of Turkey if she did not depart from an attitude
of neutrality, but now that she had departed from neutrality and had
sought and provoked a war the Turkish question would of course come
up for solution in the terms of peace, and there would arise the question
of the disposal of Turkish territory in Thrace with regard to which
Bulgaria could hardly be disinterested.   The question would of course
have to be settled in agreement with France and Russia, and the satis-

faction of Bulgarian claims would be possible, provided that Bulgaria maintained a friendly attitude to the allied Powers.

The Bulgarian Minister referred to a report in French newspapers that the Balkan *bloc* was being reformed.

I said that I longed to see it reformed, but I knew the difficulties. So far as I was aware, discussions were not proceeding between the Balkan Governments. I desired very much to see them all come to an agreement, and I should urge it strongly if I was sure that discussions between them would remove difficulties, and not emphasize them. The case for Serbia at the end of the Balkan Wars had been that the Great Powers had shut her off from the Adriatic, and that there was a large Serb population on the west kept apart from her, and therefore the Great Powers ought not to restrict her on the east. But if, as a result of the present war, Serbia obtained access to the Adriatic and a large acquisition of territory to the west of her inhabited by Serbs, the settlement of the Macedonian question should thereby be made more easy, and I saw very favourable possibilities as a consequence of this war.—I am, etc.,

E. GREY.

Mr. des Graz to Sir Edward Grey
(Received February 1)

NISH,
February 1, 1915.

I saw Serbian Prime Minister yesterday evening before receiving Petrograd telegram No. 113 of January 28, and your telegram No. 50 of January 30.

I explained that I wished to have his views on situation privately and unofficially.

Prime Minister began by saying that after late Serbian successes, and feeling that there might be further Austrian attack, he had endeavoured to arrange an *entente* with Roumania and Greece, each country to cede something to Bulgaria. Idea as regards Greece would have been some small portion of Mesta Valley, which would allow Bulgaria to build railway to Ægean Sea. Suggestion has been that Roumania should speak at Sophia, but it had come to nothing, as Roumania had replied that she did not wish to appear to threaten Bulgaria.

If Roumania, Greece, and Serbia were entirely of one mind Bulgaria could do nothing, and he thought that key of situation was at

Bucharest rather than at Sophia. He still hopes that Greece will join in the war if called upon, and also Roumania possibly.

When I approached question of Serbian concessions to Bulgaria he said that he had heard of conversations in Paris between French Minister for Foreign Affairs and Russian Ambassador, and I gather that there had also been some conversations between M. Sazonof and Serbian Minister at Petrograd. He had also heard, though with no certainty, that Greece had been offered Smyrna.

He said that for Serbia to concede more than Vardar line was impossible. In order that good and not harm might result, arrangements must be based on possibilities. Neither Serbian Parliament nor King nor Army could contemplate ceding more. There was even now some agitation over mere idea that such concessions were intended. He spoke of land having been Serbian before conquered by Turks, and of sacrifice of blood which its recovery had cost Serbia. He added that Greece was in the same position as Serbia, and that she fully realized danger to herself of that territory becoming Bulgarian. He went so far as to say that it might mean ruin of Serbia, and that there were people who might, if so, prefer patched-up peace with Austria to ceding that part of Macedonia (my telegram No. 51 of last year, last paragraph). He also touched on the possibility of his resignation.

Line I took naturally was general aspect of the situation and future interests of Serbia, for, as he knew, the only idea of the Powers was to prevent possibility of her being overwhelmed by superior forces, and to assure her future.

Mr. des Graz to Sir Edward Grey
(Received February 1)

Continued.

I have no reason to doubt the sincerity of Prime Minister. He has always held the same language. Hitherto he had not gone farther in speaking to me than to mention possible rectification of frontier. Everyone here, I am informed, civilians and soldiers, is a politician, and there has always seemed to me danger that by indisposing and discouraging Army, their power or will of resistance against enemy will be impaired proportionately.

Very confidential.

Prime Minister said that Bulgarian pretensions would never have been what they are but for grave mistake made by Russia in having held out at Sophia hopes of large concessions early in the war.

The following documents will help to illustrate still further my own personal views at the time about the things that had to be avoided, and the difficulty of steering Allied diplomacy through it all, when at first three and, after Italy joined us, four Governments had all to consult each other by telegrams and come to a unanimous opinion on questions often of great delicacy and complexity.

Sir Edward Grey to Sir R. Rodd

FOREIGN OFFICE,
February 2, 1915.

SIR,—Having heard that the German Government had informed the Italian Government, through diplomatic channels, that France, Russia, and England had offered Greece Constantinople and the Ægean Islands in Italian occupation, as well as part of the coast and mainland of Asia Minor, I took the opportunity, after dinner at the Italian Embassy last night, of telling the Italian Ambassador that Constantinople never had been mentioned to Greece, and it was absurd even to suggest that any such offer had been or could be made to Greece. It was ridiculous to suppose that Russia would agree to Constantinople being handed over to another Power. Also, I had stipulated, in all negotiations with Greece, that there must be no mention of the islands in Italian occupation. No offers to Greece had yet materialized, because they were all conditional on the participation of Greece in the war. It was true that we had contemplated the possibility of the acquisition by Greece of some of the coast and a reasonable amount of hinterland in Asia Minor, where there was a large Greek population, such as at Smyrna; but, even so, I had been careful to avoid any geographical definitions that would encroach upon the part of Asia Minor in which we knew that Italy had a special interest.

The Italian Ambassador said that he realized that the report about Constantinople being offered to Greece must be absurd. The only criticism he had to make, and that was purely personal, for his Government had not mentioned this point at all, was that Italy might have hoped for expansion in the direction of Smyrna. Germany could not be entirely ousted from Asia Minor, and therefore Italy could not expand in the direction of Konia, where German influence was already predominant.

I remarked that the only part of Asia Minor away from the Persian Gulf in which we had a vested interest was in the Smyrna district, where we had the Smyrna-Aidin railway, and therefore any concession made in the neighbourhood of Smyrna was made at our expense more than at that of any other European Power. I told the Ambassador that I had carefully avoided in any negotiations, however provisional and conditional, foreclosing any of the questions of which he had spoken to me on behalf of his Government at the beginning of the war; so that these questions were kept open for agreement.—I am, etc.,

E. GREY.

Sir Edward Grey to Sir H. Bax-Ironside
FOREIGN OFFICE,
February 6, 1915.

I observed to Bulgarian Minister to-day that the financial advance to Bulgaria had been concluded at Berlin, and I knew at such a moment some conditions must have been attached to it by Germany. I would not ask him what these were, as it might be an embarrassing question.

But sooner or later, I said, British troops would be in Balkan theatre of war, and probably Russian, and perhaps French troops also. There was still in this country real feeling and sympathy for Bulgaria, and it would be matter for great regret to us if British and Bulgarian troops were in direct conflict. I believed the Bulgarian people would have the same feeling as regards Great Britain and Russia. I wished to say, therefore, that I hoped the Bulgarian Government would not be drawn so far on the side of Germany and Austria as to make this conflict inevitable.

The Bulgarian Minister entirely reciprocated this sentiment. He spoke with emphasis of the feeling in Bulgaria for Great Britain, dating from Mr. Gladstone and continuing now, and of the feeling for Russia as the liberator. He regarded it as impossible that Bulgaria should ever fight with either.

He urged strongly that the Triple *Entente* should, to secure the attitude of Bulgaria, promise the Enos-Midia line and a definite line in Macedonia to be conceded if Bulgaria remained neutral, with a further line in Macedonia to be conceded if Bulgaria participated as an ally. He spoke also of the importance of Cavalla.

He knew nothing of conditions of the loan, and spoke throughout only personally, but suggested that Bulgaria, having undertaken very onerous concessions to obtain the loan originally, might have secured the present advance by threatening to cancel these if the advance was not given.

I said if there were no new conditions attached it was a simple matter, but a report had reached me, though not from an authentic source, that the condition Germany intended to impose was that Bulgaria should range herself on the side of Germany and Austria. Conversation, though frank, was very friendly.

Sir Edward Grey to Sir H. Bax-Ironside

FOREIGN OFFICE,
February 13, 1915.

Bulgarian Minister has informed me that no political conditions of any kind are attached to the advance that Bulgaria has arranged in Berlin. He expressed his great satisfaction at this, and I said that I was glad to hear it.

Referring to what he had said the other day as to the promise of territory to Bulgaria, I pointed out to him, speaking privately and personally, that I was as favourable to Bulgaria getting districts that were Bulgarian as I was to Serbia getting districts that were Serbian. I was in sympathy with the national aspirations of Bulgaria on national lines. But to make a promise of territory at this moment without knowing how Bulgaria would receive that promise would be to run the risk of arousing the apprehensions of Serbia and getting nothing in return. If Bulgaria would say that, if she were assured of getting certain territory at the end of the war, she would participate in the war, say, against Turkey, it might be easier for the three Powers to make her a promise. They could then tell Serbia that, though they had promised to Bulgaria something that Serbia was reluctant to concede, yet they had received in return a promise of support that would assure Serbia gains of territory inhabited by Serbs to the north and west, and therefore the three Powers had made a good bargain in Serbia's own interest. But it would not be fair to Serbia to make to Bulgaria a promise that King Ferdinand and the Bulgarian Government might put in their pocket without giving any pledge.

Bulgarian Minister said that the Bulgarian Government would not go against the opinion of the Bulgarian people, and if the leaders of the Opposition knew that an offer had been made Bulgarian Government would have to take it up, and at any rate their neutrality till the end of the war would be completely assured.

He also said that Russia gave it to be understood in Sophia that she was hostile to King Ferdinand. In this she made a great mistake, as King Ferdinand was an element in Bulgaria; his position was bound up with the success of Bulgaria, and he ought not to be treated as irreconcilable.

Sir Edward Grey to Sir F. Bertie

FOREIGN OFFICE,

February 13, 1915.

My telegram No. 29 of to-day to Sir H. Bax-Ironside.

You should inform Minister for Foreign Affairs, and say that for the moment I believe it would be better to take this line at Sophia rather than to make any promises, which would not be effective till the German offensive against Russia has been exhausted. As far as I can judge from official *communiqués,* the German offensive in the Vistula and in the Carpathians has been stopped with enormous losses to Germans, and will no doubt be stopped in the Bukowina and East Prussia when the Russian troops now retiring before superior numbers have reached strong positions and reinforcements. Till then Bulgaria will be immovable by us.

My information is that the Germans have endeavoured to bluff the Balkan States into a belief that the present German offensive will be crowned with final success, whereas the real German opinion is that Germany must lose unless she has succeeded in securing a peace before Russia has armed her vast reserves of men.

Meanwhile, whatever we say at Sophia that is favourable might be made known to leaders of opposition in Bulgaria.

It is suggested that threats at Sophia against King Ferdinand at this moment may stimulate him to commit Bulgaria to Germany and Austria.

Sir Edward Grey to Sir G. Buchanan

FOREIGN OFFICE,
February 15, 1915.

Your telegram of 14th February: Bulgaria.

I agree that something should be said at Sophia, but I am very apprehensive of the danger of making promises at Sophia that will destroy Serbian moral without securing support or even neutrality of Bulgaria.

I fear this may be the effect of communications that Russian Minister for Foreign Affairs proposes at Sophia and Nish. If my fear is well founded, the effect of these communications would be disastrous.

I should much prefer a joint communication in substance as follows:

"Russia, France, and Great Britain are not unsympathetic to Bulgarian aspirations in Thrace and Macedonia, but Bulgarian attitude has not hitherto been of a character which would justify the Allied Powers in urging the Serbian Government to make territorial sacrifices to Bulgaria of a kind which would enable latter to realize her national aspirations.

"The Allied Powers cannot make promises to Bulgaria without being assured of her attitude; they are therefore obliged to ask Bulgarian Government whether, and on what conditions or guarantees, they would be prepared to pronounce themselves on the side of the Allies, and to declare that the armed forces of Bulgaria should cooperate with the Allies."

Sir G. Buchanan to Sir Edward Grey
(Received March 2)

PETROGRAD,
March 1, 1915.

Reply which you made 25th February to a question in House of Commons on subject of Constantinople and Straits [1] was incorrectly given in Russian Press, and caused considerable uneasiness in Russian public opinion as to attitude of His Majesty's Government towards realization of Russia's aspirations. Although correct text of what you said has quieted public, this feeling has not been altogether allayed. Minister for Foreign Affairs tells me he is receiving many letters from members of the Duma and others expressing anxiety on the subject,

[1] House of Commons, February 25, 1915.

and that the Emperor had even written on a telegram recording your words a minute to the effect that he did not quite understand their meaning, and that he wished Minister for Foreign Affairs to explain them to him at his next audience.   Minister for Foreign Affairs said that he, personally, was perfectly satisfied with assurances which you had given Russian Ambassador (see your telegram No. 1075 of 20th November), and with what you said in your telegram No. 1015 of 12th November, to me, but that since then Russian public opinion had been moving fast, and would be now satisfied with no settlement which did not give Constantinople to Russia.   He had been always, as I was aware, in favour of neutralizing Constantinople, but this idea did not commend itself to Russian public, and he would be obliged to yield to their demand for its actual possession.   In the meantime, in order to allay uneasiness of public, who were incapable of reading between the lines of your reply, he would be very grateful if you could take an early opportunity of saying something that would clearly show that His Majesty's Government favoured a settlement of question of Constantinople and Straits that would accord with views of Russian Government and aspirations of Russian people.

Sir Edward Grey to Sir G. Buchanan

FOREIGN OFFICE,

March 2, 1915.

Your telegram No. 235 of 1st March: Russia and Constantinople.

I thought that in expressing our entire sympathy with what Russian Minister for Foreign Affairs has said I should entirely satisfy Russian public opinion.   I cannot be expected to be more Russian than Russian Government, and am much disappointed that there is disappointment in Russia.   The statement I have made was exceedingly well received here, and no narrow construction has been placed upon it.

I think this should be explained to the Emperor without delay.

If a more definite statement than what I have already said in public, or have said to Russian Minister for Foreign Affairs, is desired, I think it must be discussed also with the French Government.

It is one of the most important of the terms of peace, which are all to be settled in common, and the French Government cannot therefore be left out of the discussion.   Indeed, I have gone rather far in saying as much as I have about Constantinople and Straits without previous consultation with French Government; but I felt that, as in years now long past Great Britain had taken a lead in opposing Russian aspirations, we should, now that our views have entirely changed, take a lead in sympathy with them. You should speak to Minister for Foreign Affairs without delay.

Sir Edward Grey to Sir H. Bax-Ironside

FOREIGN OFFICE,

March 25, 1915.

SIR,—I reminded the Bulgarian Minister to-day of what I had said before: that it was difficult for the three Powers to make an offer to Bulgaria, but that, if she was ready to co-operate with us, provided that she was assured of getting the undisputed zone of the 1912 Treaty with Serbia and the Enos-Midia line, she ought to say so to the three Powers. I thought that if Serbia realized her aspirations on the west and Bulgaria had co-operated with the Allies, these terms could be arranged. But if Bulgaria was not ready to co-operate, the opportunity of making an arrangement might pass.

The Bulgarian Minister spoke of changes impending in the Bulgarian Government, which he regarded as favourable. He again impressed upon me that there would be no danger of an offer such as I had described being refused if it were made known to the leaders of the Opposition in Bulgaria: it would then be impossible for the members of the Government to refuse it.

He spoke also of the question that could be settled direct between Bulgaria and Roumania. He spoke, too, of Cavalla, about which I could make no promise.—I am, etc.,

E. GREY.

CHAPTER XXVII

(1915)

ALLIED DIPLOMACY IN WAR (*continued*)

The Balkans in 1915—The Menace of Bulgaria—Impossibility of appeasing her—The Intractability of Serbia—German Counter-offers—Some Typical Despatches—The Adherence of Italy—Russian Objections—French and British Representatives—Negotiations with Roumania—Further Despatches—An Ugly Feeling in Russia—Dark Days—Making the Best of Things.

WE have now got to the spring of 1915. Diplomacy in the months that followed was occupied with negotiations on the proposed entry of Italy and Roumania into the war, with attempts to get Greece to enter the war both to help Serbia and because the help of the Greek Fleet was desired by the Admiralty in the Mediterranean. The menace of Bulgaria hung like a cloud over the Balkans; Greece quite naturally desired to be assured of the neutrality of Bulgaria before she would commit herself to action. If Bulgaria were to attack Serbia, the Serbians must be swept away, hard pressed as they were already in their struggle with Austria. The addition of a war with Bulgaria must be fatal to them. But, beyond all other adverse circumstances, the situation was dominated by the appalling disasters to the Russian Army that continued all through the summer. It was these that made all the diplomacy of the Allies in dealing with Bulgaria just futile waste of time and effort.

Never were dice so heavily loaded against anything as against Allied diplomacy in 1915. The Germans were able to make larger and more unreserved offers to Bulgaria without consulting anybody. The Central Powers were fighting Serbia, and were under no obligations to Greece. The Allies were under obligation to treat Serbia as an Ally and Greece as a friend. They could not promise concessions to Bulgaria at the expense of Greece or Serbia without the consent of those countries. And neither Serbia nor Greece would agree to any concessions. Greece would not entertain the thought of giving Bulgaria access to the sea at Dedeagatch. On Greece the Allies could put no pressure; she had not, so far, needed any help from the Allies and was under no obligation to help them. With Serbia is was different. The Allies had not brought her into the war; that had been forced upon Serbia by Austria, in spite of all the Allies could do to prevent it. Serbia was under obligation to the Allies for help given; but for their presence in the war Serbia must be crushed; her only hope of survival lay in an Allied victory. In that event Serbia would not only survive intact, but would get large acquisitions of Slav territory at present held by Austria. These gains would have been made possible only by the efforts and sacrifice and victory of the Allies. They would, in effect, have been won for them by the Allies. We were, therefore, entitled to press Serbia to make the concessions to Bulgaria that were essential to the safety of Serbia and the common cause.

Serbia was quite intractable. In vain I pointed out that France, Britain, and Russia had no troops to spare and could send none to help Serbia; that an attack by Bulgaria must be fatal to her; that if she would only concede what was necessary to secure Bulgaria's friendship there was every prospect of a victory in which Serbia would gain far more than she was now being asked to concede; whereas, if Bulgaria were unreconciled and attacked her, Serbia would lose not only the glorious future prospect, but everything that she now had. It was all in vain. The Serbian Minister closed one conversation with me by saying they would all rather die than let Bulgaria have Monastir. A preference for death put an end to all argument, and I became respectfully silent. My efforts were futile, and the only result of giving advice was a report that I was anti-Serb. The statement that we could send no troops to Belgrade, though I had Kitchener's word for it and the truth was self-evident, was attributed to want of good-will on my part. Even with all the stern realities of war about them, it remains true that many people would rather have fine words and false hopes than the truth which is unacceptable.

The utmost, then, that we could say to Bulgaria was, that if it came to be in our power to win great gains for Serbia, we should make it a condition of her acquiring those gains that she should concede what we thought fair claims of Bulgaria. This still left it open to Serbia to say that she would rather not have the new gains than give up Monastir. About Greece we could say only something of the same kind, but more vague and indefinite, such as that, after victory, we would offer Greece what might make her willing to concede something to Bulgaria.

German promises, no doubt, could be and were more

downright than this, so that, other things being equal, they would be more attractive to Bulgaria. But other things were not equal. The war was going badly against Russia. The attraction of a promise is not its size, but the prospect of its being fulfilled. Our bird offered to Bulgaria was not only a smaller and duller bird, but it was receding more and more into the bush. The bird offered by Germany was not only a bigger and brighter bird, but seemed to be coming nearer and nearer to the hand.

I remember, on one occasion, saying to France and Russia that, with the military situation so adverse, it was of no use to make offers at Sophia; but I did not adhere to this line. There was nothing except dignity to be lost by trying at Sophia, and we all tried. The more desperate the situation, the more frantic grew the promises. Let it not be supposed, however, that while there was agitation there was speed. All the Allied Foreign Ministers were active in making proposals, but someone had an objection to make to everything that was proposed, and the Allied Ministers at Sophia had to wait till they all received joint instructions.

It should be borne in mind that, as the Russian reserves increased, Germany could influence Bulgaria if need be by threats as well as by promises. At the last moment, when only Germany was in a position to threaten, Russia tried the effect of a threat; this was equally futile, and Bulgaria came out on the German side and Serbia was for the time crushed.

The following documents will give some idea of the

general line taken and of the difficulties during the spring and summer of 1915:

Sir Edward Grey to Sir G. Buchanan

FOREIGN OFFICE,

March 22, 1915.

Your telegram of 21st March.

You should tell Minister for Foreign Affairs that I appreciate his objection to a triple guarantee, and that was why I said in my telegram to you that an assurance about Roumanian ships of war was really one to be given by Russia alone. I am prepared to take the line he suggests as regards Roumania.

But I must appeal to Minister for Foreign Affairs not to use any threat to Bulgaria about Burgas. It would resemble what Germany did to Belgium. We could not be a party to a forceable break of neutrality, and it would make our position very invidious if any Ally acted to any country as Germany did to Belgium.

I agree that it would be desirable to give assurances at Sophia now, and I will await Russian *aide-mémoire;* but there should be no threat to violate Bulgarian neutrality; that would spoil everything.

You should offer my most cordial congratulations on the capture of Przemysl and the success of the Russian arms. The value of this to the common cause is very great indeed.

Sir Edward Grey to Sir R. Rodd

FOREIGN OFFICE,

May 26, 1915.

Now that Italy has joined,[1] I am of opinion that the moment may be opportune for the British Minister to speak a word in Sophia.

I am told that the Opposition in Bulgaria and the Bulgarian people in general are favourable to us, but are disappointed by the fact that no offer has been made to Bulgaria from our side.

Fair terms for Bulgaria would be: cession to her of the part of Macedonia that includes Monastir (this cession to take place when Serbia obtained Bosnia and Herzegovina and a portion of the coast of the Adriatic); cession to Bulgaria of the Enos-Midia line in Thrace;

[1] See infra.

and the Allies to use their influence to assure Cavalla to Bulgaria, if Greece obtained compensation in the region of Smyrna.

I have been in communication with Paris and Petrograd on these lines for some time, and both Governments now concur.

As Italy is now our Ally, you should give this information to Minister for Foreign Affairs.

Sir Edward Grey to Sir F. Bertie

FOREIGN OFFICE,

July 7, 1915.

Your Excellency should inform Minister for Foreign Affairs that we have been carefully studying the views of the French Government conveyed in your telegram No. 422 of 28th June (No. 892 of 22nd June). We fully recognize the advantages of a strong and definite policy by means of which the immediate entry of one or other of the Balkan States into the war can be secured. Nor can we dispute that at this moment the adhesion of Bulgaria might be the most valuable of any. But we are compelled to ask our Allies to weigh carefully the following considerations: To guarantee to Bulgaria, by the use of force in the last resort, possession of territories in Macedonia and Thrace now occupied respectively by Serbia, which is fighting with us as an Ally, and by Greece, which has displayed a not unfriendly neutrality, constitutes a proceeding for which no defence can easily be framed.

I have before indicated the serious consequences I anticipate from such a course in disheartening Serbia, and in uniting against us the whole of Greece, including the party of M. Venizelos, with the probability of producing a conflict between Greece and Serbia on the one hand and Bulgaria on the other. It would, however, be reasonable to inform Serbia and Greece that the acquisition of certain other territories after the war must depend upon their willingness to cede to Bulgaria such territories as we may agree to name, and to inform the Bulgarian Government that we have taken this step. At the same time we regard it as imperative that a definite guarantee of the immediate entry of Bulgaria into the war should be secured if these sacrifices are to be pressed on Serbia and Greece. We think, therefore, that our first step should be to reply to Bulgaria in the following terms:

"The Entente Powers recognize with pleasure the friendliness in tone of the Bulgarian reply to their proposals of 29th May, and they are quite prepared to give further explanations in accordance with the request of the Bulgarian Government. Before doing so, however, they would wish to be assured that, in the event of those explanations proving satisfactory to the Bulgarian Government, they may count on immediate military action by Bulgaria against Turkey. Without such an assurance it is obvious that time would be merely wasted in further negotiations. For the same reason they suggest that it would be desirable for the Bulgarian Government to state what explanations the Bulgarian Government would regard as satisfactory."

The representatives of the Allied Powers at Sophia should also be instructed to point out, when presenting this note, that the Entente Powers are quite determined to force the Dardanelles. Whenever this is accomplished, which may be at any time, it may not be possible for the Entente Powers to offer such good terms to Bulgaria as at present. Time is therefore of great importance. They should communicate the substance of the above note to the parties in Bulgaria who are favourable to our cause.

Sir Edward Grey to Sir C. des Graz

FOREIGN OFFICE,

July 20, 1915.

Serbian Minister has spoken to me of the importance of keeping M. Pashitch informed of negotiations that affect Serbia.

I cannot make official communications except in consultation with the Allies, but I think that M. Pashitch ought to know that, on reviewing the situation on my return to the Foreign Office in the light of all that has passed while I have been away, I have formed a very strong opinion on the needs of general policy, both in the interest of Serbia and in that of the Allies generally.

Complete victory over Germany and Austria is essential to secure the interests of Serbia. Failure on the part of the Allies to defeat Germany and Austria would make the position of Serbia intolerable, for Germany and Austria have already promised to Bulgaria far more at the expense of Serbia and Greece than the Allies could ever think of proposing. These promises by Germany and Austria have been made, we understand, in return for Bulgarian neutrality only, and, of course, without thought of any compensating advantages whatever to Serbia or Greece. Events of the last two months make it clear that the co-operation of Roumania and Bulgaria, one or both, on the side of the Allies would be most desirable in the interests of success in general and of Serbian interests in particular. I am very doubtful whether this co-operation can be obtained. If we do not obtain it we shall continue the war without it; but the struggle will be prolonged. If, however, it should be apparent now, or in the near future, that the co-operation of either Bulgaria or Roumania can be obtained on conditions that would leave Serbia after the war with her aspirations for Bosnia and Herzegovina and wide access to the Adriatic realized, the strategic position of her capital immensely strengthened, and general position altogether superior to what it was when Austria attacked her, I think that it would be the height of imprudence and most unreasonable for Serbia to refuse to the Allies her consent to make reasonable concessions either to Bulgaria or Roumania in return for their co-operation. Unless the Allies had intervened in this war, Serbia, left to herself, must have been crushed by Austria, and I think it is due to the Allies, who are fighting, amongst other things, not only to prevent Serbia from being crushed, but to ensure her a greatly enhanced position, that Serbia should not refuse to the Allies such concessions as may be necessary to secure general and complete victory, and thereby Serbian interests. Bulgarian co-operation would, during the war, secure Serbia against a large Austro-German offensive.

I should like you to place these considerations privately and verbally before M. Pashitch, explaining to him that it is at the moment the best response I can make to the appeal of the Serbian Minister to keep in touch with M. Pashitch.

Sir Edward Grey to Mr. O'Beirne

FOREIGN OFFICE,

July 28, 1915.

Your telegrams of 25th July.

The acquisition of the uncontested zone by Bulgaria is ultimately dependent on Serbian compensation in Bosnia, etc. We can only ask Serbia to cede her Macedonian provinces in return for compensation elsewhere. But the Allies can, and if necessary will, refuse to recognize any extension of Serbia until she has conceded the uncontested zone, and when Bulgaria takes the field against Turkey they will arrange with Serbia for Allied forces to occupy up to the Vardar, as a guarantee to Bulgaria that the territory will be handed over to her without difficulty when the time comes. Bulgaria would, of course, engage meanwhile to prohibit formation of bands to make disturbances in Macedonia.

I agree to the formula which you suggest as regards Cavalla, and you could say that the cession of Cavalla will be a condition of any Greek extension in Asia Minor.

As regards Roumania, the position is that the Roumanian Government are willing to enter into a political agreement forthwith, but that they cannot bind themselves to take the field at a fixed and early date, in view of the actual military position. The contention seems reasonable, and His Majesty's Government are pressing the Russian Government to enter into such a political agreement. Roumania's claim to the Pruth-Theiss boundary would be recognized, while she would, *inter alia,* be expected to meet Bulgarian wishes in the Dobrudja and to discuss military combinations. But it must be remembered that it will be important to keep Roumania's military preparations against our enemies as secret as possible, and therefore any approach to Bulgaria could only be hypothetical in form.

Sir Edward Grey to Sir C. des Graz

FOREIGN OFFICE,

July 26, 1915.

SIR,—In conversation with me on the 21st instant, the Serbian Minister volunteered his willingness, if the concession of the line of the Vardar would secure Bulgarian support, to press this view on his Government.

I thanked him for his good-will, but said that I thought the offer of the line of the Vardar would not be sufficient to secure Bulgarian support, and that this could not be secured with a promise of less than the uncontested zone in Macedonia.

The Serbian Minister said that the uncontested zone, as interpreted by Bulgaria, was a thing that Serbia never could concede. Serbia would rather stand alone against the shock of an Austro-German offensive. She knew that she risked everything in this war, but her promise of such a concession would simply lead to war between herself and Bulgaria.

I let the Minister see what I had said to you in my telegram No. 285 of the 20th instant.

M. Boshkovitch called again on the 22nd instant, and was asked whether the above really represented his view, because, if the Vardar line was the utmost concession that Serbia would make, it was, as I had already told him, useless from the point of view of Bulgaria. The Serbian Minister replied that he certainly considered that his Government would not agree to any concession in excess of what he had mentioned to me, and, as it would not lead us any further, he would like to withdraw his offer to press it on his Government.

M. Boshkovitch observed that he was regarded in his country as the champion of Serbian rights in Macedonia, and spoke of the part he had played throughout the Balkan troubles in support of those rights.

He was informed that this made it all the more desirable to convince him of the point of view of His Majesty's Government, which was that the possession of the rest of Macedonia (contested and uncontested zones) other than that of the territory up to the Vardar line, should be left to Anglo-Russian arbitration at the end of the war, provided that Serbia received large territorial compensation elsewhere. He should not forget that, in the event of a resumed German offensive against Serbia, Bulgaria would very possibly join in the attack, and that in this case the Allies would be too occupied with Turkey to come to Serbia's assistance. If the claims of Serbia to Macedonia were so strong as he represented, it was fairly safe to assume that the result of the arbitration would be to give to Bulgaria only a comparatively narrow strip across the Vardar, which would probably include Monastir, as the Bulgarians seemed so anxious to have that district.

M. Boshkovitch replied that he could not support a proposal that the possession of the whole of Serbian Macedonia should be submitted to arbitration at the end of the war, as this might affect Serbia's vital interests; but he suggested that a line might be drawn in Macedonia the cession of which he would recommend to his Government. Such a line, he said, might run from Bragalnitza, south of Perlepe (to which he did not seem to attach great importance) down to Monastir.

He was then asked whether he would support such a solution at Nish. The sacrifice involved would be largely a matter of sentiment, as guarantees would probably be forthcoming that there would be no unfair discrimination from the economic point of view on the Bulgarian portion of the Vardar Railway, nor a Bulgarian military menace from the ceded territories, while Serbia would thereby earn the gratitude of this country, and we might be willing that she should sign the treaty of 5th September.

M. Boshkovitch welcomed this proposal, and finally agreed to support some such solution as the above, provided that Great Britain and Russia took the initiative at Nish, since he was unwilling himself to propose it to his Government. He would, however, urge his Government to accept the proposal once it had been made, and added that, although his influence in Macedonian questions was, perhaps, 80 per cent. in the scales, yet there was no certainty of his Government giving way. Before, however, telegraphing to his Government he must know a little more definitely what were the probable limits of the territory which Serbia would be asked to surrender.

M. Boshkovitch finally observed that, as things now stood, there appeared no use in informing you of the conversation which he had had with me on the 21st instant.—I am, etc.,

E. GREY.

Mr. O'Beirne to Sir Edward Grey
(Received August 21)

SOPHIA,
August 20, 1915.

My telegram of 19th August.

Information which has reached me from various quarters during the last two days all points to Bulgarian Government being very near to coming to decisions of policy unfavourable to our cause.

The feeling generally prevailing here is that the time has come when Bulgaria must choose between two courses of action—either to attack Turkey, thus joining the side of the Allies, or to attack Serbia, thus committing herself to the side of the Central Powers, and there are indications that the Government is inclining to the latter course. Reported fall of Kovno has, it is needless to say, made a deep impression in the governing and military circles, giving rise to anticipations of a coming disaster to Russian arms.

I fear that, even if Serbia were at once to consent to cede uncontested zone, and we could announce that we were prepared to occupy up to Vardar, there is now only but a faint chance that these inducements would be sufficient to bring Bulgaria into the field on our side. The elements most favourable to us have, during the last few days, become so impressed with Germany's military strength that they would hesitate to take the course which would expose Bulgaria to a German attack.

It is thus rapidly becoming the main question whether Bulgaria can be restrained from attacking Serbia. There is undoubtedly a large section of opinion in this country which would be strongly opposed to such a policy and realizes the disastrous consequences to which it would lead. The danger is, however, real, and has come distinctly nearer in the last few days. It is thus very important that Serbia should be, if possible, induced to see that, even though there may be little prospect for the present of obtaining Bulgarian co-operation, it is nevertheless necessary for her own safety to make concessions in Macedonia which would cut the ground from under the feet of the party here which favours an aggression upon her. Such concessions would offer the only possible chance of forming a Balkan block which could constitute a barrier against a German descent on the Balkans.

(Sent to Petrograd, Athens, Nish, and Bucharest.)

Negotiations of a different nature were proceeding during the spring of 1915. Italy expressed her desire to join the Allies, but even this negotiation was not quite a simple matter. Russia foresaw difficulties and apprehended that the addition of Italy would introduce complications or conflict of interests that would weaken the unity of the Allies:

Sir G. Buchanan to Sir Edward Grey
(Received March 3)

PETROGRAD,
March 3, 1915.

M. Sazonof said to-day he would not regard without misgivings entrance of Italy upon scene at a moment when her naval and military co-operation has lost most of its value. Any fresh collaboration would complicate peace negotiations. Intimacy and confidence existing between the three Allies was essence of their strength, and if a fourth Power attached itself to their concert there might be danger of its trying to disunite them for its own personal profit.

M. Sazonof is accordingly of opinion that, if Italian Government offer their help, Powers should evade giving a definite answer, while giving a most friendly form to the discussion.

France and ourselves took the view that these apprehensions were in themselves exaggerated, and that, even if they were not, the advantage of gaining Italy as an Ally far outweighed the disadvantage of any complications. To repel the Italian overture seemed to us the height of folly. My own view was expressed in the following despatch to Bertie:

Sir Edward Grey to Sir F. Bertie
FOREIGN OFFICE,
March 4, 1915.

Petrograd telegram of 3rd March repeated to you.

You should inform Minister for Foreign Affairs that I cannot share this (the Russian) view.

The common object of France, Great Britain, and Russia is to finish this war as quickly as possible on satisfactory terms. The participation on our side of Italy and Balkan States would enormously facilitate this object; it probably would, in a comparatively short time, effect the collapse of German and Austro-Hungarian resistance.

I cannot see how the collaboration of Italy or Balkan States would impair confidence and intimacy existing between the three Allies.

If Italy or any other Power demanded, as price of co-operation, conditions that appeared to Russia likely to impair a settlement in her favour of question of Constantinople and Straits, Great Britain and, I presume, France also, would support Russia in resisting such conditions; and, in any case, no conditions for co-operation of any Power would be agreed to except by France, Great Britain, and Russia, in consultation and agreement with each other.

It must also be remembered that if co-operation of any other Power is offered to and refused by the three Allies, the Power refused may go to Germany, who will readily offer attractive conditions.

This telegram is being repeated to Sir G. Buchanan with instruc-

tions to join his French colleague in representing this point of view
to Russian Minister for Foreign Affairs, if French Government agree.

The French simultaneously and independently expressed the same view, and Sazonof pressed no more objection of principle. The details of the negotiation were
not easy. If Italy was to take the risk of war, she must
know where she would be at the end of it. Her claims
might overlap the aspirations of Serbia, or even Greece.
We did not want to dishearten Serbia in her uphill
struggle with Austria, nor to alienate Greece by an agreement with Italy that might be regarded as made at the
expense of the legitimate aspirations of either of the two
smaller countries. It was the question of territory where
the bulk of the population was Slav that was the most
difficult and delicate in this negotiation, and in protecting
this interest Russia naturally took the lead. There were
difficulties and delays, but it was essential to the Allies
that the negotiations should succeed; conditions were
agreed, and Italy entered the war against Austria. This
is why and how another secret treaty came to be made.

Let it be remembered that, about this time, the war
took a turn most unfavourable to the Allies and that
Italy entered the war at a moment when clouds were
gathering and the prospect getting darker.

About the same time Roumania entered on negotiations
of the same kind with the same object as Italy. It was
understood that these two countries had been in close
touch and had intended to enter the war on the side of
the Allies at the same time. But the Russian defeats in
Galicia began to be serious before the negotiations be-

tween Roumania and the Allies were concluded. Roumania held her hand, while she watched with increasing concern the Russian reverses and the ever-growing magnitude of the disasters to the Russian Armies. With Russia almost prostrate and Bulgaria waiting her opportunity, it became dangerous for Roumania to depart from neutrality. The French and British Armies had been unable to press the Germans hard enough to take the pressure off Russia in her hour of distress; they evidently could not help Roumania. If she entered the war now she risked a single-handed fight with Bulgaria, added to all the forces that Germany and Austria might be able to spare after the victories over Russia. One day, in the summer, the Roumanian Minister came to tell me that, in the view of his Government, it was not safe for Roumania to fix a date for joining the Allies. The truth of this was so evident and our inability to help Roumania, if she got into difficulties, was so complete that I could do nothing but acquiesce. I could not even reproach Roumania for her decision, much less attempt to alter it in face of all the facts. The only thing to be done was to accept the thing with a good grace and to let the negotiations be suspended, but to keep alive the goodwill which had inspired them in order that, when the war took a more favourable turn, this might be renewed. We succeeded in doing this—it was little enough, and a very disappointing result; but it was all that was possible in 1915.

Worse, however, far worse, than the reaction of the Russian disasters on Roumania or Bulgaria was their effect in Russia itself. It was not only the material loss of armies, guns, and munitions of all sorts; there was the moral effect on public opinion in Russia. Russia had relieved the pressure on France and Britain in 1914 by the entrance of her armies into Germany. Now France and Britain, held in trench warfare on the West, could make no corresponding advance. There was a tendency in Russia to think that her Western Allies were saving themselves at her expense.

The two following despatches from Petrograd, sent, one in the earlier and one in the latter part of the summer of 1915, explain this.

Sir G. Buchanan to Sir Edward Grey
(Received June 25)
PETROGRAD,
June 24, 1915.

Abandonment of Lvov, and fact that Russian Army continues to retreat, in order to avoid useless sacrifice of lives, which want of ammunition entails, is increasing public discontent with the management of the war. Important meetings of deputies of the Duma are being held to consider the situation, and if the Duma itself has not been already convoked it is for fear that, under present circumstances, such violent attacks would be made on Ministers as to produce serious crisis. It will, however, I believe, be convoked later on. Prime Minister, I am credibly informed, recently tendered his resignation to the Emperor, on the ground that, with Government constituted as it is at present, he could not be responsible for what might happen. His Majesty declined in flattering terms to accept it, and a few days later resignation of the Minister of the Interior was announced.

From what the President of the Duma tells me I gather that the other Ministers will be obliged to resign, but chief difficulty seems to be to replace Minister of War, whose position is seriously compromised. The Emperor, with whom I had a conversation at the launching of the latest Russian Dreadnoughts, does not apparently share uneasiness with which so many of his subjects regard military outlook. He spoke with cheerfulness of the future, and of his determination to carry on war till Germany was crushed. On my remarking, in reply to the reference which he made to the recent reconstruction of His Majesty's Government, that in Great Britain all party difference had been forgotten, and that the present Ministry represented a coalition of all the best intellects in the country regardless of their political opinions, His Majesty said that this was the only course to follow in a crisis like the present.   Minister of Agriculture, most influential member of Government, told me on same occasion that evacuation of Galicia caused him but little concern, as that province was only source of embarrassment for Russia. From what he had been told by competent member of New Munitions of War Committee, he believed that in a couple of months army would have shells in abundance.

Other persons occupying high positions have also given me same assurance, but former favourable forecasts respecting the ammunition have so often proved illusory that one cannot count upon accuracy of the present one. There must, in any case, as military attaché has already reported, be a serious shortage in rifles for months to come, and the crucial question at present is how Russian Army is going to get on during intervening months. Situation may become critical, as it is difficult to see where Russian Army can make a permanent stand against the overwhelming superiority of the German artillery.

I regret to say that the public is accusing France and Great Britain of not making more pronounced effort to relieve pressure on this front. The President of the Duma told me the other day that he was trying to explain real situation in West to those deputies who held that France was to blame; but he regretted to say that the feeling was growing that the French were not pushing home their offensive with sufficient vigour, nor assisting Russia with shells, of which they had such an abundance.   He assured me that no complaints were made against Great Britain; but I fear that this is not entirely true.

Sir G. Buchanan to Sir Edward Grey
(Received August 20)

PETROGRAD,
August 19, 1915.

News that Kovno has either fallen or is on the point of falling creating something almost like consternation amongst the pessimists of Petrograd, who seem convinced that Brest-Litovsk line will have to be abandoned, and that road to Petrograd will be opened. Some of them, including even certain members of the Duma, appear to regard situation as lost and are talking of separate peace. I am told many reactionaries are in favour of peace, and that German influences at Court are working in the same direction and warning the Emperor of the danger of revolution.

It is only at Petrograd that such talk would be tolerated, and nothing would be more calculated to bring about revolution than an attempt to conclude peace. Japanese Ambassador, who has just returned from Moscow, tells me, in spite of strong feeling of resentment against the Government, everybody is determined to fight the war out. This determination is, I believe, shared by the Emperor and great majority of the nation.

Situation is, however, very serious, and what preoccupies me most is the idea that is gradually permeating populace that Russia is being deserted by the Allies. Leading Russian journalist asked me to-day whether I had represented the gravity of the situation to His Majesty's Government, and whether I could do nothing to hasten offensive on our side. I replied that, though I had reported the state of feeling here, I would never suggest such an offensive movement in the West until it could be made with good prospect of success. Russian public must be made to understand that if we attempted it before we were ready we might meet with a disaster which would leave Russia at Germany's mercy.

Although statement I recently gave Press gave good impression, I fear Russian public, in their present state of nervous tension, will not listen to anything which we may tell them ourselves of what we are doing. I have discussed the subject with several persons, and have come to the conclusion that the only way to check the movement which may, if it is allowed to continue, cause serious prejudice to Anglo-Russian relations would be to attach competent Russian journalist to our army in France and to French army, and to our army in Gallipoli. If right men could be found, and they given reasonable facilities, such as those Washburn received on this side, they would be able to render us service which Washburn has rendered Russia and interpret Great Britain and her Army to Russian public.

These were terrible days for men in the position of the Tsar and Sazonof, but they stood firm to their Allies.

THE MARQUIS IMPERIALI
Italian Ambassador in London, 1910-1921

They were dark days for us all. The following record of a conversation with the Italian Ambassador gives a glimpse of the situation.

Sir Edward Grey to Sir R. Rodd

FOREIGN OFFICE,

September 14, 1915.

SIR,—The Italian Ambassador asked me to-day what information I could give him on the general situation, saying that the Italian Ministers in some foreign countries sent such gloomy reports to the Italian Government on the general situation, expressing views which he himself did not share, that he was anxious to know what I thought of it.

I said that my information was that people in Germany regarded with dismay the prospect of another winter campaign, and were now much less confident of being able to force a satisfactory peace before the winter. They had failed in the hope of getting Russia to make a separate peace. The expectation that they entertained a month ago of capturing a large part of the Russian Army had not been fulfilled, and, though they might get Vilna, and even Riga, which were thought to be in danger a month ago, they had lost much time lately in the East, where it was becoming more difficult for them to advance, and also more difficult for them to retire.

In reply to a remark from the Ambassador that we could hardly expect to bring the war to an end before the winter, I said that I agreed; but if, in the autumn, the Germans reached a position in which they wished to have peace, and did not know how to get it on the terms they had once considered satisfactory, the situation would become increasingly favourable to us.

The Ambassador asked me about the Dardanelles.

I said that we had no bad news from there, but progress had been very slow for some time, and I admitted, in reply to a statement to that effect from him, that there had been many casualties in the actions that took place last month.

He then spoke of the London conversations with Count Metternich which the German Government had lately published, and observed that they bore out entirely what my attitude had always been: that we would not take part in any aggression against Germany. He said that Prince Lichnowsky had been entirely convinced of this, and had reported to his Government that our presence in the Triple Entente was a guarantee against aggression.

I confirmed this entirely, and said that we had always made it quite clear to France that an aggressive war against Germany would have no support from us, and France, I knew, had genuinely wished to avoid war.

The Ambassador observed that the publication of the conversations with Count Metternich showed that, so far from its being our intention to isolate Germany, it was Germany who aimed at the isolation of Great Britain.

I said that this would no doubt have been the result if we had entered into an agreement in the terms that Germany desired.—I am, etc.,

E. GREY.

In conversations of this kind it was a matter of course to make the best of things, to speak of what was hoped, and not of what was feared; but in intercourse at home anxiety could not be concealed, and when alone one sometimes knew what it was to have to resist "the fear that kills, and hope that is unwilling to be fed."

CHAPTER XXVIII

(1915)

ALLIED DIPLOMACY IN WAR (*continued*)

Greek Opinion in 1915—The Landing at Salonica—Venizelos's Attitude—An Equivocal Position—Venizelos's Resignation—Greece and Serbia—Refusal to help Serbia—Destruction of the Serbian Army—Plans for its Recuperation—A Reflection after the Event—The Entry of Portugal—Our Japanese Ally.

WITH the imminence of a Bulgarian attack on Serbia the need for Greek co-operation entered upon a new and urgent phase. Greece had an alliance with Serbia. It had been assumed that this alliance covered only wars between Balkan States. If so, there had been no obligation for Greece to go to war to help Serbia against Austria; but there would be an obligation to help Serbia against an attack by Bulgaria. The Western Allies and Russia had nothing to do with the alliance between Greece and Serbia, but they were anxious to give Serbia all the help they could. They therefore pressed upon Greece her presumed obligation to support Serbia against Bulgaria. Greek opinion was not unanimous about the obligation; to fight Bulgaria would involve Greece in a war with the Central Powers. The letter of the treaty might require Greece to fight by Serbia's side against Bulgaria, but did the spirit of the treaty require Greece to take part in a war in which the conflict between Serbia and Bulgaria was only a secondary matter? Such we imagined to be the reason of Greek hesitation. To overcome this, and to secure Greek help for Serbia, it was proposed to send French and British troops to Salonica to support the Greek Army in repelling the Bulgarian attack upon Serbia.

Venizelos, then Prime Minister at Athens, was willing, but, in view of the division and hesitation in Greek opinion, it was proposed to make a formal protest against, while giving every facility for, the landing of French and British troops at Salonica.

I had been strongly opposed to any landing of our troops in Greece, except with the good-will and consent of the Greek Government. In war many things are done that would not be done in peace, but there are some things that even the compulsion of war cannot justify, and we had contended in the case of Belgium that the forcible violation of neutral territory was one of these. To land troops as was proposed, with the good-will of the Greek Government, would indeed be no parallel to the German violation by force of the Belgian neutrality that Germany had bound herself by treaty to protect; but I objected to even a formal protest being made. This would be a shabby subterfuge that would deceive nobody, but would give the appearance of a violation of Greek territory. When everything was arranged the resignation of Venizelos was brought about by the division of opinion in Greece. The arrangements for landing French and British troops at Salonica were too far advanced then to be cancelled.

The following document will show what happened:

Sir F. Elliot to Sir Edward Grey
(Received September 22)

ATHENS,
September 22, 1915.

Telegraphic.

My telegram of 21st September.

M. Venizelos proposes to suggest to the King, as an inducement to fall in with his views, that, in the event of a successful campaign against Bulgaria, the Greek Army might join the Allies in operations against Constantinople. He thinks this will be an attractive bait, but His Majesty would never consent to advance into Hungary, nor would this be agreeable to the army or the country.

My Russian colleague fears that suggestion of Greek co-operation against Constantinople may again raise opposition at Petrograd, notwithstanding primary necessity of securing victory.

Sir Edward Grey to Sir F. Elliot

FOREIGN OFFICE,
September 22, 1915.

Your telegram of 21st September.

Lord Kitchener is at the moment absent from London on military business. He returns this evening, and the situation, as put by M. Venizelos, will be discussed with him.

My personal impression is that it is not possible for us to send a military force to Greece immediately, but that it might not be ruled out as impossible later on. You can tell M. Venizelos this.

Meanwhile, I am impressing privately on Roumanian Prime Minister the necessity for an understanding between Greece, Roumania, and Serbia.

You should let M. Venizelos know this for his own information only at present and should say to him that it is essential he should remain in office.

I do not believe there is a prospect of Austria and Germany being able to detach large forces to attack Serbia, and the situation is likely to improve.

Sir Edward Grey to Sir G. Barclay

FOREIGN OFFICE,
September 22, 1915.

Mobilization in Bulgaria makes it urgent to consider question of a defensive understanding between Roumania, Serbia, and Greece. You should ask M. Bratiano privately to let me have his views on this. Without some understanding between these three States there will be great risk of absolute confusion in the Balkans, which will enable Austria and Germany to play off one State against another, and treat the interest of each as counters in the German game. On the other hand, an understanding will prevent Austria and Germany from getting opportunities of interference. For Germany is getting weaker in men and money; all our information shows this to be so in spite of her temporary successes against Russia, which are themselves exhausting to her. An understanding between Balkan States will make invasion of the Balkans too formidable a task for Austria and Germany to attempt. But if Bulgaria is to attack Serbia while Greece and Roumania remain doubtful and quiescent, Austria and Germany may see the opportunity of achieving with only a small force of their own a success which would be quite beyond their power if Bulgaria was kept from joining them or kept neutral by the influence of Greece and Roumania.

Sir F. Elliot to Sir Edward Grey
(Received October 3)

ATHENS,
October 2, 1915.

I read to M. Venizelos this morning paraphrases of your telegrams of 1st October, and left them with him to show the King. My French colleague, who was with me, read him similar telegram, but nothing so categorical as your telegram. M. Venizelos was pleased, but he is in a most nervous and excitable condition, and news that French had arrived at Salonica made him even more intractable than he had been yesterday. Before consenting to their disembarkation without more than a protest, he required from French Minister a declaration of reason for their coming, which he will give in terms of one of the telegrams he received from Paris, and, further, a declaration to the following effect:

"On occasion of passage of Allied troops through Salonica French

Government declare they have no intention of encroaching on sovereign rights of Greece or of interfering in administration of the country."

M. Venizelos said that wherever we went we acted as if the place belonged to us, and he must safeguard himself against this being done in Salonica. A telegram which was brought to him, and to which I shall devote another telegram, added fuel to the fire. My French colleague said he could not make required declaration without instructions, but that he would telegraph for them, and M. Venizelos was eventually brought to say he would send instructions that troops were to be allowed to land under protest to-morrow, by which time he was assured reply of French Government would have arrived. He also laid stress on the necessity of troops doing no more than pass through Salonica and Greek territory.

The suspicion of us, which has now become ingrained in all classes of population, has actually laid hold of M. Venizelos himself.

Before our troops arrive off Salonica I shall be required to make a similar declaration, and I request authority to do so.

With regard to officers at Salonica, M. Venizelos admitted that I had spoken to him generally of their being sent, but said he had expected to be informed of their arrival beforehand—an expectation which I confess I shared with him.

His Excellency would express no definite opinion on your telegrams until he has seen the King this afternoon.

Sir F. Elliot to Sir Edward Grey
(Received October 3)

ATHENS,
October 2, 1915.

My French colleague, having received instructions that French Government regard offers to Bulgaria as lapsed in consequence of mobilization, and are ready to join Serbia and Greece in maintaining Treaty of Bucharest, communicated them to M. Venizelos this evening in my presence. His Excellency, who had seen the King and had recovered his self-possession, was greatly pleased, and asked that our troops should be sent to Salonica and landed as soon as possible. He read to us protest which he was addressing to French Minister against violation of Greek neutrality involved in demanding passage of troops before *casus fœderis* with Serbia had arisen, but at the same time he told us that orders had been given at Salonica not only not to oppose landing, but to offer every facility, indicating west side of harbour as part set apart for Allied troops. Turning to me, he said that since French Minister, in his declaration, had spoken of arrival of "Allied troops," and since His Majesty's Government had such an objection even to a formal protest, he would make no further protest than that addressed to my colleague.

Minister of Communications would arrive at Salonica to-morrow, and he requested that Allied officers should address themselves to him and should endeavour to avoid all causes of friction.

Sir Edward Grey to Lord Bertie

FOREIGN OFFICE,
October 6, 1915.

Circumstances have been seriously changed by the resignation of M. Venizelos, who had asked Allies to land troops at Salonica. He may apparently be succeeded by a Government that will adopt a policy of neutrality, and may not favour, and even may oppose, the presence of Allied troops.

We cannot send more troops to Salonica till this situation has been cleared up, and in view both of the political and military aspects of the situation His Majesty's Government are decidedly of opinion that it would be dangerous to send troops through Greek territory into the Balkans without being assured of the co-operation of Greece. It is therefore essential to come to a definite understanding with Greece before incurring further liabilities and risks in the Balkans.

You should explain this view to Minister for Foreign Affairs, and inform him of the instruction sent to Sir F. Elliot in my telegram No. 852 of to-day to Athens, repeated to you, and ask Minister for Foreign Affairs for his views.

Sir Edward Grey to Sir F. Elliot

FOREIGN OFFICE,
October 6, 1915.

Withdrawal of our pecuniary assistance does not necessarily follow on resignation of M. Venizelos. So long as Greece is ready actively to support Serbia in resisting Bulgarian aggression we are prepared to help financially, whatever Government is in power in Athens, and you should let this be known.

Sir Edward Grey to Sir F. Elliot

FOREIGN OFFICE,

Telegraphic.   *October* 6, 1915.

The resignation of M. Venizelos after we have sent troops to Salonica at his request has placed us in a very difficult position, which must be cleared up.

You should ask for an audience of the King, and should be careful to explain that your audience has nothing to do with the internal crisis caused by the resignation of M. Venizelos; that it is entirely alien to our thoughts to interfere with the internal affairs of Greece, or to criticize any action taken by His Majesty.

You should explain that some British troops have already been sent to Salonica on the understanding that Greece intended to support Serbia against Bulgaria in accordance with what were believed to be treaty obligations, and that the co-operation of British and French troops would be welcome to and was desired by Greece to enable her to support Serbia.

This is the understanding on which Allied troops are now present in Greek territory.

You should impress upon His Majesty how urgent it is that we should know clearly what the views of Greece are in this respect, that we may be able to decide what use can be made of British and Allied troops to support Greece and Serbia against Bulgaria, and you should ask the King to authorize M. Venizelos or his successor to inform us frankly and fully on these points.

Sir Edward Grey to Sir F. Elliot

FOREIGN OFFICE,

Telegraphic.   *October* 6, 1915.

Please inform the Senior British officer at Salonica that he should confidentially warn all officers there to be very careful in their dealings with the Greek authorities, and particularly to avoid all possibility of giving offence or the appearance of high-handed action in dealing with the necessities of the situation.

Sir Edward Grey to Lord Bertie

FOREIGN OFFICE,

October 14, 1915.

MY LORD,—M. Cambon came to see me this morning, expressing great anxiety lest we were not going to fulfil the engagements which, he said, we had entered into to send troops to Salonica, in accordance with the understanding arrived at when M. Viviani and M. Augagneur were in London, and on the strength of which M. Viviani had made his speech on the 12th instant. M. Cambon asked me whether it was true that we were not sending to Salonica any more troops than those already there, whereas we had promised to send our share of the 150,000 with France to help Serbia.

I said that the 150,000 had been promised with France at the request of M. Venizelos, in order to enable Greece to fulfil her treaty obligations and to support Serbia. If Greece would not fulfil those obligations and co-operate with us, I held that we were under no obligation to send this particular force. I had always told the Serbian Minister that we would send what help we could, but it must be dependent on the consent of Greece. At the meeting with M. Viviani and M. Augagneur it had been made clear that it was not safe to send a force into the Balkans without being assured of a base at Salonica, of which we could be assured only if Greece would co-operate. This, at any rate, was my recollection.

M. Cambon asked me whether we had now ceased making any preparations to send the troops agreed upon.

I said that, on the contrary, in our view the situation in the Near East was so anxious that we were preparing transports and making all preparations with the least delay possible for sending the troops that had been agreed upon between General Joffre and Lord Kitchener; but these troops would not be available immediately, and could not arrive for at least two or three weeks, and the place of disembarkation and the use to be made of them must be decided according to circumstances.

M. Cambon asked me whether the 200,000 troops we had promised conditionally to Roumania and Greece were additional to the Anglo-French 150,000 or included them.

I said that I could not answer authoritatively without consulting Lord Kitchener, but I wrote down my personal view as follows:

"We are preparing to despatch without delay to the East the contingent of troops promised. Where these troops will be disembarked, and the use to be made of them, will be decided in consultation with the French military and naval authorities. The 200,000 troops promised, on certain conditions, to Roumania and Greece include the 150,000 and are not additional to them."

With this M. Cambon seemed satisfied, and he took a copy of it.

In the afternoon, after having shown the Prime Minister what I had written, and having its accuracy confirmed by him, I wrote to M. Cambon to confirm it. It was subsequently shown to Lord Kitchener, and read to the War Committee in the evening.

M. Cambon appeared to be very much afraid that I was going to say something in the House of Commons in the afternoon, especially with regard to the number of troops, which would be inconsistent with what M. Viviani had said on the 12th instant.

I showed him, in the statement that I was to make, the passage about sending troops to Greece and Serbia.

He said that it was quite satisfactory.

In the course of conversation I observed to him that it was precisely because I did not consider that we should be committed to send troops into Serbia without the co-operation of Greece that I had urged that, in any formula used by M. Viviani in his speech, the words "support of Greece and Serbia" should be used, and not "Serbia" alone; but the formula that M. Viviani had actually used was not the same as either formula that had been shown to us.—I am, etc.,

E. GREY.

It is only necessary to add that when Greece drew back and would not admit an obligation to help Serbia by arms, the French and British troops could not serve Serbia. The Serbian Army became a refugee in Albania: for the present, there was nothing to be done except to convey the Serbian Army to some place away from the scene of conflict, where the Allies could help it to re-cuperate and be refitted. My own view at this point appears in the following despatch:

Sir Edward Grey to Lord Bertie

FOREIGN OFFICE,
December 6, 1915.

MY LORD,—M. Cambon told me to-day that the French Cabinet were strongly of opinion that the Allied forces should be kept at Salonica; that the French military authorities, including General Joffre, believed it to be possible to defend Salonica; and that he was instructed to ask that the British Cabinet should reconsider the matter.

I replied that of course I would report this at once to the War Committee, which was to meet at five o'clock this afternoon; but I could not refrain from expressing my personal opinion, founded upon that of our military advisers. Our 10th division was in Serbia. We should have withdrawn it long ago, but it was kept there to support the French force, which General Sarrail had not so far withdrawn. According to our information Bulgarian and German forces were concentrating for an attack, and it was probable that our 10th division would be sacrificed. The German and Bulgarian forces would then concentrate for an attack on Salonica; and the Greek troops would not defend their frontier, in the absence of any agreement that our troops should be withdrawn. Our troops in Salonica were defenceless. The total Allied forces sent to Salonica would be 150,000 men, for we were fulfilling our promise to send 90,000. What the French Government were now asking was, in my opinion, that we should sacrifice 90,000 British troops, which would no doubt include the sacrifice of the 60,000 French troops; we should then not have sufficient troops to defend Egypt against further attacks; and the French Government were therefore asking, first, that we should sacrifice 90,000 British troops in Salonica, and then that we should sacrifice Egypt. It was a tremendous sacrifice to ask us to make; and for what object were we to make it? It would not help Serbia, for the Serbian Army was now dispersed in Albania and was past help.

Personally I was prepared to sacrifice any part of our Eastern Empire in order to support the Allied line in the West; and I personally should be against withdrawing any troops from France or Flanders that would weaken that line; for, as long as we held that position and succeeded there, the Germans could not win. But now we were being asked to sacrifice 90,000 men and Egypt uselessly.

This was only my personal opinion, but I founded it upon what our military authorities said.

When I was told, as M. Cambon did tell me, that General Joffre considered that Salonica could be held, I could not help feeling that General Joffre overlooked the political difficulty of getting Greece to agree to give up the positions necessary to defend Salonica. In my opinion, if orders were given at once to the Franco-British forces in Serbia to withdraw to Salonica, and we then said to Greece that we were prepared to withdraw all our forces and evacuate Salonica on condition that Greece undertook, pending the withdrawal of our forces and after their withdrawal, to defend her own frontier, and at once allowed the Franco-British forces to occupy temporarily the defensive positions at Salonica necessary to protect their embarkation, an agreement would be come to with Greece, by which the whole Franco-British force, or the greater part of it, would be saved. I did not believe that these forces could be saved in any other way.

M. Cambon admitted that he was much impressed by the military arguments, and inclined to my view; but he said that he was bound to discharge the mission given to him by his Government.—I am, etc.,

E. GREY.

Looking back on it all, my criticism is that it would have been better to face the facts, ugly as they were, and to recognize that, with the military situation as it was, neither threats nor promises on our part would influence Bulgaria's decision. Coinciding as these did with military disasters, they gave an impression of weakness, not of strength; and pressure on Serbia or Greece to make the only concessions that would be attractive to Bulgaria irritated these two countries without moving them. I knew that King Ferdinand had a close grip on Bulgarian policy; I had no personal knowledge of him, but my estimate was that he was the sort of man who was bound to believe that Germany would win. He had the reputation of being the cleverest diplomatist in Europe, but of taking very little account of moral factors. These he would leave out of account in his political calculations. Anyone who did this was sure to overestimate German power and to underestimate the strength of the forces that were opposed to it. If he believed in German success, then Bulgaria had everything to gain by siding with Germany, and everything to lose by remaining neutral, or, still worse, by joining the Allies. The presumption was that the only question in King Ferdinand's thought was not which side to take, but at what moment to join Germany and Austria in the attack on Serbia. Something of this I expressed at least once to the Bulgarian Minister in London, and then I was met by the emphatic assurance that the opposition element in Bulgaria would be able to assert itself and carry the day, if only offers from the Allies sufficiently attractive were forthcoming. Other people who knew Bulgaria urged the same view. It is pathetic to reflect what a belief many people had in the efficacy of words to compensate for military defeats; the pressure, therefore, upon Allied diplomacy to be active at Sophia was very persistent. It was evident that we should be blamed in the long run if we did not succeed in preventing Bulgaria from entering the war, and if we did not try we should be blamed still more for not trying. It would hardly be worth while now to wade through the morass of Foreign Office papers in order to decide which of the Allied Governments or Foreign Ministers comes best or least badly out of the record of this diplomacy. My impression is that, as far as dealings with Bulgaria are concerned, the French record in 1915 would be the best. They never were hustled out of a sound scepticism, and they were the least prone to make suggestions or to raise objections to the suggestions of others—objections that were bound to result in compromise, complication, and delay.

Bulgaria passed the first year of the war in watching its course and in receiving offers from both sides; then, when the Russian armies were driven back and seemed to be defeated beyond the power of recovery, and when our last attack in Gallipoli had failed, Bulgaria entered the war on the Austro-German side.

A word must be said about our dealings with Portugal. Portugal was our oldest Ally. My impression is that from the beginning she was ready, if we asked, to enter the war on that footing. But it seemed unreasonable to us to expose Portugal to the risks of war, unless our military or naval authorities considered that action on her part could be of material assistance to us. Her commerce would suffer on the seas, even her colonies might be raided by German cruisers or auxiliaries, and protection against these risks would be an additional liability and burden on the British Fleet. For some weeks, therefore, after the outbreak of war, it seemed better that Portugal should remain neutral, and that we should make no demand upon her that was inconsistent with that neutrality. In the autumn, however, both the British and French Armies came to be in urgent need of field-artillery. The Portuguese had some excellent guns, and Kitchener told us that it was essential to get these for use on the French front immediately. It became my business to get the guns. The Portuguese were willing that we should have the guns, but they belonged to the Government, and for a Government, as distinct from a private firm, to supply guns to a belligerent is an unneutral act. If Portugal departed from neutrality she wished to do it with the full status of an Ally at our request. We made the request, and Portugal entered the war.

I have already spoken[1] about the entry of our other

[1] See supra, p. 103.

Ally, Japan, into the war. From one point of view that was simple enough. The seizure of Kiao-Chau by Germany, after Germany had joined in ordering Japan out of Port Arthur, had laid the foundation of hostility to Germany. The association of the German Emperor with the doctrine of the yellow peril could not have been pleasant to Japan. Japan was exposing herself to no risks by entering the war against Germany—unless, indeed, the end of the war was such an overwhelming victory for Germany, that British naval power was destroyed and German naval power left supreme. Even in that improbable contingency Japan would, during the war, have possessed herself of the only German naval base in the Far East. She was beyond the reach of annoyance by Germany during the war and of effective attack by Germany after the war, whatever the result of the war might be. Germany could not trust Japan in the war, and the whole of Germany's colonies in the Pacific were at the mercy of Japan.

Sentiment for the British alliance, just resentment against Germany, and material interest were all therefore on the side of Japan entering the war; and Japan was ready.

For us this was a delicate matter, owing to the vital importance of relations with the United States. This has been dealt with in the chapters devoted to those relations.

CHAPTER XXIX

(1916)

THE END OF OFFICE

THERE is no need to spend time over the details of what was done in 1916. Much of what happens under pressure of the exigencies of war has little abiding interest. There were two secret treaties which have not yet been mentioned, that were made in the earlier part of the war, and that were important. One was the promise to King Hussein that Arabia should be an entirely independent Moslem State. This was the only one of these secret treaties that was due to British initiative and for which we had a special responsibility greater than that of any other of the Allies. Some of the subsequent complications that arose in Asia Minor after the war were due not to this first promise to the Arabs, but to other things of the same kind of later date, of which I have no inside knowledge.

235

The Franco-British-Russian secret agreement about spheres in Asia Minor was due to French initiative. The following despatch will show how it began.

Sir Edward Grey to Sir F. Bertie

FOREIGN OFFICE,

March 23, 1915.

SIR,—M. Cambon informed me to-day that M. Delcassé had observed that, as the question of Constantinople and the Straits, which was the chief question affecting Russia, had now been disposed of, it was rather for France and Great Britain to discuss other questions respecting Asia Minor. M. Delcassé, therefore, proposed that there should be an unofficial discussion, either verbally or in the form of private letters about French and British desiderata. It might take place either through Your Excellency in Paris with M. Delcassé, or between M. Cambon and myself here.

I agreed to this, and said that it would be better that the discussion should be between M. Cambon and myself. The Cabinet here had not yet had time to consider our desiderata, and they would have to be discussed with the Cabinet, and referred to it from time to time. I said that we had already stipulated that, when Turkey disappeared from Constantinople and the Straits, there must, in the interests of Islam, be an independent Moslem political unit somewhere else. Its centre would naturally be the Moslem Holy Places, and it would include Arabia. But we must settle what else should be included. We, ourselves, had not yet come to a definite opinion whether Mesopotamia should be included in this independent Moslem State, or whether we should put forward a claim for ourselves in that region.

M. Cambon said that the whole subject had better be discussed unofficially in the way now proposed.—I am, etc.,

E. GREY.

I was not very anxious to carve up Asia Minor in advance: if we won the war, spheres of interest would have to be defined; but the thing seemed rather premature: what we needed first was to concentrate on winning the war.

Presently, however, the Russians advanced into Asia Minor and announced that they must not be expected at the end of the war to withdraw from what they had conquered. This opened up the whole question, as it was not certain that the limits of Russian advance had yet been reached. The French pointed out, with undeniable force, that this made it urgent for France and Britain to come to a definite agreement with Russia about spheres of interest in Asia Minor. We agreed. We stipulated for Mesopotamia as a British sphere, and left the French and Russians to settle the boundary between these spheres. I never regarded this treaty as entailing any obligation on us, except to fulfil a promise to give the Arabs independence. There was no obligation on us to occupy or administer Mesopotamia, but it was desirable to make sure that other European Powers would not push into Mesopotamia and down to the Persian Gulf.

The last days of office in 1916 were made tiresome by Greek complications. British military authorities, certainly Kitchener, had never liked the Salonica adventure. They regarded it as a dissipation of force and strength and the submarine warfare made the line of communication precarious and costly. The operations in that theatre were political rather than military strategy. The Allies had the never-failing good-will of Venizelos and his supporters, but there was another party in Greece that was averse to Greece joining the Allies. I was ready to offer Greece every inducement to join us voluntarily, but I was opposed to coercing her to do so. We could not be sure of safeguarding her against the consequences. The Allies had been totally unable to protect Serbia, but they were in no way responsible for the dangers to which Serbia was exposed. Roumania had suffered, but she had come voluntarily into the war, and the responsibility for the consequences of her doing so did not rest on the Allies.

If, however, we dragged Greece in against her will, and were then unable to protect her if she got into difficulties, the consequences would lie heavy on the conscience of the Allies. This sort of burden would be a disaster that we had not yet incurred. While this matter was pending, the Asquith Coalition Government resigned. Before describing this exit from office it may be of interest to supplement what has already been written about the war by some appreciation of the part taken by two or three prominent persons and some account of detached incidents that stand out in my memory.

The following letter is from Lichnowsky. It bears no date, except the day of the week, but it was received by me on August 1, 1914. It has no intrinsic importance now, and I cannot say to which in particular of many suggestions of mine it refers, but it is given as an example of the spirit in which we worked together to avoid war:

9 CARLTON HOUSE TERRACE, S.W.,
Saturday.

DEAR SIR EDWARD,—I have immediately communicated the contents of our letter to Berlin and hope that the result may prove satisfactory.

If we succeed once more in avoiding European war, it will, I feel sure, be due essentially to your help and statesmanship.—Believe me, dear Sir Edward, yours sincerely,

LICHNOWSKY.

Lichnowsky has necessarily shared the misfortunes from which he tried so earnestly and so sincerely to save his country. He had been the trusted agent of the German Government in keeping the peace of Europe in 1912-13 at the Conference in London. He knew how easily the crisis of 1914 might have been solved by similar methods after the Serbian reply to the Austrian ultimatum; but the German Government would neither use him nor agree to the method of Conference. Do his countrymen yet recognize not only how clear he was of any responsibility, but the debt that is owed him for his efforts for peace during the whole of his Embassy in London? We, at any rate, remember him gatefully for having tried to avert a war that has been a calamity for everyone, victors as well as vanquished.

To pass to Mensdorff, the Austro-Hungarian Ambassador, the spirit in which negotiations were conducted between us on both sides is shown in the following despatch which he addressed to Count Berchtold, the Austro-Hungarian Foreign Secretary, a few days after war had broken out, and while he was still awaiting his instructions in London:

Count Mensdorff to Count Berchtold

LONDON,
August 7, 1914 (*Evening*).

Long conversation with Grey. He is very bitter about the attack on Belgium, and complains especially of the manner in which everything in Berlin has been delivered into the hands of the military, so that he could absolutely never be sure, while he was negotiating, where the authority lay in Berlin.

Grey is in despair at the shattering of his efforts to keep the peace. About the war he said to me again and again, "I hate it, I hate it." He went all over the ground of our labours together in former years to keep the peace during the Balkan Conference. He said he had earnestly

hoped that, when the fearful danger of this moment had been sur-
mounted, peace might be assured for years to come. "I was quite ready,
if ever Russia had been aggressive—it was not likely that France
would be—to stand by Germany and (I hoped) that we might come
to some sort of understanding between the Powers." [Words in inverted commas in English.] Now all that was destroyed, and the uni-
versal war, with its terrible and sinister consequences, had broken out.

I believe that the attack on the neutrality of Belgium has ruined
everything, combined with the bid for the neutrality of England, which
he has made public in his Blue Book, and which has greatly angered
him.

For the rest, he spoke again of the incalculable consequences of
this world-war. "It is the greatest step towards Socialism that could
possibly have been made. We shall have Labour Governments in every
country after this." [Words in inverted commas in English.]

I should like to send you the very interesting (English) Blue
Book as a supplement to this despatch. It is in every respect from
beginning to end of the utmost importance historically. To illustrate
Grey's characteristics and his earnest anxiety to keep the peace, I should
like to call attention to a passage in No. 111 (telegram to Goschen of
July 31) in which he says he has informed Lichnowsky that if it were
clear that Germany and Austria were striving to keep the peace, he
would support them in Petersburg and Paris, and would go so far
as to declare that, in case Russia and France proved obdurate, the
British Government would wash its hands of the consequences (thus
the Entente Powers would be left to their fate). Otherwise he made it
clear that, if France were involved, England must be drawn in.
(Translation).

The despatch contains some other sentences not bearing
upon my own negotiations with Mensdorff, but it has been
published in full in an Austrian Red Book. The French
Ambassador, Paul Cambon, was a patriotic Frenchman
working for one end—to serve and preserve the position
of France in times of difficulty and danger. He wanted
peace, because he knew that war must be hazardous for

France, but he felt that tame submission would be fatal to her. His great knowledge and experience had made his judgment mature; he felt the ground carefully before he ventured on it or advised others. He was above all petty manœuvres, and, even if they had not been foreign to his own nature, his experience would probably have made him despise them as things that are of no real value in the long run and that defeat the objects and destroy the credit of those who employ them. I felt safe with him: he wanted British policy to support France, but he would never use it for a passing advantage in a way that would result in his losing touch with it and forfeiting our confidence. He knew also that he could trust us entirely in this respect. What we said to him would govern what we said to others, and *vice versa;* perhaps he was sometimes impatient that we did not promise more. All of us have constantly to choose in life between the risks of saying too much or saying too little; sometimes he may have thought me over-nice and cautious in preferring the chance of exceeding to the risk of disappointing expectations; though he never expressed criticism, I sometimes felt that he was critical. He appreciated my loyalty to the Entente with France in diplomacy, but now and then I felt that he would have liked a little more partisanship. Possibly, too, there is always a certain limitation of touch between a man whose whole time and life has been given to one sort of work so that his personality has become absorbed in it, and one to whom that work, though temporarily absorbing, is new and must be transitory, and whose personality lies outside it. Cambon was always cordial, but we were officially rather than personally intimate. Of all our numberless conversations in eleven years, I remember only one in which the human element broke through and dominated.

It was during the worst days of the retreat from Mons, when it seemed as if Paris must fall and the victory of the battle of the Marne was not foreseen. There seemed nothing encouraging to say about the military situation and immediate prospect in the West. I said what I could. The Russian advance was beginning and presently must help us, and some other obvious banalities. Cambon sat silent while I spoke and then, his spare frame tense with emotion, he said, "Il y a aussi la *Justice*." There was nothing theatrical or even dramatic in manner or tone, but the word "Justice" was spoken with an emphasis and ring of indignation and conviction that gave a sense of impact, of something stronger than armies. No one but a Frenchman, who had in his own person known 1870, could have thus spoken.

Cambon stayed on in London till after the victory, then he retired. The gratitude of the British Foreign Office, and of myself especially, is due to him for his conduct of affairs with us. I esteem it great good fortune that, during the whole of my time at the Foreign Office, the French Embassies in London and Berlin were filled by Paul Cambon and by his brother, Jules Cambon. Everything that passed through their hands was dealt with on a high and sagacious plane.

In the very early days of the war, before any disaster had occurred, someone remarked to me that it was very patriotic of the Conservative Party to support the Liberal Government, when the war might be a triumph that would give the Liberal Government an assured lease of power for many years.

It was amazing to me that anyone should be capable of such a reflection or of thinking at such a time in terms of party politics at all. By May 1915 it was apparent that the Liberal Government could not carry the burden alone, and Asquith resolved that a Coalition Government must be formed. He announced this decision and accompanied it by a statement that there would be no change at the Foreign Office. This was done without previous consultation with me or any other colleague, but I too felt that a Coalition was necessary, and I was prepared to stay at my post till I was no longer wanted. The forming of the Coalition Government, however, caused one very disagreeable personal incident. Bonar Law, as spokesman of the Conservatives, made it a condition that Haldane should be excluded from office. I felt this to be intolerably unjust, and my feeling was expressed in the following letter to Asquith:

Sir Edward Grey to Mr. Asquith

F.O. LONDON, S.W.,
Wednesday, May 26, 1915.

MY DEAR ASQUITH,—It had, as you know, been my intention not to remain in the Government unless Haldane were included in it.

I need not enter into the reasons that have made it impossible for me to give effect to my personal preference at this moment.

I think, however, that it should be known how extraordinarily unjust are the attacks that have been made upon Haldane in certain quarters. I understand that he has been accused of intriguing with Germany behind the back of his colleagues; of weakening the Army, more particularly by reducing the artillery; and of opposing or obstructing the sending of an Expeditionary Force to France. The true facts are that he has had no dealings with German authorities that were not undertaken either at the request or with the full knowledge and consent of his colleagues, including particularly myself. It was due to the work done by him in the War Office that there was an Expeditionary Force of a certain strength, and with a full equipment of artillery, ready to be sent abroad; but for his work, this Force would not have been available at a moment's notice. The effective artillery was strengthened, and not diminished, while he was in the War Office. Probably, inside the War Office, he laid it down that no orders were to be given for the despatch of the Expeditionary Force to the Continent without the authority of the Cabinet; but no doubt your recollection will confirm mine that, in council, he was one of those who most strongly advocated the despatch of the Expeditionary Force, when necessary, and no proposal to send it abroad met with opposition from him at any time. The Territorials and their organization, which has proved such an invaluable strength in this emergency, were created by him. He brought the Army to the very maximum of strength in numbers and equipment which his colleagues were prepared to propose to Parliament, and which Parliament was prepared, as far as I can judge, to sanction before the war. Throughout the last ten years there is no colleague from whom I personally have, in policy, received more consistent encouragement and support. He possessed, and I believe possesses in a peculiar degree, the confidence and good-will of the soldiers who worked with him in the War Office, some of whom hold the highest commands in the field.

That, after this, Haldane of all people should have been singled out for the special sort of attack that has been made upon him, and accused of lack of patriotism or public spirit, is an intolerable instance of gross ignorance, or malice, or of madness. His friends gratefully recognize that the larger part of the Press has never associated itself with these charges, and has expressed due appreciation of his work. The authors of such attacks are probably incorrigible, and incapable either of fairness or of knowledge; but I do not think that this moment should pass without the public—some of whom have been misled by the constant reiteration of the attacks, but who are fair-minded—knowing what Haldane's record of service in the last ten years is, in the opinion of his colleagues, and I would speak particularly for myself—that of one of the most patriotic, public-spirited, and devoted Ministers and most loyal colleagues who have ever sat in a Cabinet.—Yours sincerely,

E. G.

I had an interview on the matter with Bonar Law, but he would not be moved from the condition his party had made, and it was evident that, unless we acquiesced in the exclusion of Haldane, a Coalition Government could not be formed. To form it was essential: and we acquiesced, though I expressed my regret a few weeks later in an answer in the House of Commons. I know that Asquith felt about it as I did, and, though at the time it seemed that we could not do otherwise under the stern necessity of war, the thing has left a scar.

Something more about persons should be said. One of the most exasperating features of working in close contact with remarkable men is the defects of those who have great qualities. The very greatness of the qualities makes the defects so plain and so provokingly inconsistent. We are all apt to be conscious of each other's shortcomings. This is not because we have none of our own; our own may be even worse than those of others; but they are not the same, and we see most clearly the faults from which we are ourselves free. Equally exasperating is the perception that those who are free from the defects that we deplore are often without the qualities that we admire. In war we must have the men with the qualities essential to success. We cannot have the benefit of these great qualities without the defects that accompany them. In the torrent of criticism that has been poured forth it would appear sometimes to be forgotten that the war was won.

In the conduct of it many mistakes were made, and it is right that these should be exposed for warning to those who come after us. But when this has been done, this question remains to be answered about everyone who took a foremost part in it. Did he contribute something without which the war would have been lost, and which but for him would not have been forthcoming?

Kitchener is an example of what is meant. His conception of work was that it must be a one man job. He shouldered the responsibility, and did the work of a Titan; but he did not realize that general responsibility must be shared with the Cabinet, and strategic responsibility with the most independent and expert military brains, organized in a General Staff and working with him. When the Cabinet insisted on such a General Staff he abided loyally by this decision, which he accepted; but he seemed to regard it rather as a supersession of himself than as an addition of strength. Nor did he realize that for an Army such as he was raising, the whole industries of the country must be organized for war, and that this could not be done inside the War Office.

Yet no one but Kitchener measured the dimensions of the war with such prescience; no one but he foresaw how great would be the need for men, and from the first moment he prepared accordingly. He inspired the country with the magnitude of the military need, and gave it confidence. It may be that before his end came all that was in his power to contribute to winning the war had been given. But without that contribution the war might have been lost, or victory rendered impossible.

Little has been said so far, in this narrative of the war and of the week that preceded it, of the two most important figures in the Liberal Cabinet, Asquith and Lloyd

George, and to close without some words about each would be a great omission.

Abuse would not be too strong a word for the criticism that has been levelled at Asquith as War Prime Minister, and people have been led to overlook much for which they have reason to be grateful. The inference that a man who is prone to put off decision is incapable of taking it, is quite untrue of Asquith. He was not disposed to go to meet the occasion and take it by the forelock, but when it came to him he faced and grasped it; and when a decision was taken there was no hesitation or compromise in announcing it, no wavering in standing by it. His courage was never shaken in adversity. Kitchener selected him as the one colleague in whom, to use his own phrase, he had never seen the least sign of being "rattled" in the desperate days of the retreat from Mons. Asquith had the confidence, even the attachment, of Kitchener in a way that no one else in the Government had them. This understanding between the two men holding places so important at such a time was an asset of value, and those who knew Kitchener will realize how exceptional it was for his confidence to be given so quickly to a civilian with whom he had never worked before. This could only be because there were in Asquith some qualities that attracted and inspired confidence in the soldier.

Asquith took no trouble to secure his own position or to add to his personal reputation. When things were going well with his Government he would be careful to see that any colleague got credit, if he were entitled to it, without regard to whether any credit would be given to or left for himself. On the other hand, if things were going

badly he was ready to stand in front and accept all responsibility: a colleague who got into trouble was sure
that the Prime Minister would stand by him. These
qualities are happily not unique, but Asquith possessed
them in a rare degree.

It was this that did so much in the agitating days at the
end of July to keep the Cabinet together, that made the
final decision firm, and that kept things steady in the first
shock of disaster. Had it not been for Asquith the outbreak of war might have found us with a Cabinet in disorder or dissolution, impotent to take any decision; and
when the German armies seemed to be carrying all before
them there might have been oscillation, resort to sudden
change or rash expedients, that would have spoilt the
chance of recovery. There is much more that a friend
would wish to say about Asquith, but it is no part of this
book to give character sketches or personal descriptions
of men or colleagues, except in so far as these are necessary to explain the part they took in the events narrated.
Were it not for this limitation a reference to Lloyd
George might develop into abnormal proportions of great
variety. What follows will deal only with my impression
of his work in those two years while we were colleagues in
the war.

His fertility and resource were wonderful; his energy
was never depressed by difficulties or daunted by adversity; his spirit was always high. His activity sought any
point of importance, where he thought something was not
being done that needed to be, or where he saw his way
to set right what was wrong or to give a new impulse.
When munitions ran short and he had realized what the

needs were and how they would grow, he made the question his own, though it then belonged entirely to the War Office. Kitchener's principle and practice was to leave the work of other people alone, and to tolerate no interference from others with what he regarded as his job. When he found the activity of Lloyd George entering his department he barred the way. The torrent of Lloyd George's activity foamed against the obstruction, and for a time was delayed; but it ended by sweeping before it that part of the War Office that dealt with munitions and depositing it elsewhere. In short, a separate Department of Munitions was formed, and Lloyd George's method was to get things done by searching out the ablest men for his purpose, wherever they could be found, and throwing them into the work. Critics said that he made chaos, but out of it came a department and the Munitions, and but for Lloyd George the country would not have been organized as soon as it was for the work of making munitions.

Lloyd George was eminent and invaluable in war work at home, but many others both in the Liberal and in the first Coalition Government did manful and effective work each in his department. If one more name is to be selected it should be that of Runciman at the Board of Trade; not only because his special aptitude, experience, and knowledge made his work in that Department efficient and valuable; but because it has received so little recognition. We had not time to know much of what each department was doing, and the history of the work of the Board of Trade must be written by someone with knowledge;

but we knew enough to appreciate something of its activity and of the difficulties that were being overcome.

It was interesting, after the Coalition Government was formed, to observe the impression made upon Conservatives; those who had hitherto regarded us from the angle of opposition, and who now saw us as colleagues. After one Cabinet at which some important Board of Trade subject had been the staple of discussion and which had been handled by Runciman with conspicuous ability, I happened to walk away in company with a Conservative colleague. "We used," he said, "to wonder why you put Runciman in important office: now we *know*."

The scene of catastrophe that overwhelmed us at the first outbreak of war before a battle had been fought, was succeeded by a feeling of intense indignation, when the accounts, some of them from neutral sources, began to reach us of the conduct of German troops in Belgium. The feeling then was of being up against something abominably and incredibly evil, that had been let loose upon us. As the war went on the outburst of German hatred against England, the treatment of British prisoners, and other incidents strengthened and deepened this feeling. But the intention is to end this book not on a note that will stimulate recrimination or feelings of vengeance on any side, but rather to draw such conclusions as may be helpful to future peace. These will be given in a concluding chapter: before closing this one let me touch on one or two lighter incidents.

The fighting services, whether in peace or war, have always been able to retain the relief of humour. It seemed at first, to people at home, as if this would be

Photograph by Reginald Haines

THE RIGHT HON. D. LLOYD GEORGE

impossible. How, for instance, were comic papers such
as *Punch* to find material for jokes in war that would not
jar on public feeling? The thing was done. There was
an ingenious humour in writers and draughtsmen that was
a genuine alleviation. Grief and distress will for a time
darken life, and may permanently dominate it, but human
nature, if it is not so maimed as to be utterly crushed, will
find relief in the common happenings of life. There was
laughter sometimes even in the Cabinet, and two stories
in which I played a part may be worth giving.

The French had formed a huge Cabinet of concentration. M. Briand was Prime Minister, but the Cabinet
contained men of great age.

M. Clemenceau, then approaching eighty years, was
not included. It was said that when asked the reason for
his exclusion, he had replied, "Je suis trop jeune." To
greet this Cabinet Asquith, Lloyd George, and I went to
Paris. We attended a meeting of it, and there beheld
with great interest and respect the living forms of men
whose names had been familiar to us in our youth as of
high repute in French politics. It was a very large
Council; the proceedings were complimentary and formal
rather than important, but there was some discussion, and
it was naturally all in French. Such part as was taken
by us was left to, or, it would be more correct to say, thrust
upon myself. Asquith would not, Lloyd George could
not, and I *had* to speak French.

In French I know my vocabulary to be limited, my
grammar to be imperfect, and my genders to be at the
mercy of chance; further, I am told that my accent is

atrocious.   But with my back really against a wall, something relevant could always be made forthcoming.

When the Council was over, and we three British Ministers were safely outside, Lloyd George said to me: "You know, your French was the only French that I could understand."   If this suggests to a mocking spirit a doubt whether the French Ministers understood it, I can reply that on other occasions when I have had to speak French, I have had proof that it was intelligible even to French ears.

There were many of these visits to Paris.   On another occasion it was Arthur Balfour, Lloyd George, and I who went together.   We crossed to Boulogne and entered the harbour close to a hospital ship, lighted throughout and on the point of starting for home.   After we reached Paris we heard that the hospital ship had struck a mine and had sunk on the route by which we had come.   The next evening we were taken back from Calais to Dover, as being presumably safer.

Having always been immune from sea-sickness, the condition of the waves did not preoccupy me, and there being no light to read by and my companions having disappeared, I found myself thinking of mines and wondering what the explosion and shock would be like.

When we were all three safely seated in the railway train at Dover the following interchange of experiences took place, which may serve as a gauge to varying degrees of immunity from sea-sickness:

E. G.: "I couldn't help thinking about mines on the way over."

Ll. G. (wearily): "Oh! I was feeling much too bad to think of mines."

A. J. B. (with convincing emphasis): "I *longed* for a mine."

In May 1915 I was told that it was imperative for me to go away to rest my eyes completely for six weeks. I did so, and at the end of the period the trouble was pronounced to be quiescent, and I returned to the Foreign Office. I had however, written to Sir Francis Blake, then Chairman of the Liberal Association in my constituency, to say that I should not again stand for the House of Commons. There was to be no public announcement of the fact; this was not necessary nor opportune, as there was no prospect of an election, and the war-time was not suitable for choosing new candidates; but an announcement was to be made, whenever it became desirable for the constituency to prepare for a new election. A year later the change was precipitated in a very unexpected way. There is a rule of the Constitution that not all the Secretaries of State may be in the House of Commons at one time. The presence of Kitchener as Secretary of State for War in the Coalition Government complied with this rule; all the other Secretaries of State were in the House of Commons. On the death of Kitchener it was the general wish, as well as that of the Prime Minister and himself, that Lloyd George should go to the War Office. To make this arrangement comply with the rule, one of the other Secretaries of State must leave the House of Commons or must resign and give place to a peer. Asquith suggested to me, in conversation, that the difficulty might be solved by my going to the House of Lords. I did not respond, and he did not at first press the request; but, as the difficulty persisted, he wrote asking me seriously to consider the suggestion. As I had decided not to seek election to the House of Commons again, there was no reason for refusing to leave it at once, except that the constituency to which, for over thirty years, I had owed so much would be put to the trouble of a sudden bye-election. This inconvenience could not stand in the way of a public necessity—indeed, it scarcely was an inconvenience, for in Sir Francis Blake there was a successor on whom both parties in the constituency would agree to choose to support the Coalition Government. So the change was made: it enabled me to continue work at the Foreign Office for the time, but I did not regard it as going to a new sphere of activity. It was a corollary of the previous resolve to retire from the House of Commons, which had contemplated withdrawal from political life altogether.

The knowledge that failing sight would soon make political work more laborious than ever, and the feeling that after the war there must be a new order of things to be dealt with by fresh minds, combined to confirm this resolve.

To answer a question for the last time and then to walk out of the House of Commons, never to enter it again, after an unbroken membership of every Parliament for more than thirty years, marks the conclusion of the most important part of a man's life, and I felt it so to be; but the change did not come as I had often imagined it in bygone years. There was no sense of a leap into freedom, for I was still in office; and, if there had been freedom, what would it have been worth in the midst of the fury and desolation of war?

A friend has reminded me that one day, as we came away from a War Council, late in November or early in December 1916, I said to him, commenting on what had passed there, "Lloyd George means to break up the Government." This happened in no long time. Lloyd George forced a crisis by resigning; the Liberal members of the Government held a separate meeting with Asquith to decide what course should be taken. The opinion in favour of resignation was unanimous. Whether we were all of the same opinion for the same reason, I cannot say. My own view was clear: the present position was very unsatisfactory; people were not working well together, and the Government was not receiving from the country the confidence and support that were essential to make it efficient. The only thing to be done was for the Government to clear up the situation by resigning. One of two things must then happen: either a new Government under a new Prime Minister would be formed, or, if this proved impossible, it would be demonstrated that there was no alternative to the Asquith Coalition Government. In this event, that Government must be given a fresh start by the country with the support that was at present being withheld from it and with the cordial co-operation of all who again took office in it.

The first of these two alternatives, if it were possible, was preferable. I, at any rate, was at the time very tired and anxious to be relieved of office. I was in fact, though

I did not know this at the time, on the brink of a violent attack of illness that laid me up completely before the end of the month and lasted for some weeks.

It was on Monday, December 11, 1905, that I had gone to Buckingham Palace to receive the seals of office. It was on Monday, December 11, 1916, that I went to Buckingham Palace to give up the seals—a curious coincidence of date and day of the week.

Here let this narrative stop. Appreciation or criticism of what was done in the war in 1917 and 1918 must be left to those who were in the Government then and to the soldiers who served under it.

After the Peace, more especially in the last two years of the Lloyd George Government, its proceedings and conduct of affairs stirred me with indignation and despair such as I have never felt about any other British Government; but this has no bearing on either the recollections or judgment of what passed when we were in office together.

Once more, in 1919, I undertook an official position and went as British Ambassador on a special mission to Washington. To describe the object of this visit would require an excursion into questions of the Peace, outside the scope of this book. So far as public work was concerned, the mission was useless, for President Wilson was struck down by illness before I landed in America and he transacted no business—not even with his own Secretary of State.

I had entered upon official duties again with great reluctance and only under pressure: it was a revelation to find how pleasant even an official post can be made by hospitality that is accompanied by kindness, in which formality disappears in cordial sincerity. The aspiration that the mission would be of use as regards the completion of the Peace Treaties was disappointed; the hope that it would be a pleasant experience was more than fulfilled. Though an account of it would not be relevant here, it remains a vivid, a delightful, and a grateful memory. It has also left the conviction that an understanding based on common ideals between Britain and the United States is possible in a greater degree than between any other separate countries or nations.

CHAPTER XXX

THE FOREIGN OFFICE

The Foreign Secretary's Routine—A Typical Day's Work—The "Boxes"—At the Office and Afterwards—Debates in Parliament and Afterwards—The Qualifications of a Foreign Secretary— Recording Conversations—A Current Delusion—Informing the Cabinet—Public Men and Office—The Loss of Freedom—A Quotation from Bacon.

THE organization and mechanism of the work at the Foreign Office as a whole has been described in Mr. Algernon Cecil's chapters in the *Cambridge History of British Foreign Policy*,[1] and it would be superfluous to go over the same ground here. It may be of some interest, nevertheless, to give some account of the part taken by the Secretary of State, who, for the sake of brevity, shall be referred to as the Minister. The methods of one Minister differ no doubt from those of another; what follows must therefore be understood to apply only to my own practice, though it is written in the third person. It will represent the proceedings of a normal day, when the work of the Foreign Office is large in amount, but when there is no great crisis to disturb the usual routine. The sample of twenty-four hours shall begin with the arrival of the Minister at the Foreign Office at or soon after 11 a. m. On arrival, if

[1] Vol. iii, ch. viii.

no arrears have been left over on the previous day, he finds only one box: it contains copies of the telegrams that have come in and been deciphered since the Office as a whole finished its work the day before. These he reads, and presently the Under-Secretary comes to his room. If any of the telegrams are urgent the Minister discusses them with the Under-Secretary; settles the line on which they should be dealt with. It may be that one or two of the telegrams render it desirable for the Minister to see one or more of the Foreign Ambassadors or Ministers: he sees the Private Secretary, who makes his appointments for the afternoon, arranges for him to see in succession foreign representatives whom he wishes to see, or who have asked to see him, British representatives, who are at home on leave, and any other persons whom he ought to see or interview.

Meanwhile the Under-Secretary has got to work on the papers that have been sent to him from the Assistant Under-Secretaries. Such of these as are deemed to be of sufficient importance or interest for the Minister to see are sent up to him. They arrive in wooden boxes covered with red leather; these boxes are of various shapes. Some are square, some are oblong and narrow, some are short, some are deep, some are shallow, and they are in different stages of renovation, preservation, and dilapidation; occasionally one seems to be new. Each box has a label protruding from it on which is printed the official title or name of the Minister, and also the name of the official from whom it comes. When the Minister has read the contents he reverses the label, locks the box, and returns it to the official who sent it.

Amongst the papers that are sent will be the telegrams that the Minister has already seen, but a copy of each will be affixed to a large sheet of thick paper on which minutes are written.   All the papers will, if they require it, have a minute by the head of the department specially affected, another by the Assistant Under-Secretary in whose group of departments this one is, and finally one by the Permanent Under-Secretary.   In some cases no action is required; a despatch, for instance, from a British Embassy or Legation abroad may be interesting for the information it contains, but may not require any action; in many other cases the way in which the matter should be dealt with is not open to question.   In such papers the Minister simply adds his initials in red ink to the last minute on the paper.   On other papers, which he thinks require it, he writes his own comments or instructions, sometimes writing textually the words of the telegram that he wishes sent.   If a paper presents much difficulty, especially if it should lead to difference of opinion in the minutes, the Minister perhaps reserves it for personal discussion with the Under-Secretary or one of the officials with special knowledge of the subject.   When once he has initialled his own or any other official minute the Office is authorized to carry it out, without further reference to him.

To return now to the time-table.   About 1.30 the Minister goes away to lunch; about three o'clock he returns, and much of the afternoon is taken up with conversations. The appointments made for him are spaced in time according to the estimate of the business to be discussed at each.   A conversation of importance with a Foreign

THE FOREIGN SECRETARY'S ROOM AT THE FOREIGN OFFICE

Ambassador may last half an hour; when it is over the Minister sends at once for his shorthand writer and dictates a condensed summary of the talk. If the matters discussed are fairly simple, the Minister may have two or three successive interviews with different Foreign Representatives, and then dictate the separate records one after the other. But it is better to dictate the record of an important conversation immediately it is over. Practice gives facility in distilling quickly for a dictated record the essential points, even of a long conversation, but much that is not essential has to be eliminated. Throughout the afternoon important business must not be hurried, but all must be done with as much despatch as possible, or the appointments will get into confusion. If there has to be an important interview, space is cleared for it.

Meanwhile, in such interstices of time as the interviews allow, the Minister deals with the red boxes of papers that are reaching him. Between five and six o'clock he will have some tea brought in; it refreshes but does not make a break in the work, unless it be to look at an evening paper. The Minister remains at the Office on easy days till about six, but more often till seven o'clock. The work that he has not finished or that the Under-Secretary sends up later goes to increase the pile that is sent to the Minister's house. There, after dinner, or when he comes home after dining out, he works at the papers, till such time as he goes to bed. By his bed he places the papers that he has not yet done, and when he wakes, say about 7 a. m., he resumes work in bed, spending an hour or more upon it before coming down to breakfast at 9 o'clock. From breakfast till 11 a. m. there is opportunity for reading the newspapers and private correspondence.

This would be a fair sample of a full day, leaving ample time for meals, for some pleasure reading or society after dinner, and also for sleep, the rest of the time being fully occupied but without undue pressure. When, however, the Minister has to attend a debate in Parliament, he has to make up somehow for the time thus taken away from his Foreign Office work. One of his most depressing moments is after a long Foreign Office debate in the House of Commons. The debate may have begun at four o'clock and ended at eleven. It will have been necessary for him to sit through it and to speak, possibly to make a difficult and important speech. When the debate is over he enters his room at the House of Commons and sees the pile of red boxes that have accumulated. The boxes have labels of three colours: red implies urgent, and white ordinary business; green is intermediate. The Minister sorts out the urgent work, condenses it into one or as few boxes as possible, and takes it home with him to work upon at night. The rest he leaves to be taken back by messenger to the Foreign Office next morning, where it will greet him on his arrival as arrears of work belonging to the previous day. It is absolutely essential to avoid the accumulation of long arrears of work; they can never be overtaken, and they greatly impede the smooth and efficient working of the Office.

In my own experience I was very conscious of the admirable way in which the immense and multifarious business was handled by the officials at the Foreign Office:

if that were not well and regularly done the Minister's position would be distracting; he owes it to the Office, in return, to deal with what comes to him in a manner that may make it as easy as possible for him to be well served.

Three qualities of mind may be mentioned as specially needed for the transaction of business.

1. A power of rapidly seizing the important or decisive points in the papers submitted to him.

2. A habit of switching his mind to the angle of vision that takes account of the environment of each subject. He has to pass quickly from continent to continent. One subject may be considered without regard to any other Power; another requires the susceptibilities or interests of other Powers to be borne in mind, and so forth with great variety.

3. The power to dismiss from the mind papers disposed of, but to recall at once, when papers come before him again, perhaps weeks later, what was the last point with which he dealt. To each paper, as it reaches him, there are attached previous papers, if there be such, that give the history of the affair; but it is well to be able to remember without having to reread documents that have been considered before.

What has been said so far applies to the transaction of the ordinary work. On the larger questions of policy thought must work, not on any one paper or at any stated time, but frequently and when the tide of the mind is in flood; and the handling of these will depend on temperament, character, judgment, and much else besides the mental qualities necessary to efficient transaction of business.

Conversations with Foreign Ambassadors are so important that some further comment on them may be given. They provide a courteous, elastic, and comparatively informal way of discussing difficult questions. Diplomatists become trained to conduct, to remember, and to make a concise but adequate record of important conversations. It is an important part of their professional equipment. A Minister for Foreign Affairs who is not trained for the career of a diplomatist must acquire the power by practice. After leaving the Foreign Office the Foreign Ambassador goes to his Embassy and there makes his record of the conversation into a despatch to his Government. The Minister dictates his record, reads in type what he has dictated; the Office, by prefixing "Your Excellency," gives the record the form of a despatch to the British Embassy in the country concerned. It may afterwards appear as such in a Blue Book and be scrutinized as if it were a document of which every word had been carefully weighed and considered. As a matter of fact, the words used have probably had to be improvised in the talk and the record is a recollection of them, as perfect as the Minister's memory can make it.

The Minister often feels that it is easier to remember what he has said, and his own words, than to remember those of the Ambassador; but he must strive to record the one as faithfully as the other. He must also resist the temptation to alter or improve his own part in the conversation. On reflection, the Minister will often see how something of his own might have been much better said: how effective something would be that it did not occur to him to say at the moment. All these suggestions of *l'esprit d'escalier* must be quelled. The record may some day be published, and it would be unfair to the Ambassador to represent him as having listened to words or arguments that he did not in fact hear.

It is reported, I think, that Dr. Johnson, when writing accounts of debates in Parliament, said that he took care not to let the Whig dogs have the best of it. The Minister on his side, and the Ambassador on the other, are each exposed to the sort of temptation to which Johnson succumbed; perhaps it would be more appropriate to say the partiality in which Johnson indulged, for he never succumbed to anybody or anything. I only remember one instance in which I ever saw at the time the record that an Ambassador made of a conversation with me. In such records as saw the light afterwards I never once had occasion to feel that my words had been misrepresented or that justice had not been done to what I said. I hope the same may be felt by those of whose conversations I made record.

One delusion in connexion with these conversations never came to my knowledge at the time. Had I heard of it, it would have been summarily disposed of. In the room at the Foreign Office there was a large screen behind the writing-table at which I sat. I vaguely assumed that it had been put there to protect some predecessor from draughts. I did not know it, but I never felt the room at the Foreign Office to be my home or anything but a place for work, and so long as the furniture did not impede work I did not interfere with it. A few years after I had left Office, one, who had been on the staff of the American Embassy and who had become a personal friend, told me that it was assumed in the American Embassy that there was a shorthand writer behind the screen.

The notion that an Ambassador talking with me should have been placed surreptitiously at this disadvantage was very repugnant to me; the notes of the shorthand writer could of course have been produced in favour of my record, if it was questioned, and against the Ambassador. Indeed, the suggestion opened up a vista of possible unfairness. For eleven years I had apparently lain under this imputation without knowing it. If the Embassy really believed that there was a shorthand writer concealed behind the screen, it is surprising that no Ambassador ever suggested that he should be shown the notes of his conversation. Had I been an Ambassador and believed that a Foreign Minister was treating me so, I should have considered the possibility of bringing my own shorthand writer and so either have put the practice on equal terms or made an end of it.

Had I known of the suspicion at the time, the screen that was guilty of causing it would have had short shrift. I kept nothing behind it but an atlas.

Members of the Cabinet are kept in touch with the current work of the Foreign Office to a far greater extent than with the work of any other department. Certainly, while I was at the Foreign Office, other Ministers could find information about every matter of importance in the papers that were circulated to the Cabinet. The record of the conversation with Cambon in January 1906 about consultations between British and French General Staffs

THE NEW HOUSE, FALLODON
(Rebuilt 1923)

is the only exception of importance that I remember. This is dealt with in previous chapters.[1]

Copies of the official telegrams received are sent every day in a printed paper to each Cabinet Minister. They are sent in a small box or pouch. The paper is confidential, and must not be left about. The Minister may keep it or burn it; but my own practice, and probably that of most Ministers, was to read the paper, replace it and relock the box with the label reversed, which then returned to the Foreign Office by messenger, or, if the Ministers were absent from London, by post. I found that, as a rule, my colleagues read and followed with interest the information sent to them, but some youthful curiosity arose in the Foreign Office to know whether certain Ministers read what was sent to them. To satisfy this, the paper of telegrams, instead of being left loose, was sent in the pouch enclosed in an envelope. I knew nothing of it at the time, but I was told afterwards that in one instance at least the box or pouch was returned with the envelope inside unopened—to the delight, no doubt, of the enterprising clerk who had made the experiment.

The feelings of a Minister in high office vary presumably according to the temperament, the tastes, and the circumstances of each individual. Ambition, which has its worth as an incentive to public work, is restless when out of office, seeks it, and is not long content with any but the highest. Many men, however, like office for the sake of the interest and work. Lord Ripon, a man of too much public spirit to be moved by selfish or

[1] See supra, Vol. I, Chapter VI.

jealous personal ambition, once expressed to me his own experience about it. He said that the day of going out of office, after being in it for a few years, seemed to him the happiest day of his life. For a few months this mood continued, then he found himself beginning to take an interest again in public affairs; and, after a year or so of freedom, the only question with him was what office he would be given when his party came into power once more.

There is an interesting comment made by Gibbon on the voluntary retirement of Diocletian:

It is seldom that minds, long exercised in business, have formed any habits of conversing with themselves, and in the loss of power they principally regret the want of occupation.

This, more commonly than ambition or love of power, is the reason why men so often cling to office or to public life "even," as Bacon says, "in age and weakness which require the shadow."

I had not sought or even desired office. I knew that it meant the sacrifice of pleasure. A man may know this, and yet not be without a feeling of elation when he enters the room of the Secretary of State for the first time as head of a great office. Much of the work is interesting, but interest is often checked by the mass of it; and often one is obliged to turn from a subject of absorbing interest and importance to a bundle of papers that are insufferably dull. More and more, as the years went on, I chafed at the life of restraint. Within grasp, if I chose to leave office, was life in a country home, with leisure for books, endless opportunities for observing the natural life of birds and beasts, the beauty of trees, the delights of a garden, the ever-varying and ever-recurring seasons, leisure for sport and exercise. For me there would be no want of occupation; the mind would be active outwardly and inwardly: it might even come to me to write a book of some merit, the outcome of observation, feeling, and thought.

This contrast with the life of office was more and more present to me. I longed to be free, and looked forward to a day when I might obtain my discharge. But, once in office, a man can hardly give up for no reason; he waits for the time, which is ordinarily only a few years, when his party goes out, or till some point of difference makes resignation seem a duty. The end of office may come in either of these ways at any time, and for this he waits.

Cecil Rhodes once advised a friend to "do the comparative." He explained how he applied this counsel to himself. When things were going badly with him, he reflected how fortunate he was to be a citizen of the British Empire, with scope and opportunity for great and imaginative policy. He contrasted this with what his lot would have been had he been limited to the career open to a citizen of a small State.

The man who is galled by office finds ample compensation in the scope of the work so long as he believes that he can do that work well; but he may doubt whether the place could not be better filled by someone else, and therefore whether he is sacrificing his freedom to good purpose. Even then he can silence complaint by "doing the comparative" and reflecting that the restraints of office are no more than everyone, great or small, has to submit to, if he is under the necessity to earn a living.

Nevertheless, there will come a sense almost of indignity in office. The Minister not only loses his freedom, but his privacy, and there is a feeling of servitude as well as of honourable service. Bacon's essay "Of Great Place" comes to mind. All his essays read well, but they are not of equal value. The best are those that are written with feeling born of experience. The essay "Of Great Place" is one of these, and a quotation from it may fitly be given here:

Men in Great Place are thrice Servants: Servants of the Soveraigne or State; Servants of Fame; and Servants of business. So as they have no Freedom: neither in their Persons; nor in their Actions; nor in their Times.

CHAPTER XXXI

CONCLUSION

IF this narrative has succeeded in giving a true impression of the course of events that led to Britain's part in the war it will have made the story a simple one.

It will have shown a young man going to the Foreign Office in 1892, with no experience of foreign affairs and little or no prejudices for or against particular foreign countries. At first, he is impressed by the hostility of France, and disposed to meet it with firm resentment; but he also becomes conscious of the discomfort of depending upon Germany. After three years he leaves the Foreign Office, feeling very dissatisfied with Britain's position, but without any clear view as to a new departure in policy. The impression made upon him by the course of foreign affairs in the years that ensue has been described. He is in Opposition, an onlooker and a commentator only, with no share in policy; but he follows the course of foreign affairs as closely as he can. The knowledge gained by his three years at the Foreign Office from 1892 to 1895 makes what he reads about current events intelligible and interesting to him.

After an absence of ten years he returns to the Foreign Office, this time as Secretary of State. He finds the situation quite changed from what it was when he left the Office in 1895. France, one of the nations that were most hostile to Britain, has become a friend. The other once hostile nation, Russia, is the Ally of France. French influence, which before had sought to combine that of her Ally against Britain, now works for good relations between Britain and Russia. Ten years before, war with France and Russia had seemed almost certain to come: now this menace has entirely disappeared; where there was this black cloud on the horizon, there is now the fair prospect of assured peace.

The new Secretary of State enters office with a determination not to let this part of the sky be clouded again. But he realizes that the points of friction with Russia are such that they must be overcome by an agreement with Russia that will put an end to suspicion and intrigue. This he proceeds to effect.

It would be quite wrong to infer that this point of view was the result of pro-French or pro-Russian sentiment. In so far as sentiment or feeling had any part in the matter, this was due solely to a preference for friendship instead of quarrels. But the real base of opinion was not sentiment, but a reasoned conclusion that war with France and Russia had been a real danger for Great Britain, and was something to be steadily avoided.

It would also be untrue to suppose that anti-German sentiment had anything to do with this policy. I was not only ready, I desired, to be on good terms with Germany; but the increasing challenge and menace to Great Britain of the growing German naval programme was an adverse influence on British feeling towards Germany. It had also the effect of making French and Russian friendship seem more than ever desirable.

Meanwhile, German policy tests the friendship with France. There is no choice but to sacrifice this friendship, or to strengthen it and to prepare for the contingency of supporting France against a German attack. This is done, but Britain remains unpledged; and when Europe is on the brink of war in 1914 British opinion, official and other, is divided and uncertain. Then the German invasion of Belgium pushes the British Empire wholesale into the war.

This is, I believe, the main and central truth of British policy and action, and whoever does not accept it and looks for the truth about us elsewhere is failing to understand British psychology; moreover, he will make mistakes about us in the future. Nations are always making mistakes because they do not understand each other's psychology.

Von Tirpitz suggests [1] that the same sort of warning ought to have been given to Germany in 1914 as was given by Lloyd George during the Agadir Crisis in 1911. This assumes that we had a steady intention of going to

[1] *My Memories*, p. 253.

war with Germany. That was not the case. Our attitude, and the attitude of different members of the Cabinet, varied with the various phases of German policy. In 1911 Lloyd George acted on his own initiative; in 1914 he and others were not disposed to take that initiative; they were, indeed, prepared to resist such an initiative being taken at all, until Belgium was invaded. Then they felt differently. Von Tirpitz's suggestion given above is that of one who has learnt nothing about us.

For us, there is one outstanding reflection; it is that of the great danger we escaped—the danger of sitting still while Germany conquered Europe. We should then have found ourselves dependent upon Germany—dependent, that is, upon the disposition that von Bülow describes, and the mentality that von Tirpitz illustrates. How we escaped this danger has been told; but it was an escape that to any student of British politics may well seem unexpected. The general dislike, in Britain, of continental war, the still pervading belief that we are an island and could stand aside, all this made heavily for inertia. In addition there was the distraction of party controversy over home affairs. Any keen observer would have been disposed to predict that we should not promptly and unanimously enter a continental war that seemed to have its origin in a dispute between Austria and Serbia. Anyone familiar with the War Office before 1905 might have thought himself safe in predicting that if a continental war did come suddenly, we should be found without an expeditionary force organized and equipped to take part in it. Any such prediction would not have been fulfilled, but it would have been plausible—for up to 1905 we had never possessed anything like the organized preparation for war that was made between that date and 1914.

The escape, however, was narrow and the danger very real. What is the moral to be drawn from it? The moral, to some people, seems obvious—it is to prepare public opinion better beforehand and to have a bigger Army. To such people the reply is that what may seem to them obvious is in fact no more possible now than it was before 1914. British public opinion cannot be manipulated to make up its mind to war beforehand. Look at the present trend of opinion in 1925. The country has already settled down again to dislike and distrust of alliances that may commit it to the unforeseen.

As for keeping up an expeditionary force of continental size, not even a Conservative Government dare risk its majority by doing so. It would mean asking the House of Commons to vote an enormous military budget in addition to the sum required to maintain the strongest Navy in the world. Not along these lines of a vastly increased army and continental alliances is safety to be found.

To what, then, are we to look?

Not to better preparation for a state of things similar to that of 1914, but to a policy that shall prevent that state of things from recurring; not to military preparation ourselves, greater than our people will approve or can afford, but to a policy that may discourage the growth of armaments elsewhere; and this policy is as good and as essential for other European nations as it is for Britain.

Such a policy will be the outcome of right thinking about the war, but much of the talk to which the war has given rise is useless; it leads nowhere. If we are to profit by the experience of the war, let our thoughts travel on lines that lead to useful conclusions.

First, let us discard what is worth little more than gossip, even if some of it be true.

For instance, I was told on good authority upon the outbreak of war that Isvolsky, when it seemed as if the unexpected resistance of Belgium might upset German plans, said in Paris, "C'est ma guerre." It was some time since Isvolsky had been Foreign Minister at St. Petersburg: Foreign Ministers, when they leave their foreign offices and go to Embassies, cease to control general policy. Isvolsky's boast, had it been true, would have been criminal; as it was vain and empty, it was merely disgusting.

On good authority, also, I was told that before the Austrian ultimatum to Serbia was launched, the German Ambassador at a European capital had said that an ultimatum would be sent, and that it would be couched in such terms as to make war certain.

Just after the outbreak of war I was told that a few years before, a German of position had said to a distinguished Frenchman that Germany would have to crush France again. The Frenchman demurred, saying that France did not want war and would not give the opportunity. The German replied, "We shall let loose Austria on Serbia: that will bring war with Russia, and then France the Ally will have to come in." There is always a temptation to think that behind important events there is some great secret, and that a chance remark or indiscretion has revealed it. It is better to resist this tempta-

THE LIBRARY AT FALLODON
(New House)

tion: to indulge it is more likely to lead us off than on to the track of true conclusion.

There is another line of discussion which also leads nowhere, which is, indeed, a blind alley for thought. The talk about "old diplomacy" and "new diplomacy" is little better than useless chatter. In so far as it leads people to look for safety in new methods, it is a positive hindrance and mischief. It was not the old diplomacy that was to blame for the war. What is diplomacy? Either there is no such thing or it is something that exists in all dealings of men with each other. Business men use it in transactions with one another, the negotiations of Federations of Employers with Trade Unions, and of one Trade Union with another, are full of it; men on every committee use it. It is called "diplomacy" when Governments, which are the executive committees of nations, are dealing with each other, because it then has certain forms. Representatives of Governments call each other Excellency, and so forth, but the game they play is fundamentally the same as if they were called Tom, Dick, or Harry. The honest man could and did play it as honestly in Diplomacy as the honest man in business or on the executive of a Trade Union. The dishonest man will be no more honest in a new diplomacy than in the old. In so far as changes of method, as openness and frankness, are the outcome and expression of a change of purpose and spirit among nations, they are good and welcome; but, if they are this, they will come naturally without forced talk about them. If they are not this, they will be an illusion and deception. New methods may even be dangerous, and influence the public and excite public passion more quickly and irretrievably than the old methods.

Are those who look for safety in the new diplomacy quite sure that a new diplomacy would not have precipitated war before 1914? Pause to consider this question. It was the quiet methods of the diplomatists, notably those of Jules Cambon, that staved off war in the Agadir Crisis of 1911. We must look for a new spirit and purpose among nations, not to a change of method, to secure better things.

The same caution applies to overmuch concentration upon the question of war-guilt. Let us suppose, what personally I believe to be true, that there was a thing called Prussian Militarism, which believed force to be all that really counted in and controlled human affairs. That this militarism considered the moment in 1914 favourable for war, and was glad that Austria should not be restrained, for it welcomed rather than feared the consequences. If this was so, no one in Germany was strong enough or in a position to control this thing; its spirit was in diplomacy and everywhere. The German people at large did not desire war, but they had the memory of three successful wars on which their Empire had been founded; they believed their Army to be invincible and irresistible; they had not that fear and dread of war that would prompt resistance to the idea of it. When war actually came, it was acclaimed in Germany with an enthusiasm that existed in no other country.

Let us suppose all this truthfully said, and that we have satisfactorily settled the question of war-guilt for 1914 and placed it solidly upon Prussian Militarism. We have still to ask ourselves the further question whether, if war had not come in 1914, it could have been indefinitely postponed or altogether avoided? With Europe an armed camp, every nation feeling impelled to measures of defence, and every measure of defence by one nation construed by some other nation as a prospective aggression, could peace have been preserved much longer?

At this point, if thought is to progress, we must not let it stop at the determination of war-guilt in 1914; we must enlarge it to consider the condition to which Europe had then been brought.

Every country had been piling up armaments and perfecting preparations for war. The object in each case had been security. The effect had been precisely the contrary of what was intended and desired. Instead of a sense of security there had been produced a sense of fear, which was yearly increasing. Europe was afraid of the German Army. Germans encouraged in themselves and in others the belief that the German Army was invincible; but even they were becoming apprehensive that in a few years, when the armaments of their neighbours were perfected, even Germany might be afraid. Britain was not afraid of the German Army, because she believed herself to be an island that was out of the reach of any continental army; but the great increase of the German fleet made her watchful, and she no longer felt at rest; indeed, she felt decided uneasiness at the thought of isolation.

Such was the general condition of Europe; preparations for war had produced fear, and fear predisposes to violence and catastrophe.

People in Allied countries may say with truth that Germany, by forcing the pace in military and naval armaments, was more than anyone else responsible for this evil state of affairs. It was her policy of exclusive alliances and armaments after 1870 that produced this result. The truer this comment is, the more force does it give to the conclusion that follows from it. If the Allies, victors in the last war, pursue the same policy that Germany pursued after 1870, precisely the same untoward consequences will follow. Allied exclusive alliances and armaments will produce counter-combinations and armaments—A German-Russian alliance, this time, instead of a Franco-Russian. The notion that Germany can be kept permanently disarmed by temporary expedients, such as foreign missions of control, is an illusion.

Time is going on; several years have passed since the Armistice; human affairs do not stand still; people should be asking earnestly, on what course is Europe moving? Is it on the old lines again, or is it on new lines that may lead to new security and not to the old fear?

People tell us that in Germany there is no change; that her policy will still be of the von Bülow, and her mentality of the von Tirpitz, type. If that be so, things are indeed hopeless, for every conciliatory overture to her will be interpreted as a sign of weakness, as something of which advantage can be taken.

Our proposal for a naval holiday in shipbuilding before the war was purely and simply common sense. It was not inspired at all by apprehension that we might drop behind in the naval competition; on the contrary, it was based on the assumption that we *must* keep our standard margin over the German Fleet and on the knowledge that we would and could do so. This naval superiority had been life or death to us ever since we became dependent on world trade; we must either keep it or die. Germany had become the most powerful nation in Europe, and could remain so without naval superiority over us. She had the right to build a big Navy, if she desired, but she had not the same incentive as we had. It would not be we who would first give up in the competition; our financial position was strong, and if the competition were pushed to extremes it would not be our finance that would crack first. The naval competition was, therefore, one in which Germany could not win. Who is not, therefore, sensible that she should agree to a naval holiday in shipbuilding and lessen the burden on us both of an expenditure from which, in the long run, she could gain nothing?

So far as we can judge, our proposal was attributed to any motive but the true one. It was regarded as a sign that we were weakening in the competition, or as an insolent attempt to put pressure on Germany to stop building a big fleet. Its effect was to encourage the hopes or stiffen the determination of Germany in naval construction.

Von Tirpitz [1] now attributes our readiness to make agreements with Germany about the Bagdad Railway and the Portuguese colonies to the increase of the German Fleet. The growing strength of that fleet was, he thought, making us more conciliatory. It was I who negotiated

[1] *My Memories,* by Grand Admiral von Tirpitz. English translation, p. 209.

and initialled the last versions of those two Agreements. The whole transaction was in my hands, and I *know* that the growth of the German Fleet had nothing whatever to do with my attitude. The sole motive was a desire to show that we were ready to meet German aspirations, wherever we could reconcile them with British interests and engagements. The challenge of the German Fleet was making it more difficult, and not more easy, to be conciliatory; it distrusted Germany, and was undermining both the power and the good-will of those who wished to be friendly to her.

I would even hazard a guess that Germans such as Metternich, who knew something of Britain, must have warned Berlin that the big German Fleet policy must have a reaction on Anglo-German relations, exactly the opposite of what its German authors supposed. Apparently they did not believe this then: do they see it now?

It has not been possible for me to read all the second edition of von Bülow's book (published when he apparently thought Germany was winning the war), or the book of von Tirpitz, but I have been made acquainted with their general tenor. It is quite clear that if this remains the policy and mentality of Germany, Europe will be forced again into the same unhappy course as before 1914. Germany is, in numbers and efficiency combined, potentially the strongest country in Europe. For the present she is disarmed, but in the long run there can be no security in Europe without a Germany that is working genuinely for peace. If the present and rising generations there have learnt nothing from the experience of the war, then indeed the Allies, particularly Belgium,

Britain, and France, cannot help themselves; they must adopt the policy of Bismarck after 1870, make themselves secure for the new future in the old way and try to avoid the mistakes of Bismarck's successors. But this will be a last resort, and almost a counsel of despair. It rests on an assumption which ought not to be accepted till it is clear that there is no better hope.

The immediate responsibility, however, for exploring what is possible, for initiating and giving the tone to new European policy, rests rather with the Allies, who were victors, than with Germany. It is for these to make the new start in the better way and to give Germany her chance of joining in it.

The lesson of European history is so plain. It is that no enduring security can be found in competing armaments and in separate alliances; there is no security for any Power unless it be a security in which its neighbours have an equal share.

All this, it may be objected, is so obvious as to be commonplace—something of which nations must all have been aware for many generations, though they have not acted on it. The fact that, though possessing this knowledge, they have not hitherto acted upon it, is represented as proof that they cannot and will never do so. We are therefore invited to discard such reflections as are made in this chapter as being counsels of perfection, which could be of no use in practical politics.

This line of argument is, in effect, based on the assumption that nations are incapable of learning by experience. There is much in history that supports this view, but the tendency to pessimistic acceptance of it is checked by the reflection that man has, in fact, ascended from savagery to civilization, and that this ascent has been possible only because men, individually and collectively, have been capable of learning by experience. The Great War has been the most tremendous experience in the history of civilized man, and the assumption that he has learnt nothing from it except to prepare for and to make another war is unreasonable. It is not in accord with his past progress. It can only be true if he has ceased to learn, and, if that be so, he will not only cease to progress, but will dwindle and decay; for he cannot be stationary.

Another aspect of this thought is that man, in common with all animate and perhaps "inanimate" nature, continues to exist by his power to adapt himself to changed and changing conditions. As long as he can do this, he goes on; if he ceases to be able to do it he will drop out, as many forms of animate life have dropped out in geological periods of time.

To-day civilized man is confronted by immensely changed conditions. They are due, in the main, to his own discoveries in the region of science. In the last hundred years he has eaten more fruit of the Tree of Knowledge than any previous generation of which there is record. He has acquired unprecedented power over the processes of nature. He can move by air, land, or water with hitherto unheard-of speed. He has facilities for incessant communication that heretofore have been unknown. Whether he will control the use of all these things so as to make them serve and not injure his physical and mental capacity and welfare is a speculation that goes beyond political enquiry. "Knowledge comes, but wisdom lingers," wrote Tennyson, at a time when thought was being enlarged and exhilarated by the discoveries of science. In one respect, however, these discoveries confront man with a definite political problem. "War" is the same word as it was a century ago, but it is no longer the same thing. It used to imply a contest between armies; it will henceforth, by common consent, mean the destruction by chemical agencies, of the crowded centres of population; it will mean physical, moral, and economic ruin. It is necessary therefore that, by common consent, war should be avoided.

Can it be avoided, and, if so, what are the means to that end?

The most effective change would be that nations should dislike each other a little less, and like each other a little more; but this aspect takes us into regions of moral or religious speculation. Nations cannot help disliking what they do not understand.

Yet it should be possible for them, after the last war, to find at least one common ground on which they should come together in confident understanding: an agreement that, in disputes between them, war must be ruled out as a means of settlement that entails ruin; that between nations, as between individuals, the risk involved in settlement by law or arbitration is preferable to the disaster of force. "Learn, or perish" is the rule for nations as for individuals: by evident necessity, though the justice of it may seem inscrutable, one nation or one individual cannot be saved by separate virtue. A wise individual cannot escape being involved in misfortunes due to the unwisdom of his countrymen; one nation may learn, but may yet be involved in the misfortunes of a Continent that does not learn.

The future, the life of European civilization, will depend upon whether a wiser and more instructed spirit prevails now than it did before the experience of the Great War; if it does not, our present civilization will perish, as others have done before it, and the future progress of mankind will depend on the rise of something new, some human agency outside Europe and perhaps not of European race. If, however, such a spirit does exist, then some things that have hitherto been unattainable aspirations may, and indeed will be, accomplished.

Rightly considered, this will not lead to the conclusion that under no circumstances are nations to use force. The internal peace of every country depends upon the knowledge that force is available to uphold law. The greater the consensus of opinion in any country that force should be used for this purpose, the less occasion there will be for the use of force, and the more settled and sure will be the internal peace of that country. So it is with the community of nations. Only a general consensus of opinion not to be lawless, and to prevent any nation from being lawless, will ensure world peace. No great country will contribute anything to that peace by saying that there is no principle whatever for which it will stand up, if need be, by the use of force.

There will be no secure peace till the Great Nations of the world have a consensus of opinion among them sufficient to inspire confidence that they will stand by each other to avoid, to suppress, or to localize and insulate war. Little concrete advance has yet been made. People in Britain, and even more in the Dominions, are as yet somewhat shy of defining exactly what obligation, or pledge, they have undertaken by signing the Covenant of the League of Nations. The United States have hitherto declined to give any pledge or undertake any obligation. Governments cannot go ahead of public opinion, and public opinion is not as yet decisive, but here and elsewhere it is not indifferent. This is good, for indifference is the only state that is incompatible with hope.

The public mind is much exercised by a desire to restrict armaments. It seems to be understanding that competition in armaments does not lead to security. The next stage is for it to realize that only a sense of security will prevent growth of armaments. When this stage is reached, the public will be unmistakably face to face with the problem of how to produce this essential feeling of security.

To solve this problem will require the concentrated effort of all the Great Nations in concert, and if this is to be forthcoming, it will be necessary for them to understand that the solution of this problem is the supreme need of civilized Mankind.

APPENDICES

APPENDIX A

SIR GEORGE GREY (GRANDFATHER OF VISCOUNT GREY)

(From the Memoir by M. Creighton, D.D., Bishop of London)

THROUGHOUT his life nothing gave him keener pleasure than the companionship of the young. His ready sympathy and his unfailing good humour made him beloved by them, and his entire simplicity of character made it no effort for him to interest both himself and them by his conversation. His readiness to feel and to express his feelings about the little incidents of private life contrasted with the caution and reserve of his public career. He had a boundless sense of fun, quick observation, and untiring interest. He would take as much pains to answer a boy's question as he would to study a political problem. There was no sense of unbending in his intercourse with those younger than himself. All was entire frankness, and he was as ready as they were to be amused or interested. "One of my earliest recollections," writes a lady who knew him in her girlhood, "is the delight with which the announcement that Sir George was coming was ever hailed, and the devotion—for I can call it nothing else—which his bright and joyous presence excited in all our hearts—a delight only equalled by his goodness and kindness to us all in the midst of all his work."

First and foremost, he devoted himself to the care of his seven grandchildren, to whom he was a constant companion and friend. He had no difficulty in establishing with them entirely free and open intercourse. The old man of eighty might be seen leading his granddaughters in a gallop over the greensward, his laugh mingling joyously with theirs. He delighted to watch them in their games, to plan picnics and expeditions for them, and laughed with good-humoured resentment at their endeavours to take care of him, and guard him against possible colds or rheumatism. He read classics with his grandsons in their holidays, and keenly watched their progress in learning. Every morning he would gather his granddaughters together, and read with them some English classic, a play of Shakespeare, or a novel or poem of Scott. He read with fire and spirit which entranced his listeners, and made them sigh when the hour was at an end. Their youthful sallies amused him; their interests were his. They claimed his advice and help in anything that was near their heart. He was never impatient of their presence, or irritated by their solicitude. In his last illness he was anxious that the children should not discontinue their sports, or be made to keep quiet on his account. As he lay in pain upon his bed, he was cheered by the sound of their voices as they played lawn-tennis under his window, and, if he did not hear them, would ask that they should not cease their games through fear of disturbing him. (Pp. 58-59, and 126-127.)

APPENDIX B

SPEECH BY SIR EDWARD GREY ON THE ANGLO-FRENCH AGREEMENT IN THE HOUSE OF COMMONS

(Hansard, June 1, 1904, p. 516)

SIR EDWARD GREY (Northumberland, Berwick):
The House is indebted to the noble Lord, not only for
a very clear and comprehensive survey of the scope and
details of the Agreement, but more especially for the closing
part of his speech, in which, in a lofty tone, he sketched what
ought to be the ideal state of relations between the different
great nations of Europe in the process of their expansion in the
world at large. Why we especially welcome that is that in the
convention that is now before us we have, to a degree which
we have never had, at any rate for a very long time, a proof
that an ideal of that kind is not entirely separate from practice. There are two ways in which we may look at this Agreement. I admire the way in which the noble Lord, discussing
it from the point of view of profit and loss, held that the scales
have been delicately adjusted, and pointed out how the concession was so evenly balanced that the scale inclined neither one
way nor the other. I do not propose to discuss the Agreement
from the point of view of a bargain between two Governments; but, if I did, I do not think I should be quite so confident as the noble Lord is that the balance of the scales is so
equally adjusted. There is, no doubt, a good deal to be made
out of the Agreement, if you look at it from the point of view
of a bargain between the two countries. I admit that it is a
considerable gain, as the noble Lord has contended, that our
hand in Egypt is to a considerable extent freed; but I do not

293

think it is as free a hand as we are giving in Morocco; and when the noble Lord instances the progress of our trade in Tunis, he might have mentioned another Agreement with regard to Madagascar, which suggests a very different picture of what British trade might be in Morocco. Again, the rights which France sacrifices in Newfoundland were limited, admittedly limited, though the extent of the limitation was always the subject of debate. But the rights which we give up in return for the French concessions are absolute. There are many criticisms of that kind to be made, and I do not mention these in order to discount the effect of the Agreement, because I think it is entirely wrong to look at it as a bargain between the two countries. I am not going to pursue the question which country has got the most. If it be the case, as I think it is, that France has gained a great deal, both sentimentally and materially, under this Agreement, I do not grudge it in the least. A great deal certainly she has gained with our good-will, and in consequence of our concessions, and that will be a matter for satisfaction to both countries.

But the real point of view from which we ought to look at the Agreement is the point of view of general policy. I do not think it is an expression of general policy so much as an expression of general sincere good-will towards each other on the part of both nations. That is the spirit in which the House will desire that the Agreement as a whole should be regarded; and if they will study the Agreement closely they will see how much more important the agreement is in the spirit in this case than in the letter, especially with regard to the future. Take Article 9, for instance, of the Agreement, which relates to Egypt and Morocco: "The two Governments agree to afford to one another their diplomatic support in order to obtain the execution of the clauses of the present declaration regarding Egypt and Morocco." The words "declaration regarding Egypt and Morocco" are in themselves somewhat vague, and the phrase "diplomatic support" is again vague. Everything depends on the spirit and not upon the letter; but

it is precisely because so much does depend on the spirit that
there are, in that clause alone, great opportunities, looking
to the probabilities of future politics, for the two nations
using the Agreement, by a liberal interpretation of that article,
to draw closer to each other. There will be continual opportunities of befriending each other under that one clause alone,
if it be interpreted in the spirit in which I believe the Agreement is conceived.

The notable feature of this Agreement is that, although it
is drawn up between ourselves and France, it deals with the
interests of third parties—with the interests of Morocco, for
instance, and with the interests of Siam. I think that is rather
a novel way of dealing with the interests of third parties; but,
when you are dealing with the interests of those countries
which are in a position of minimum stability, I have always
been an advocate for the great European nations who have
joint interests dealing directly with each other and not leaving
their interests to be settled by intrigue or diplomatic strife at
the Courts of the Powers. It is much better that they should
be frank with each other; and, to take the noble Lord's illustration, I hope that what the Government has done in regard
to Morocco and Siam may be used as a working model, when
favourable circumstances arise, in the case of Persia, China,
and other places where we have interests of the same kind. It
is true that this Agreement does begin by setting out that the
Governments concerned do not mean to disturb the *status quo*
in Egypt or in Morocco. It has hitherto been the case that
whenever two Governments laid special stress upon their desire
and intention to maintain the *status quo* it was really meant
that the *status quo* was in imminent danger of being disturbed.
I agree, of course, that in all good faith it is the desire of both
parties to this Agreement to see the *status quo* maintained in
Morocco; but Morocco itself is not a party to this Agreement,
and nobody looking towards the future can help fearing that
the *status quo,* as far as Morocco is concerned, is not one which
it is in the power of Europe to maintain. It is essentially so

unstable that you cannot contemplate with confidence that the *status quo* will be maintained. What this Agreement does, therefore, is to prescribe and preserve the policy of friendship between the two countries in the event of that *status quo* being disturbed, and that I think is a great advantage. Both with regard to Egypt and Morocco, and with regard also to Newfoundland, we have all felt that there has been danger for years past of our relations with France being disturbed by events which were beyond our control and beyond the control of the French Government. These three questions alone have been like mines that have drifted into the sea of our diplomacy, and have made navigation very difficult and perilous, and made us feel that there has been real danger, even with the best intentions, of an explosion taking place which might endanger the relations of the two Governments. I cannot say that these questions are removed by this Agreement, but their explosive character is taken away. There is no longer a danger that the relations of the two Powers will be disturbed by these questions, and that is an enormous gain.

When we come to the Agreement as it stands, it would seem very simple—so simple that it has been asked, quite naturally — Why has it not been arrived at before? The noble Lord was careful in his speech to explain that, whatever credit he took for the Government for having made this Agreement, that credit was not taken at the expense of their predecessors. It was a natural reserve for him to make, because the present Government have been in power, I think, for two years, but for thirteen out of the sixteen years preceding their predecessor was Lord Salisbury's Government. Now, Lord Salisbury was not averse to making graceful concessions. He was, I think, willing at any time to make not only commercial, but territorial concessions if by doing so he could secure favourable relations with our European neighbours. So far from criticizing that, I will say I am sure that sober reflection even now, and perhaps still more in the future, will always be ready to place that to Lord Salisbury's credit. He would not have been averse to an Agreement of this kind, had it been possible sooner. I do not think it was possible that it could have been made two years ago. I doubt whether any Government in this country could, a few years ago, have with confidence recommended to the House of Commons or to public opinion in this country the concessions we have made in this Agreement. I doubt also whether the French Government would have ventured to recommend to their Chambers, or to their country, the concessions which they have made in the present Agreement. The fact is that this Agreement means really a change of policy which is common not only to ourselves, but to some other nations in Europe as well. Other things have happened in the last few years that were not possible some time ago. Europe was some time ago divided into two, I will not say hostile, but certainly not friendly, camps—the Triple Alliance and the Dual Alliance. There has been a tendency to obliteration of the hard-and-fast lines between those two camps. Italy has made her own arrangements with France directly. Austria has made her own arrangements with Russia directly. There has been a tendency to more direct inter-communication, more direct settlement, and this has been more favourable to a frank adjustment of the relations between these Powers; and we, in our turn, have now taken part in making a sort of arrangement with a view to creating greater frankness and friendliness between ourselves and France. It would not have been possible to establish this Agreement between ourselves and France some years ago, because the atmosphere was not so favourable. We are told by geologists that our own country has gone through various changes, from a glacial epoch to a genial epoch, and that trees and plants which flourished in this country in the glacial epoch would not grow with us now, and plants and trees that flourish with us now could not have flourished in the glacial epoch. Some time ago the atmosphere between ourselves and France may be said to have been of the glacial epoch. It has happily now changed to a genial epoch.

How has the change been brought about? The noble Lord

has said that the head of the State in France and our own King have had a good deal to do in promoting the change. The Governments of the two countries have also borne their share in promoting the change. I entirely endorse what the noble Lord has said about the willingness of Lord Lansdowne to take advantage of the favourable opportunity which offered, and especially we may mention on the other side M. Delcassé as a Foreign Minister equally quick and ready to take advantage of the change. Groups of Members of this House and of the French Chamber have had something to do, through their friendly relations with each other, in promoting this change. And last, but not least, I think the Press on both sides of the Channel have had their share. Without their co-operation, I doubt whether all the efforts of other parties, whatever the intention, could have gone as far as they have done. The result of all that has been to make possible an Agreement of this kind now, which would not have been possible some time ago, and the great return to both countries for the concessions they have made in this Agreement is the good-will of each of them. It is sometimes said that good-will is not an asset on which we can rely between nations. Well, of course, it is not a thing which we can put on paper as you can put the terms of a treaty on paper. But anything written, anything expressed in definite terms, is valueless unless good-will is behind it. If there be good-will which is genuine and sincere, the mere fact that it is not expressed on paper is not of very great importance. Like all human relations, good-will and friendship may be disturbed by unforeseen events in the future; but we all feel that friction between ourselves and another nation is a great liability which entails upon us anxiety and expenditure; and I do not see why we should not count good-will between ourselves and other nations as an asset of some value. In this case especially I welcome it, because France, I think especially amongst nations, has shown, what is not common in international relations, a certain capacity for friendship. There are many nations who conduct their relations with perfect propriety and all the forms

of friendliness; but France, when she has had friendly relations with other Powers, has specially distinguished herself by
her capacity for friendship. No one viewing the relations between France and Russia since the Dual Alliance was known
to the world can fail to discover that, when France is a friend,
she is an exceedingly good friend; and, therefore, I think in the
good-will, which is not the result so much as the cause, of this
Agreement, there is an asset of real value to the two nations.
I trust the friendship for which I claim so essential a part in
bringing about the good relations between the two nations will
continue to keep these relations good. I trust the two existing
Governments and their successors on either side of the Channel,
when they have any, will also do their utmost to promote this
good-will. I think it is based upon a real recognition for the
first time, both on our part and on that of France, that we have
ceased to be aggressive Powers.

I believe, with regard to ourselves, the feeling is really
spreading in the world that we are not an aggressive Power.
[AN HON. MEMBER: "Tibet."] It may seem soon to say so.
An Hon. Member exclaimed "Tibet." I do not wish to introduce controversial topics. It may seem a little soon, a little
bold to make that statement now as to such a feeling being
abroad so soon after the comments aroused in Europe during
the Boer War; but I think there is some substance in it. Other
countries have come to realize that even those among us who
are the most watchful of the actions of other Powers and so-
licitous for our own expansion have come to look upon our responsibilities as now large enough. What the noble Lord has
so well said this afternoon about the consolidation of our resources is not new; it has been said before, but never with
much general acceptance, and never with such real sincerity of
feeling in the House before. The necessity for consolidation
and, I do not say restriction, but restraint of further expansion, has been brought home to the country, and is likely to
continue to be brought home to the country; and if there be
expansions as, for instance, in Tibet at the present moment—

if there be an exception there—I wish to remind the House of
the fact that I am dealing with the state of public opinion, not
with the action of the Government, and the mere fact of the
jealousy with which public opinion is watching the course of
events in Tibet and the apprehensions that have been expressed are further proof that public opinion is settled in the
desire that there should be restriction of further expansion and
responsibilities. Of course the coolness of our relations with
France some years ago arose out of the fact that we had an
expanding colonial empire, and France wanted a colonial empire. But now France has such an empire—no doubt to a
great extent undeveloped, but full of possibilities—and France
has come to realize that the concessions we have made in
Africa of rights indisputably ours are willingly made with the
object of enabling her to develop the power she has there.
Her claim, I understand, was put forward, not as a right to
any concession in Gambia or adjustments of territory in the
region of Lake Chad, but on the ground that we had our territory so disposed that we could freely develop even if we
made these concessions, whereas the concessions we have made
are absolutely vital to the development of the French possessions. We have made the concessions not so much from the
idea that they are a fair *quid pro quo* for the Newfoundland
arrangement, but for the inherent reason that we regard these
matters as of little importance to us and essential to France.
It is evidence of our good-will that we make these concessions to her. That is the spirit in which the Agreement has
been made, and that is the spirit in which I believe it has been
entered into by France; and in the future we shall see these
two Empires side by side in West Africa, for to a considerable
extent they will be conterminous, with an increasing development of their resources and an increase of the friendly relations between the two Powers. I welcome the Agreement,
and I hope, as the noble lord has said, the Government will
lose no opportunity of making it a working model for other
cases where it is possible to do so. I welcome the Agreement

because I believe not only will it be a working model for other cases, but because it has in it great possibilities for keeping us in contact with France, with a growth of friendly relations to the advantage of both countries, and the many points of contact in various parts of the world will not, as in the past, be occasion for dispute and debate, but will be so many opportunities for the interchange of international courtesies.

APPENDIX C

MEMORANDUM OF INTERVIEW BETWEEN SIR EDWARD GREY AND M. CLEMENCEAU, APRIL 28, 1908

FOREIGN OFFICE,
April 28, 1908.

M. CLEMENCEAU had some conversation with me at the Foreign Office this morning.

He dwelt with great emphasis upon the certainty that we should have to intervene on the Continent of Europe against any Power which attained a position of domination there, just as we had had to do in the time of Napoleon.

He said we ought to be prepared for this. He realized that conscription might not be suitable for us. Mr. Morley had explained to him how the people in this country were all actively engaged in trade, and could not give up a year or two years in order to go through military training. But he thought it might be possible for us to adopt something like the Swiss system, which would put us in a position to intervene on the Continent if need be.

He felt this to be most important. The fate of Napoleon had been decided, not at Trafalgar, but at Waterloo. And so it would have to be again in the case of any Power which attempted to dominate the Continent, if that domination was to be prevented.

I told him that the recent reforms under Mr. Haldane, though they had involved a reduction of some 20,000 men of the Regular Army, had been in the direction of giving more effective training to the Volunteers and so making them a useful part of a general organization, instead of leaving them as a rabble without any serious work assigned to them, as had previously been done. This system of Mr. Haldane offered possibilities for expansion.

I admitted that the system had not yet gone so far as to enable us to put a large force in the field, but, in considering these matters, it must be borne in mind that we intended to keep our Navy in a position of supremacy.

We had come to the conclusion, this year, that we had about twelve months in hand, during which time we might watch, not what Germany proposed to do but what she actually did. Should it turn out that she made the progress with her naval programme which was expected, we should certainly add to our building programme sufficiently next year: any Government which failed to do so would at once create a naval scare in this country, and would be swept away.

No doubt, however, people in this country felt that, as they were prepared, and I was quite sure they were prepared, to vote the necessary expenditure for maintaining the command of the sea, they should not be called upon at the same time to maintain a large Army.

M. Clemenceau said this was perfectly natural. But the Government ought to be alive to the actual situation on the Continent, and to the necessity there might be at any time for us to intervene. Under modern conditions the situation would not develop as gradually as in the time of Napoleon: things would move much more rapidly, and unless we had made previous preparations everything might be over on the Continent before we were in a position to intervene.

Such a contingency might not come soon, perhaps neither he nor I might see it. But, on the other hand, it might come any day. The German Emperor was the most incalculable factor in Europe: he was impulsive, he was sensitive as to his own prestige, and he had at his disposal enormous forces. The Emperor would certainly go on building ships, because to stop building would in itself be an admission of defeat, and therefore the tendency was for the situation to grow worse.

I said that my own view was that the Emperor was no doubt

impulsive, and that he enjoyed sensations, but that he did not desire great sensations, and I doubted whether he had the disposition to precipitate a really great crisis. I felt, however, that he should be humoured in matters which were not opposed to our interests; and this had been done in the case of the North Sea Agreement.

Further, though I was bound to admit that the situation might give rise to anxiety if untoward circumstances arose, I thought that Russia ought to be looked to as a great counterpoise to Germany on land.

M. Clemenceau said it was very desirable that Russia should become such a counterpoise. But at present she had no efficient Government and no money, and for an indefinite period she would continue to be weak. Incidentally, he remarked that, had Russia won the war with Japan, her future would have been entirely in Asia, and she would have dropped out of European politics altogether.

I pointed out that finance might, in the course of the next few years, prove a serious difficulty to Germany, and exercise a restraining influence upon her.

M. Clemenceau said he did not believe that want of money ever prevented military preparations.

He thought the Emperor would regard it as a defeat to restrict his shipbuilding, and therefore Germany would go on borrowing year after year in order to carry on her programme. Germany had not the great National Debt of France. It was true that Germany, for borrowing purposes, was anxious to be given a quotation on the Paris Bourse; but to give this would at once lead to a fall in French Government securities and a rise in German ones, so that no French Government could allow such a quotation.

M. Clemenceau then went on to say that it was curious how Germany was constantly trying to rope in France. It was always being said to the French that their interests and German interests were really alike, more alike than English and French interests were, and that a working arrangement with Germany was the right thing for the French.

I told him that I knew this was being said. We also were, of course, constantly having overtures made to us by Germany; visits of various associations, for instance, were always being encouraged or invited, sometimes to an extent which was quite embarrassing.

But I could not understand why, if Germany had really been seriously pursuing the policy of an Agreement with France, she did not make such an Agreement before the Algeciras Conference while M. Rouvier was in power.

M. Clemenceau said that Germany was always making blunders, going first on one tack, and then on another.

As an instance of the overtures constantly made by Germany to France, M. Clemenceau told me that, when he had had to make a speech referring to Alsace recently, the first person to congratulate him on his return to Paris had been the German Ambassador.

I asked M. Clemenceau whether Alsace and Lorraine were not still a bar to any real *rapprochement* between France and Germany.

He said they were a bar, and more so than ever.

I told him I had heard that it was at the mention of this that M. Etienne's interview with the German Emperor had broken down.

M. Clemenceau said this was what had happened.

The people in Alsace and Lorraine were just as French in sympathy and feeling as they had ever been. So long as this remained the case, though there might be good relations between France and Germany, and though current affairs might be adjusted in a friendly manner, there could be no settlement which would be definitive.

In the course of conversation, M. Clemenceau told me that he was impressed by the increased confidence of the generals at the head of the French Army with regard to resisting attack. But it must be remembered that acting on the defensive, though it might be the right thing to do, was not the line which had been in accordance with the temperament of the French in warfare.

It was absolutely certain, however, that France was so disposed to peace that, if there was war between her and Germany, it would be a war in which she was most clearly in the right and not the aggressor. M. Clemenceau also said that the apprehension of the German generals with regard to war was that the Emperor himself, as the War Lord, would insist upon taking the command personally.

M. Clemenceau also spoke to me about the position of Italy, and dwelt upon the importance of keeping her in good humour.

I explained that we had done our best to humour Italy in connexion with Abyssinia, by agreeing that, under the Tripartite Agreement, her share should be on our side of the country if Abyssinia went to pieces.

Lately, we had been most inconveniently pressed by Italy about the Tripoli frontier. If, as Italy desired, we made an arrangement with her about the frontier, the Turks would be sure to hear of it, and might give us trouble in Egypt. I had, however, succeeded in allaying the susceptibilities of the Italians by assuring them that, in our opinion, the place to which they attached most importance was in Turkish territory: meaning that we would not put forward any claims to this place on behalf of Egypt.

Now, we were constantly being pressed by the Italians, with regard to the arms traffic and to dues in Abyssinia, and asked to press their views upon the French; and I thought it was necessary that the French Government should co-operate in these matters if Italy was to be humoured.

M. Clemenceau touched on the subject of Macedonia, and said he did not understand our proposal about the Governor-General. It seemed to him to imply that, as in the case of Eastern Roumelia, Turkey would be deprived of the country.

I explained that we had expressed ourselves as willing to

accept Hilmi as Inspector, and that the main object to be secured was that his administration should not be thrown into confusion, and ruined by secret orders given by the Palace behind Hilmi's back to his subordinates in Macedonia.

But, of course, I realized the delicate position in which France found herself with regard to Germany and Macedonia owing to the situation in Morocco. (M. Clemenceau had previously expressed himself as very apprehensive that Germany would at some moment intervene in Morocco. He called my attention specially to the statement of Herr von Schon that, though Germany did not complain of the French action in Morocco, Germany might have to protect her own subjects if conditions arose which were not provided for by the Algeciras Act.) I had carefully abstained from pressing the French Government to take any part at Constantinople which was likely to bring them into conflict with Germany there.

We ourselves, however, could not go on taking part in a farce with regard to Macedonian Reforms, and it was necessary for us to say what measures we thought would be effective. We could not go on pretending that improvements were being made and that things were going well when the case was really quite otherwise.

(Signed) E. G.

APPENDIX D

SPEECH BY SIR EDWARD GREY IN THE HOUSE OF COMMONS ON AUGUST 3, 1914

LAST week I stated that we were working for peace not only for this country, but to preserve the peace of Europe. To-day events move so rapidly that it is exceedingly difficult to state with technical accuracy the actual state of affairs, but it is clear that the peace of Europe cannot be preserved. Russia and Germany, at any rate, have declared war upon each other.

Before I proceed to state the position of His Majesty's Government, I would like to clear the ground so that, before I come to state to the House what our attitude is with regard to the present crisis, the House may know exactly under what obligations the Government is, or the House can be said to be, in coming to a decision on the matter. First of all, let me say, very shortly, that we have consistently worked with a single mind, with all the earnestness in our power, to preserve peace. The House may be satisfied on that point. We have always done it. During these last years, as far as His Majesty's Government are concerned, we would have no difficulty in proving that we have done so. Throughout the Balkan crisis, by general admission, we worked for peace. The co-operation of the Great Powers of Europe was successful in working for peace in the Balkan crisis. It is true that some of the Powers had great difficulty in adjusting their points of view. It took much time and labour and discussion before they could settle their differences, but peace was secured, because peace was their main object, and they were willing to give time and trouble rather than accentuate differences rapidly.

In the present crisis, it has not been possible to secure the peace of Europe; because there has been little time, and there has been a disposition—at any rate in some quarters on which I will not dwell—to force things rapidly to an issue, at any rate, to the great risk of peace, and, as we now know, the result of that is that the policy of peace, as far as the Great Powers generally are concerned, is in danger. I do not want to dwell on that, and to comment on it, and to say where the blame seems to us to lie, which Powers were most in favour of peace, which were most disposed to risk or endanger peace, because I would like the House to approach this crisis in which we are now, from the point of view of British interests, British honour, and British obligations, free from all passion as to why peace has not been preserved.

We shall publish Papers as soon as we can regarding what took place last week when we were working for peace; and when those Papers are published I have no doubt that to every human being they will make it clear how strenuous and genuine and whole-hearted our efforts for peace were, and that they will enable people to form their own judgment as to what forces were at work which operated against peace.

I come first, now, to the question of British obligations. I have assured the House—and the Prime Minister has assured the House more than once—that if any crisis such as this arose, we should come before the House of Commons and be able to say to the House that it was free to decide what the British attitude should be, that we would have no secret engagement which we should spring upon the House, and tell the House that, because we had entered into that engagement, there was an obligation of honour upon the country. I will deal with that point to clear the ground first.

There have been in Europe two diplomatic groups, the Triple Alliance, and what came to be called the "Triple Entente," for some years past. The Triple Entente was not an Alliance—it was a diplomatic group. The House will remember that in 1908 there was a crisis, also a Balkan crisis, originating in the annexation of Bosnia and Herzegovina. The

Russian Minister, M. Isvolsky, came to London, or happened
to come to London, because his visit was planned before the
crisis broke out.   I told him definitely then, this being a Balkan
crisis, a Balkan affair, I did not consider that public opinion
in this country would justify us in promising to give anything
more than diplomatic support.   More was never asked from
us, more was never given, and more was never promised.

In this present crisis, up till yesterday, we have also given
no promise of anything more than diplomatic support—up till
yesterday no promise of more than diplomatic support.   Now
I must make this question of obligation clear to the House.
I must go back to the first Moroccan crisis of 1906.   That was
the time of the Algeciras Conference, and it came at a time
of very great difficulty to His Majesty's Government when a
General Election was in progress, and Ministers were scattered
over the country, and I—spending three days a week in my
constituency and three days at the Foreign Office—was asked
the question whether, if that crisis developed into war between
France and Germany, we would give armed support.   I said
then that I could promise nothing to any foreign Power unless it was subsequently to receive the whole-hearted support
of public opinion here if the occasion arose.   I said, in my
opinion, if war was forced upon France then on the question
of Morocco—a question which had just been the subject of
agreement between this country and France, an agreement
exceedingly popular on both sides—that if out of that agreement war was forced on France at that time, in my view public
opinion in this country would have rallied to the material
support of France.

I gave no promise, but I expressed that opinion during the
crisis, as far as I remember, almost in the same words, to the
French Ambassador and the German Ambassador at the time.
I made no promise, and I used no threats; but I expressed that
opinion.   That position was accepted by the French Government, but they said to me at the time—and I think very reasonably—"If you think it possible that the public opinion of Great

Britain might, should a sudden crisis arise, justify you in giving to France the armed support which you cannot promise in advance, you will not be able to give that support, even if you wish to give it, when the time comes, unless some conversations have already taken place between naval and military experts." There was force in that. I agreed to it, and authorized those conversations to take place, but on the distinct understanding that nothing which passed between military or naval experts should bind either Government or restrict in any way their freedom to make a decision as to whether or not they would give that support when the time arose.

As I have told the House, upon that occasion a General Election was in prospect. I had to take the responsibility of doing that without the Cabinet. It could not be summoned. An answer had to be given. I consulted Sir Henry Campbell-Bannerman, the Prime Minister; I consulted, I remember, Lord Haldane, who was then Secretary of State for War, and the present Prime Minister, who was then Chancellor of the Exchequer. That was the most I could do, and they authorized that on the distinct understanding that it left the hands of the Government free whenever the crisis arose. The fact that conversations between military and naval experts took place was later on—I think much later on, because that crisis passed, and the thing ceased to be of importance—but later on it was brought to the knowledge of the Cabinet.

The Agadir crisis came—another Morocco crisis—and throughout that I took precisely the same line that had been taken in 1906. But subsequently, in 1912, after discussion and consideration in the Cabinet, it was decided that we ought to have a definite understanding in writing, which was to be only in the form of an unofficial letter, that these conversations which took place were not binding upon the freedom of either Government; and on the 22nd of November, 1912, I wrote to the French Ambassador the letter which I will now read to the House, and I received from him a letter in similar terms in reply. The letter which I have to read to the House is this, and it will be known to the public now as the record that, whatever took place between military and naval experts, they were not binding engagements upon the Government:

MY DEAR AMBASSADOR,—From time to time in recent years the French and British naval and military experts have consulted together. It has always been understood that such consultation does not restrict the freedom of either Government to decide at any future time whether or not to assist the other by armed force. We have agreed that consultation between experts is not and ought not to be regarded as an engagement that commits either Government to action in a contingency that has not yet arisen and may never arise. The disposition, for instance, of the French and British Fleets respectively at the present moment is not based upon an engagement to co-operate in war.

You have, however, pointed out that, if either Government had grave reason to expect an unprovoked attack by a third Power, it might become essential to know whether it could in that event depend upon the armed assistance of the other.

I agree that, if either Government had grave reason to expect an unprovoked attack by a third Power, or something that threatened the general peace, it should immediately discuss with the other whether both Governments should act together to prevent aggression and to preserve peace, and, if so, what measures they would be prepared to take in common.

LORD CHARLES BERESFORD: What is the date of that?

Sir E. GREY: The 22nd November, 1912. That is the starting point for the Government with regard to the present crisis. I think it makes it clear that what the Prime Minister and I said to the House of Commons was perfectly justified, and that, as regards our freedom to decide in a crisis what our line should be, whether we should intervene or whether we should abstain, the Government remained perfectly free, and, *a fortiori,* the House of Commons remains perfectly free. That I say to clear the ground from the point of view of obligation. I think it was due to prove our good faith to the House of Commons that I should give that full information to the House now, and say what I think is obvious, from the letter I have just read, that we do not construe anything which has previously taken place in our diplomatic relations with other Powers in this matter as restricting the freedom of the Government to decide what attitude they should take now, or restrict the freedom of the House of Commons to decide what their attitude should be.

Well, Sir, I will go further, and I will say this: The situation in the present crisis is not precisely the same as it was in the Morocco question. In the Morocco question it was primarily a dispute which concerned France—a dispute which concerned France and France primarily—a dispute, as it seemed to us, affecting France, out of an agreement subsisting between us and France, and published to the whole world, in which we engaged to give France diplomatic support. No doubt we were pledged to give nothing but diplomatic support; we were, at any rate, pledged by a definite public agreement to stand with France diplomatically in that question.

The present crisis has originated differently. It has not originated with regard to Morocco. It has not originated as regards anything with which we had a special agreement with France; it has not originated with anything which primarily concerned France. It has originated in a dispute between Austria and Serbia. I can say this with the most absolute confidence—no Government and no country has less desire to be involved in war over a dispute with Austria and Serbia than the Government and the country of France. They are involved in it because of their obligation of honour under a definite alliance with Russia. Well, it is only fair to say to the House that that obligation of honour cannot apply in the same way to us. We are not parties to the Franco-Russian Alliance. We do not even know the terms of that Alliance. So far I have, I think, faithfully and completely cleared the ground with regard to the question of obligation.

I now come to what we think the situation requires of us. For many years we have had a long-standing friendship with

France. [An Hon. Member: "And with Germany!"] I remember well the feeling in the House—and my own feeling—
for I spoke on the subject, I think, when the late Government
made their agreement with France—the warm and cordial
feeling resulting from the fact that these two nations, who
had had perpetual differences in the past, had cleared these
differences away. I remember saying, I think, that it seemed
to me that some benign influence had been at work to produce
the cordial atmosphere that had made that possible. But how
far that friendship entails obligation—it has been a friendship
between the nations and ratified by the nations—how far that
entails an obligation let every man look into his own heart,
and his own feelings, and construe the extent of the obligation
for himself. I construe it myself as I feel it, but I do not wish
to urge upon anyone else more than their feelings dictate as
to what they should feel about the obligation. The House,
individually and collectively, may judge for itself. I speak my
personal view, and I have given the House my own feeling
in the matter.

The French Fleet is now in the Mediterranean, and the
Northern and Western coasts of France are absolutely undefended. The French Fleet being concentrated in the Mediterranean, the situation is very different from what it used
to be, because the friendship which has grown up between
the two countries has given them a sense of security that there
was nothing to be feared from us. The French coasts are
absolutely undefended. The French fleet is in the Mediterranean, and has for some years been concentrated there because of the feeling of confidence and friendship which has
existed between the two countries. My own feeling is that if
a foreign fleet engaged in a war which France had not sought,
and in which she had not been the aggressor, came down the
English Channel and bombarded and battered the undefended
coasts of France, we could not stand aside and see this going
on practically within sight of our eyes, with our arms folded,
looking on dispassionately, doing nothing! I believe that

would be the feeling of this country. There are times when one feels that, if these circumstances actually did arise, it would be a feeling which would spread with irresistible force throughout the land.

But I also want to look at the matter without sentiment, and from the point of view of British interests, and it is on that that I am going to base and justify what I am presently going to say to the House. If we say nothing at this moment, what is France to do with her Fleet in the Mediterranean? If she leaves it there, with no statement from us as to what we will do, she leaves her Northern and Western coasts absolutely undefended, at the mercy of a German fleet coming down the Channel, to do as it pleases in a war which is a war of life and death between them. If we say nothing, it may be that the French Fleet is withdrawn from the Mediterranean. We are in the presence of a European conflagration; can anybody set limits to the consequences that may arise out of it? Let us assume that to-day we stand aside in an attitude of neutrality, saying, "No, we cannot undertake and engage to help either party in this conflict." Let us suppose the French Fleet is withdrawn from the Mediterranean; and let us assume that the consequences—which are already tremendous in what has happened in Europe even to countries which are at peace—in fact, equally whether countries are at peace or at war—let us assume that out of that come consequences unforeseen, which make it necessary at a sudden moment that, in defence of vital British interests, we should go to war: and let us assume—which is quite possible—that Italy, who is now neutral—[Hon Member: "Hear, Hear!"]—because, as I understand, she considers that this war is an aggressive war, and the Triple Alliance being a defensive alliance her obligation did not arise—let us assume that consequences which are not yet foreseen—and which perfectly legitimately, consulting her own interests—make Italy depart from her attitude of neutrality at a time when we are forced in defence of vital British interests ourselves to fight, what then will be the position in the Mediterranean? It might be that at some critical moment those consequences would be forced upon us because our trade routes in the Mediterranean might be vital to this country.

Nobody can say that in the course of the next few weeks there is any particular trade route the keeping open of which may not be vital to this country. What will be our position then? We have not kept a fleet in the Mediterranean which is equal to dealing alone with a combination of other fleets in the Mediterranean. It would be the very moment when we could not detach more ships to the Mediterranean, and we might have exposed this country from our negative attitude at the present moment to the most appalling risk. I say that from the point of view of British interests. We feel strongly that France was entitled to know—and to know at once!— whether or not, in the event of attack upon her unprotected Northern and Western Coasts she could depend upon British support. In that emergency, and in these compelling circumstances, yesterday afternoon I gave to the French Ambassador the following statement:

> I am authorized to give an assurance that if the German Fleet comes into the Channel or through the North Sea to undertake hostile operations against the French coasts or shipping, the British Fleet will give all the protection in its power. This assurance is, of course, subject to the policy of His Majesty's Government receiving the support of Parliament, and must not be taken as binding his Majesty's Government to take any action until the above contingency of action by the German Fleet takes place.

I read that to the House, not as a declaration of war on our part, not as entailing immediate aggressive action on our part, but as binding us to take aggressive action should that contingency arise. Things move very hurriedly from hour to hour. Fresh news comes in, and I cannot give this in any very formal way; but I understand that the German Government would be prepared, if we would pledge ourselves to neutrality, to agree that its fleet would not attack the Northern Coast of France. I have only heard that shortly before I came to the House, but it is far too narrow an engagement for us. And, Sir, there is the more serious consideration— becoming more serious every hour—there is the question of the neutrality of Belgium.

I shall have to put before the House at some length what is our position in regard to Belgium. The governing factor is the treaty of 1839, but this is a treaty with a history— a history accumulated since In 1870, when there was war between France and Germany, the question of the neutrality of Belgium arose, and various things were said. Amongst other things, Prince Bismarck gave an assurance to Belgium that, confirming his verbal assurance, he gave in writing a declaration which he said was superfluous in reference to the treaty in existence—that the German Confederation and its allies would respect the neutrality of Belgium, it being always understood that that neutrality would be respected by the other belligerent Powers. That is valuable as a recognition in 1870 on the part of Germany of the sacredness of these treaty rights.

What was our own attitude? The people who laid down the attitude of the British Government were Lord Granville in the House of Lords, and Mr. Gladstone in the House of Commons. Lord Granville, on August 8, 1870, used these words. He said:

We might have explained to the country and to foreign nations that we did not think this country was bound either morally or inter- nationally or that its interests were concerned in the maintenance of the neutrality of Belgium; though this course might have had some conveniences, though it might have been easy to adhere to it, though it might have saved us from some immediate danger, it is a course which Her Majesty's Government thought it impossible to adopt in the name of the country with any due regard to the country's honour or to the country's interests.

Mr. Gladstone spoke as follows two days later:

There is, I admit, the obligation of the treaty. It is not necessary, nor would time permit me, to enter into the complicated question of the nature of the obligations of that treaty; but I am not able to subscribe to the doctrine of those who have held in this House what plainly amounts to an assertion, that the simple fact of the existence of a guarantee is binding on every party to it, irrespectively altogether of the particular position in which it may find itself at the time when the occasion for acting on the guarantee arises. The great authorities upon foreign policy to whom I have been accustomed to listen, such as Lord Aberdeen and Lord Palmerston, never to my knowledge took that rigid and, if I may venture to say so, that impracticable view of the guarantee. The circumstance that there is already an existing guarantee in force is of necessity an important fact, and a weighty element in the case to which we are bound to give full and ample consideration. There is also this further consideration, the force of which we must all feel most deeply, and that is, the common interests against the unmeasured aggrandisement of any Power whatever.

The treaty is an old treaty—1839—and that was the view taken of it in 1870. It is one of those treaties which are founded, not only on consideration for Belgium, which benefits under the treaty, but in the interests of those who guarantee the neutrality of Belgium. The honour and interests are, at least, as strong to-day as in 1870, and we cannot take a more narrow view or a less serious view of our obligations, and of the importance of those obligations, than was taken by Mr. Gladstone's Government in 1870.

I will read to the House what took place last week on this subject. When mobilization was beginning, I knew that this question must be a most important element in our policy—a most important subject for the House of Commons. I telegraphed at the same time in similar terms to both Paris and Berlin to say that it was essential for us to know whether the French and German Governments respectively were prepared to undertake an engagement to respect the neutrality of Belgium. These are the replies. I got from the French Government this reply:

The French Government are resolved to respect the neutrality of Belgium, and it would only be in the event of some other Power violating that neutrality that France might find herself under the necessity, in order to assure the defence of her security, to act otherwise. This assurance has been given several times. The President of the Republic spoke of it to the King of the Belgians, and the French Minister at Brussels has spontaneously renewed the assurance to the Belgian Minister of Foreign Affairs to-day.

From the German Government the reply was:

The Secretary of State for Foreign Affairs could not possibly give an answer before consulting the Emperor and the Imperial Chancellor.

Sir Edward Goschen, to whom I had said it was important to have an answer soon, said he hoped the answer would not be too long delayed. The German Minister for Foreign Affairs then gave Sir Edward Goschen to understand that he rather doubted whether they could answer at all, as any reply they might give could not fail, in the event of war, to have the undesirable effect of disclosing, to a certain extent, part of their plan of campaign. I telegraphed at the same time to Brussels to the Belgian Government, and I got the following reply, from Sir Francis Villiers:

The Minister for Foreign Affairs thanks me for the communication, and replies that Belgium will, to the utmost of her power, maintain neutrality, and expects and desires other Powers to observe and uphold it. He begged me to add that the relations between Belgium and the neighbouring Powers were excellent, and there was no reason to suspect their intentions, but that the Belgian Government believe, in the case of violation, they were in a position to defend the neutrality of their country.

It now appears, from the news I have received to-day—which has come quite recently, and I am not yet quite sure how far it has reached me in an accurate form—that an ultimatum has been given to Belgium by Germany, the object of which was to offer Belgium friendly relations with Germany on condition that she would facilitate the passage of German troops through Belgium. Well, Sir, until one has these things absolutely definitely, up to the last moment, I do not wish to say all that one would say if one were in a position to give the House full, complete, and absolute information upon the point. We were sounded in the course of last week as to whether, if a guarantee were given that, after the war, Belgian integrity would be preserved that would content us. We replied that we could not bargain away whatever interests or obligations we had in Belgian neutrality.

Shortly before I reached the House I was informed that the following telegram had been received from the King of the Belgians by our King—King George:

Remembering the numerous proofs of your Majesty's friendship and that of your predecessors, and the friendly attitude of England in 1870, and the proof of friendship she had just given us I make a supreme appeal to the diplomatic intervention of your Majesty's Government to safeguard the integrity of Belgium.

Diplomatic intervention took place last week on our part. What can diplomatic intervention do now? We have great and vital interests in the independence—and integrity is the least part—of Belgium. If Belgium is compelled to submit to allow her neutrality to be violated, of course the situation is clear. Even if by agreement she admitted the violation of her neutrality, it is clear she could only do so under duress. The smaller States in that region of Europe ask but one thing. Their one desire is that they should be left alone and independent. The one thing they fear is, I think, not so much that their integrity but that their independence should be interfered with. If in this war which is before Europe the neutrality of one of those countries is violated, if the troops of one of the combatants violate its neutrality and no action be taken to resent it, at the end of the war, whatever the integrity may be, the independence will be gone.

I have one further quotation from Mr. Gladstone as to what he thought about the independence of Belgium. It will be found in *Hansard,* Volume 203, Page 1787. I have not had time to read the whole speech and verify the context, but the thing seems to me so clear that no context could make any difference to the meaning of it. Mr. Gladstone said:

We have an interest in the independence of Belgium which is wider than that which we may have in the literal operation of the guarantee. It is found in the answer to the question whether, under the circumstances of the case, this country, endowed as it is with influence and power, would quietly stand by and witness the perpetration of the direst crime that ever stained the pages of history, and thus become participators in the sin.

No, Sir, if it be the case that there has been anything in the nature of an ultimatum to Belgium, asking her to compromise or violate her neutrality, whatever may have been offered to her in return, her independence is gone if that holds. If her independence goes, the independence of Holland will follow. I ask the House, from the point of view of British interests, to consider what may be at stake. If France is beaten in a struggle of life and death, beaten to her knees, loses her position as a great Power, becomes subordinate to the will and power of one greater than herself—consequences which I do not anticipate, because I am sure that France has the power to defend herself with all the energy and ability and patriotism which she has shown so often—still, if that were to happen, and if Belgium fell under the same dominating influence, and then Holland, and then Denmark, then would not Mr. Gladstone's words come true, that just opposite to us there would be a common interest against the unmeasured aggrandisement of any Power?

It may be said, I suppose, that we might stand aside, husband our strength, and that, whatever happened in the course of this war, at the end of it intervene with effect to put things right, and to adjust them to our own point of view. If, in a crisis like this, we run away from those obligations of honour and interest as regards the Belgian Treaty, I doubt whether, whatever material force we might have at the end, it would be of very much value in face of the respect that we should have lost. And do not believe, whether a great Power stands outside this war or not, it is going to be in a position at the end of it to exert its superior strength. For us, with a power-ful fleet, which we believe able to protect our commerce, to protect our shores, and to protect our interests, if we are engaged in war, we shall suffer but little more than we shall suffer even if we stand aside.

We are going to suffer, I am afraid, terribly in this war whether we are in it or whether we stand aside. Foreign trade is going to stop, not because the trade routes are closed, but because there is no trade at the other end. Continental nations engaged in war—all their populations, all their energies, all their wealth, engaged in a desperate struggle—they cannot carry on the trade with us that they are carrying on in times of peace, whether we are parties to the war or whether we are not. I do not believe, for a moment, that at the end of this war, even if we stood aside and remained aside, we should be in a position, a material position, to use our force decisively to undo what had happened in the course of the war, to prevent the whole of the West of Europe opposite to us—if that had been the result of the war—falling under the domination of a single Power, and I am quite sure that our moral position would be such as to have lost us all respect. I can only say that I have put the question of Belgium some-what hypothetically, because I am not yet sure of all the facts, but, if the facts turn out to be as they have reached us at present, it is quite clear that there is an obligation on this country to do its utmost to prevent the consequences to which those facts will lead if they are undisputed.

I have read to the House the only engagements that we have yet taken definitely with regard to the use of force. I think it is due to the House to say that we have taken no engagement yet with regard to sending an expeditionary armed force out of the country. Mobilization of the Fleet has taken place; mobilization of the Army is taking place; but we have as yet taken no engagement, because I do feel that, in the case of a European conflagration such as this, unprecedented, with our enormous responsibilities in India and other parts of the Empire, or in countries in British occupation, with all the unknown factors, we must take very carefully into consideration the use which we make of sending an Expeditionary Force out of the country until we know how we stand. One thing I would say.

The one bright spot in the whole of this terrible situation is Ireland. The general feeling throughout Ireland—and I would like this to be clearly understood abroad—does not make the Irish question a consideration which we feel we have now to take into account. I have told the House how far we have at present gone in commitments and the conditions which influence our policy, and I have put to the House and dwelt at length upon how vital is the condition of the neutrality of Belgium.

What other policy is there before the House? There is but one way in which the Government could make certain at the present moment of keeping outside this war, and that would be that it should immediately issue a proclamation of unconditional neutrality. We cannot do that. We have made the commitment to France that I have read to the House which prevents us from doing that. We have got the consideration of Belgium which prevents us also from an unconditional neutrality, and, without those conditions absolutely satisfied and satisfactory, we are bound not to shrink from proceeding to the use of all the forces in our power. If we did take that line by saying, "We will have nothing whatever to do with this matter" under no conditions—the Belgian Treaty obligations, the possible position in the Mediterranean, with damage to British interests, and what may happen to

France from our failure to support France—if we were to say that all those things mattered nothing, were as nothing, and to say we would stand aside, we should, I believe, sacrifice our respect and good name and reputation before the world, and should not escape the most serious and grave economic consequences.

My object has been to explain the view of the Government, and to place before the House the issue and the choice. I do not for a moment conceal, after what I have said, and after the information, incomplete as it is, that I have given to the House with regard to Belgium, that we must be prepared, and we are prepared, for the consequences of having to use all the strength we have at any moment—we know not how soon —to defend ourselves and to take our part. We know, if the facts all be as I have stated them, though I have announced no intending aggressive action on our part, no final decision to resort to force at a moment's notice, until we know the whole of the case, that the use of it may be forced upon us. As far as the forces of the Crown are concerned, we are ready. I believe the Prime Minister and my right hon. Friend the First Lord of the Admiralty have no doubt whatever that the readiness and the efficiency of those Forces were never at a higher mark than they are to-day, and never was there a time when confidence was more justified in the power of the Navy to protect our commerce and to protect our shores. The thought is with us always of the suffering and misery entailed from which no country in Europe will escape and from which no abdication or neutrality will save us. The amount of harm that can be done by an enemy ship to our trade is infinitesimal, compared with the amount of harm that must be done by the economic condition that is caused on the Continent.

The most awful responsibility is resting upon the Government in deciding what to advise the House of Commons to do. We have disclosed our mind to the House of Commons. We have disclosed the issue, the information which we have,

and made clear to the House, I trust, that we are prepared
to face that situation, and that, should it develop, as probably it may develop, we will face it. We worked for peace
up to the last moment, and beyond the last moment. How
hard, how persistently, and how earnestly we strove for peace
last week, the House will see from the Papers that will be
before it.

But that is over, as far as the peace of Europe is concerned.
We are now face to face with a situation and all the consequences which it may yet have to unfold. We believe we
shall have the support of the House at large in proceeding
to whatever the consequences may be and whatever measures
may be forced upon us by the development of facts or action
taken by others. I believe the country, so quickly has the
situation been forced upon it, has not had time to realize
the issue. It perhaps is still thinking of the quarrel between
Austria and Servia, and not the complications of this matter
which have grown out of the quarrel between Austria and
Servia. Russia and Germany we know are at war. We do not
yet know officially that Austria, the Ally whom Germany is
to support, is yet at war with Russia. We know that a good
deal has been happening on the French frontier. We do not
know that the German Ambassador has left Paris.

The situation has developed so rapidly that technically, as
regards the condition of the war, it is most difficult to describe
what has actually happened. I wanted to bring out the under-
lying issues which would affect our own conduct, and our own
policy, and to put them clearly. I have put the vital facts
before the House, and if, as seems not improbable, we are
forced, and rapidly forced, to take our stand upon those issues,
then I believe, when the country realizes what is at stake, what
the real issues are, the magnitude of the impending dangers in
the West of Europe, which I have endeavoured to describe
to the House, we shall be supported throughout, not only
by the House of Commons, but by the determination, the

resolution, the courage, and the endurance of the whole country.

Sir EDWARD GREY: I want to give the House some information which I have received, and which was not in my possession when I made my statement this afternoon. It is information I have received from the Belgian Legation in London, and is to the following effect:

Germany sent yesterday evening at seven o'clock a Note proposing to Belgium friendly neutrality, covering free passage on Belgian territory, and promising maintenance of independence of the kingdom and possession at the conclusion of peace, and threatening, in case of refusal, to treat Belgium as an enemy. A time limit of twelve hours was fixed for the reply. The Belgians have answered that an attack on their neutrality would be a flagrant violation of the rights of nations, and that to accept the German proposal would be to sacrifice the honour of a nation. Conscious of its duty, Belgium is firmly resolved to repel aggression by all possible means.

Of course, I can only say that the Government are prepared to take into grave consideration the information which it has received. I make no further comment upon it.

APPENDIX E

ADDRESS BY VISCOUNT GREY OF FALLODON AT
THE UNVEILING OF THE TABLET TO
WALTER HINES PAGE IN THE CHAPTER
HOUSE, WESTMINSTER ABBEY, JULY 3, 1923.

THE tablet that is to be unveiled to-day is in memory of one whose every word and act in great place were inspired by single-minded and earnest desire to make human freedom, as he saw it realized in democracy, prevail among the nations of the world. Walter Hines Page was an example of the truth that the strongest personalities are the outcome not so much of striving for personal success or fame, as of patriotism and of faith in an ideal. His patriotism was of the noblest kind; he loved his country both for what it was and for what he believed it could and would do for the benefit of mankind. His perception of the power of the United States, his belief in its democracy, his absolute and never-faltering trust in the will of its people to do great things and good things for the world, were part of his very being.

Surely it must be a proud as well as a happy thought for his country to remember that it inspired a faith so high, in a mind so keen and pure.

I have spoken first of Walter Hines Page as an American, because that is how, I am sure, he would have wished us to speak of him and to think of him; but it was very near his heart that there should be between his country and ours true knowledge and understanding each of the other; and there is no greater consummation to be wished for in public affairs than that the high and beneficial hopes for the world which he founded upon this should be realized.

We in this country feel deep gratitude to him; we wish

that there should be something to commemorate the sympathy and moral support that he gave us in the greatest crisis of our history. We wish his name to be remembered with regard, with honour, and with affection as that of one who gave us invaluable help at a time when our liberty, our very independence even, seemed to be at stake.

His countrymen who still cherish the names of those who helped the United States years ago in time of trial and peril will find it easy to understand what we here now feel for such men as Walter Hines Page. In all our conversations with him I felt—what I am sure many others here, who knew him, also felt—that there was between him and us a peculiarly close tie of personal sympathy. We felt attached to him by a sense of the same values in public life, by a desire for the same sort of world in which to live, by a kinship of thought, of standards, and of ideals. Therefore, while his resting-place is in his own country, which he loved so devotedly, we have wished to have a memorial here to do honour to him and to preserve for those who come after us a record and memory of his life. It is most fitting that the place for this should be Westminster Abbey—where so much that is great and honourable and dear in our history is consecrated —this Abbey, which not so very long ago, as time is reckoned in the life of nations, was as much part of the inheritance of his ancestors as of our own. In this spirit I unveil the memorial, and ask the Dean to accept it.

APPENDIX F

THE "SUGGESTIONS" OF AUGUST 1, 1914

THE following telegram from Prince Lichnowsky was published in Germany soon after the outbreak of war:

AUGUST 1, 1914.

Sir Edward Grey has just called me to the telephone and has asked me whether I thought I could declare that in the event of France remaining neutral in a German-Russian war we would not attack the French. I told him that I believed that I could assume responsibility for this.

On August 8, 1914, I was questioned about this in the House of Commons and returned the following answer:

It was reported to me one day that the German Ambassador had suggested that Germany might remain neutral in a war between Russia and Austria, and also engage not to attack France, if we would remain neutral and secure the neutrality of France. I said at once that if the German Government thought such an arrangement possible I was sure we could secure it. It appeared, however, that what the Ambassador meant was that we should secure the neutrality of France, if Germany went to war with Russia. This was quite a different proposal, and, as I supposed it in all probability to be incompatible with the terms of the Franco-Russian Alliance, it was not in my power to promise to secure it. Subsequently the Ambassador sent for my private secretary, and told him that, as soon as the misunderstanding was cleared up, he had sent a second telegram to Berlin to cancel the impression produced by the first telegram he has sent on the subject. The first telegram has been published. This second telegram does not seem to have been published.

Since the text of this book was completed, a telegram, which I addressed to the British Ambassador in Paris on August 1, has been brought to my notice and an apparent inconsistency pointed out:

Sir Edward Grey to Sir F. Bertie

FOREIGN OFFICE,
AUGUST 1, 1914.

German Ambassador here seemed to think it not impossible, when I suggested it, that after mobilization on western frontier, French and German armies should remain, neither crossing the frontier as long as the other did not do so. I cannot say whether this would be consistent with French obligations under her alliance. If it were so consistent, I suppose French Government would not object to our engaging to be neutral as long as German army remained on frontier on the defensive.

To this Sir F. Bertie replied:

I cannot imagine that in the event of Russia being at war with Austria and being attacked by Germany it would be consistent with French obligations towards Russia for French to remain quiescent. If the French undertook to remain so, the Germans would first attack Russians and, if they defeated them, they would then turn round on the French.

In these last critical days and hours every suggestion that might have a chance of avoiding or localizing war was explored. Time was getting short, and, in the effort to save it, confusion sometimes arose. My recollection of the misunderstanding that occurred on the telephone between Lichnowsky and myself is still clear, and is precisely as explained in the answer in Parliament.

I do not recollect the circumstances of the telegram to Bertie, and cannot say with certainty exactly what was in my mind when I sent it. My impression is that it implied that

WALTER HINES PAGE

the German and French armies should each, though mobilized, take no part in the war, so long as the other did not do so. But it may be that in the pressure of the time I made a suggestion without considering its full bearing, and that Bertie very justly pointed out that it was impracticable.

G. OF F.

APPENDIX G

THE ALLEGED "FAKING" OF DOCUMENTS

T HE following passage is taken from an article entitled "The Great Lie," by W. N. Ewer, in the *Daily Herald* of October 18, 1922:—

On July 24 (the day of the delivery of the Austrian Ultimatum to Serbia) Sir Edward Grey made his first peace move. He proposed that England, Germany, France, and Italy should exercise "moderating influence" simultaneously at Vienna and Petrograd (British Blue Book, Nos. 10, 11, 24). Germany agreed (Blue Book No. 18). Italy agreed (Blue Book No. 29).

But the Russian Foreign Minister flatly rejected Sir Edward's proposal.

"If," he wired to Paris and London on July 27, "it is proposed that a moderating influence should be exercised in St. Petersburg, we absolutely refuse such a suggestion."

The despatch in which that sentence occurs went simultaneously to London and Paris. It was communicated to Sir Edward Grey. Part of it is printed in the British Blue Book (No. 53).

But that damning sentence showing not Germany, but Russia, rejecting the first peace proposal, has been cut out.

It is enough. If one despatch has been doctored in order to hide an embarrassing fact, it is safe to assume that this is no solitary example but that, in the Blue Book, as in the Orange Book, a careful editor "prepared" the documents, deleting, adding, altering—in a word faking —wherever it seemed necessary for the proving of the case against Germany.

The same allegation was repeated in *The Nation* and *Athenæum*, October 28, 1922. It is drawn from a German publication entitled *The Falsifications of the Russian Orange Book*, compiled from Bolshevist sources (Die Falschungen des russischen Orangebuches.   De Gruyter & Co., Berlin and Leipzig, 1922).

All these allegations and suggestions, either as regards this document (No. 53) or any others issued by the Foreign Office, are completely unfounded.   There was no mutilation of No. 53 to my knowledge, and I never heard of the charge until long after I had left office.   From enquiries made it appears that the original document now in the Foreign Office shows that something has been cut off at the end of it.   I am convinced and am authorized to state that the document as it exists in the Foreign Office is in the actual form in which it was received there.   It is quite possible that in the communication made in London a passage was withheld to which it was anticipated we should take exception.   Such a proceeding is always within the discretion of an Embassy.   When time permits, the Embassy would withhold the communication and ask for fresh instructions; in time of great urgency, an Ambassador or high official would exercise his discretion and report home what he had done.

In the particular document (No. 53) it is worth noting that the passage cut off refers to "an answer given by the French Minister of Justice" and may therefore not have been intended for communication to us.   Whoever cut it off appears in error to have left in the previous paragraph, which, as printed, has no relevance to what precedes and is meaningless without the subsequent (detached) paragraph.   Internal evidence shows that the document was sent to the printer exactly as it was received and that it was left to speak for itself without any attempt to edit or correct it.

On the point of substance it appears that the objection taken (in the detached paragraph) was to the exercise of influence *at St. Petersburg* and on the Russian Government apart from the other Governments.   As stated in the text, the Russian Government promptly assented to the proposal of a Conference, and did not make the objections which Count Benckendorff had led me to fear they might make. The point is made clear in No. 78 in the British White Paper:—

Sir George Buchanan to Sir Edward Grey

No. 78

(Received July 29, 1914).

The Minister for Foreign Affairs (M. Sazonof) said that the Austrian Government had now definitely declined direct conversation between Vienna and St. Petersburg. The Minister for Foreign Affairs said he had proposed such exchange of views on advice of German Ambassador. He proposed, when informing German Ambassador of this refusal of Austria's, to urge that a return should be made to your proposal for a conference of our Ambassadors, or at all events for an exchange of views between the three Ambassadors less directly interested, yourself, and also the Austrian Ambassador, if you thought it advisable. Any arrangement, approved by France and England, would be acceptable to him, and he did not care what form such conversations took. No time was to be lost, and the only way to avert war was for you to succeed in arriving, by means of conversations with Ambassadors either collectively or individually, at some formula which Austria could be induced to accept. Throughout the Russian Government had been perfectly frank and conciliatory, and had done all in their power to maintain peace. If their efforts to maintain peace failed, he trusted that it would be realized by the British public that it was not the fault of the Russian Government.

As to other documents, it may be convenient to explain how there may be discrepancies between documents that originate in the Foreign Office and versions of them that are published abroad. The authentic version is of course our own document in English, but it may appear abroad translated into a foreign language and then be retranslated independently into English from the foreign language for publication in British or American newspapers and books. In such cases the unofficial retranslation is sure to contain some differences in expression from the original.

In presenting recent cypher telegrams to Parliament it is necessary to paraphrase some part of the originals in order to guard the cypher in which they were sent. With the exception of a few that have already been published, the telegrams in this book, not being of recent date, are with the permission of the Foreign Office printed without paraphrase in the exact form in which they were despatched or received.

So far as I can ascertain, all the allegations of "faking" documents which have been made against the British Foreign Office in foreign or English publications are founded either on slight discrepancies due to paraphrasing or on differences between the retranslated and the original documents. G. of F.

INDEX

INDEX

AALAND ISLANDS, i. 138; conversation with German Ambassador, i. 143.

Abdul Hamid, claim to Gulf of Akaba, i. 119; refuses Joint Commission, i. 120; courts ultimatum, i. 121; subsequent justification for British attitude, i. 122; ultimatum delivered, i. 122; yields, i. 122; overthrow, i. 168; intrigues, i. 250; deposition, i. 250.

Adrianople: Bulgarian demands, i. 251; occupied by Bulgaria, i. 253; retaken by Turkey, i. 253.

Ægean Islands, i. 261, ii. 187.

d'Aehrenthal, Baron, M. Isvolsky's view of, i. 177.

Agadir crisis, i. 210-39; *Panther* despatched to, i. 211; peace in the balance, i. 211; British attitude, i. 212; German explanations, i. 218; German military disappointment, i. 232; military conversations, i. 92-3; discussion by Committee of Imperial Defence, i. 93; conversations not binding on His Majesty's Government, i. 95; French reply, i. 95.

Akaba and Denshawai, i. 119-37.

——, Gulf of, Turkish claim to, i. 119; Lord Cromer's views, i. 120; Turkey refuses Joint Committee, i. 120; Abdul Hamid yields, i. 122; despatch to Sir F. Lascelles respecting British views, i. 126.

Albania, i. 255-61; Greek aspirations, i. 256; Austrian contention, i. 257; Russian acquiescence, i. 257.

Algeciras Conference, i. 69; M. Cambon seeks British support at, i. 69; German attitude towards, i. 70; danger of Franco-German rupture, i. 70; Lord Ripon's apprehensions,

i. 99; atmosphere of suspicion, i. 99; diplomatic support to France, i. 100; Entente Cordiale, attacks on, i. 101; French contention *re* Moroccan ports, i. 101; Casablanca, Austrian proposals, i. 101, suggested compromise, i. 106; rumour respecting British delegate's attitude, i. 102, British indignation, i. 102, despatch from British Ambassador in Paris regarding, i. 102-07; French differences with Germany, i. 103; Austrian scheme for policing ports, i. 103; French anxiety regarding British attitude, i. 105, French reassured, i. 106; successful termination, i. 109.

—— crisis, naval and military conversations, i. 68-96; crisis passed, i. 90.

Allied Agreement, i. 154.

—— diplomacy, ii. 166; in war, ii. 147-220; relations with neutrals, ii. 167; military difficulties in 1915, ii. 202.

—— post-War policy, ii. 283.

—— solidarity preserved, ii. 166.

Alsace-Lorraine, ii. 22; French sentiment, ii. 305.

Ambassadors' Conference, i. 248, 267.

America, *see* United States.

—— and the war, ii. 86-122.

Anglo-French Agreement of 1904, i. 46; German opposition, i. 75, France seeks British support, i. 70-88, British attitude regarding, 76; British indignation about current rumour, i. 102; speech in the House of Commons, ii. 293.

—— co-operation, policy of His Majesty's Government, i. 105; naval and military consultations, i. 72-76; ii. 2.

—— relations, improvement in, i. 50,

"Workhouse fever," ii. 60.

World predominance: Germany's aims, ii. 29.

END OF VOL. II